RAPE

WEAPON OF WAR
AND GENOCIDE

RAPE

WEAPON OF WAR AND GENOCIDE

Edited and Introduced by
Carol Rittner and John K. Roth

PARAGON HOUSE

First Edition 2012

Published in the United States by

Paragon House
1925 Oakcrest Ave, Suite 7
St. Paul, MN 55113
www.ParagonHouse.com

Library of Congress Cataloging-in-Publication Data

Rape : weapon of war and genocide / edited and introduced by Carol Rittner and John K. Roth. -- 1st ed.
　　p. cm.
　Includes bibliographical references and index.
　Summary: "Its chapters by experts in genocide studies, this book, which includes key documents and discussion questions, concentrates on diverse historic and contemporary atrocities to focus the challenges to male behavior, international law, and political action that arise from the agony of rape used as a weapon of war and genocide"--Provided by publisher.
　ISBN 978-1-55778-898-6 (pbk. : alk. paper) 1. Rape--Political aspects--History. 2. Rape as a weapon of war--History. 3. Sex crimes--Political aspects--History. I. Rittner, Carol, 1943- II. Roth, John K.
　HV6558.R37 2012
　364.15'32--dc23
　　　　　　　　　　　　　2012012878

The paper used in this publication meets the minimum requirements of American National Standard for Information Sciences— Permanence of Paper for Printed Library Materials, ANSIZ39.48-1984.

Manufactured in the United States of America
10 9 8 7 6 5 4 3 2 1

For current information about all releases from Paragon House, visit the website at http://www.ParagonHouse.com

To

Myrna Goldenberg

You hear me speak. But do you hear me feel?
—*Gertrud Kolmar, "The Woman Poet"*

It has probably become more dangerous to be a woman than a soldier in armed conflict.

—*Major-General Patrick Cammaert, former commander of United Nations peacekeeping forces in the eastern Democratic Republic of Congo*

Contents

INTRODUCTION

One of Many

Carol Rittner and John K. Roth

> I shared my testimony hoping that this book will spread my
> message farther than I could ever do myself. The international
> community should help us to rebuild our hopes and dreams.
> —*Jeanette Uwimana*

Rape: Weapon of War and Genocide is about experiences and predicaments that are as important and fundamental as they are violent, heartrending, and discouraging. Therefore, this book's contributors thank you for opening its pages. Courage and fortitude will be needed to cope with the darkness they contain, but the hope is that the effort will be worthwhile because it will inspire solidarity with women such as Jeanette Uwimana, who is one of many.

Uwimana's life is distinctive, her story deeply personal, but as a woman who has experienced rape as a weapon of war and genocide, she has many sisters. Before genocide engulfed her native Rwanda in the spring of 1994, this Tutsi woman, born on April 2, 1972, lived in Butare and then in Kigali, her country's capital. She married her husband, Diogene, on November 28, 1990. Soon they had a daughter and, three years later, a son. As 1994 began, says Uwimana, "we had a very good life."[1] A few months later, her life changed devastatingly and forever.

On the night of April 6, 1994, Rwanda's President Juvénal Habyarimana (b. 1937) was killed when unknown assailants shot down his plane as it approached Kigali.[2] That event triggered attacks against Rwanda's Tutsi minority by extremists in the Hutu majority.[3] Rivalry and hostility between Tutsis and Hutus had a long and complicated history, but these ethnic groups also lived side-by-side. Friendships and marriages that brought them even closer together were not unusual. Unfortunately, such relationships were insufficient to prevent a Hutu-led genocide during a 100-day period from April 6 to July 16, 1994. It took the lives of an estimated 800,000 to 1,000,000 Tutsis and moderate Hutus. Uwimana's husband and daughter were among the murdered.

During the genocide, between 250,000 and 500,000 women and girls, mostly Tutsi, were raped. In Uwimana's case, being one of many meant that she was not raped once but multiple times and often by gangs of Hutu men. "During this period," she says, "I felt like I was no longer a human being, and I wanted to kill myself. But I couldn't do it, since I still had my son to care for."[4] More than 67 percent of the women and girls raped during the Rwandan genocide were infected with HIV and AIDS as a result.[5] Not only was Uwimana one of many who became HIV-positive but also her son, who survived the genocide, and at least one of the three children born to her after she remarried, tested the same way. When her second husband—he, too, was HIV-positive—died in November 2005, Uwimana became, for the second time, one of the 50,000 widows of the genocide.

"I experience a lot of trauma all year long," Uwimana says, "especially during the annual mourning period for the genocide in April each year. My stomach, my head and my private parts ache a lot. Sometimes my private parts start bleeding without a reason. I live in constant fear, wondering who will take care of my children if I die." When she sums up her testimony by adding that "my life is hard," her understatement speaks volumes.

Jeanette Uwimana is one of many, but she is also one of not-so-many because she survived genocidal rape and decided to share her story. She hoped that by including her testimony in a book, her message will spread "farther than I could ever do myself." Her dream is that the people who read about her, who receive her testimony, will learn about what happened in Rwanda and be moved not only to "rebuild . . . hopes and dreams" when such atrocities take place but also to prevent and resist such disasters before they do their worst.

Invitations, Messages, and Goals

In preparing for this work, we sent an invitation to the writers who have contributed to the book you are presently reading. Our message went to authors who have expertise in genocide studies and gender issues as well as detailed knowledge of specific times, places, and circumstances where rape has been a weapon of war and genocide. It said: We invite you to participate in a book project that is under way. We hope very much that the project will interest you and that you will accept the invitation to work with us. We are under contract with Paragon House to produce a volume dealing with rape as a weapon of war and genocide. We envision a wide readership for the book, but we also hope that it will find a home in college and university courses in a variety of fields: history, ethics, gender studies, Holocaust and genocide studies, to name a few.

The book, we went on to say, would contain chapters that combine documents and essays. Thus, each invited contributor was asked to identify a brief document that would be reproduced in the book—a relevant survivor testimony, for example, an excerpt from an important United Nations document, or part of a genocide-related trial transcript. The selected documents, we urged, should be especially important for students and others who may come to this book without extensive prior knowledge about its topics but with a desire to expand their awareness of and engagement with them. To advance those aims, the contributors were asked to integrate the selected documents with essays that addressed these questions:

- What is important and moving about the document you selected?

- From your point of view, what do you most want your readers to know and to grapple with as far as the document and the book's topic, rape as a weapon of war and genocide, are concerned?

Thanks to the generosity of President Michael A. MacDowell of Misericordia University (Dallas, Pennsylvania) and Dean Jan Colijn of The Richard Stockton College of New Jersey, who both kindly provided necessary funds, the authors accepting our invitation traveled to Philadelphia in early March 2010 and participated in a seminar that further focused the book project. When the seminar concluded, the plan was to complete the manuscript about six months later, but new developments in the contributors' research as well as events that kept unfolding, particularly in the Democratic Republic of Congo, created unavoidable delays. At Paragon House, our steadfast editors Gordon L. Anderson and Rosemary Yokoi worried that the delays might make the project out-of-date. Unfortunately, when rape as a weapon of war and genocide is the topic, research, reflection, and calls to action about that catastrophe are scarcely ever out of date, at least in the sense that this devastating scourge shows no signs of ceasing any time soon, and it remains much more than a topic of merely historical interest. Rape continues to be a weapon of war and genocide, but the book *Rape: Weapon of War and Genocide* seeks to resist that reality. Depending on how its readers respond, the book, we hope, may spread its message farther than any one of its authors could do alone.

The Book's Focus and Scope

As the chapters in this book reveal and explain, rape consists of violent acts as varied as they are heinous and destructive. No definition of terms can state adequately what constitutes rape as a weapon of war and genocide. Nevertheless, it is important at the outset to indicate how the key terms in the book's title are intended to work. First, then, consider that this book primarily concentrates on violent armed conflicts—wars between or within nations—that have been or continue to be genocidal.

Debates swirl about the best ways to define *genocide*, but widespread agreement exists that the United Nations 1948 Convention on the Prevention and Punishment of the Crime of Genocide established a fundamental understanding: namely, that *genocide* at least refers to acts—including but not restricted to outright killing—that are "committed with intent to destroy, in whole or in part, a national, ethnical, racial or religious group, as such."[6] It is no accident that the Genocide Convention was enacted in the wake of World War II. Genocide does not take place in a nonviolent vacuum; arguably, war is a necessary though not sufficient condition for it. War is not inevitably genocidal, but when genocide happens, war typically triggers it and becomes the context and even the justification for it. In some circumstances—Rwanda comes to mind—war and genocide are scarcely separable, but each case has its particularities, and no single size fits all as far as the relationships between war and genocide are concerned.

Likewise, no single size fits all as far as the relationships between rape and war are concerned or, more specifically, those between rape and genocide. This book underscores that rape, in varied ways, has long been a weapon in warfare. Rape has also accompanied genocide, which existed long before the Jewish jurist Raphael Lemkin (1900-1959) coined the term *genocide* while the Holocaust, Nazi Germany's genocide against the Jewish people, raged during World War II. But especially in the second half of the twentieth century and continuing now in the twenty-first century, *rape-as-policy*—intentional and systematic uses of rape as a weapon of war and genocide—has loomed larger and larger. This book traces that gruesome development in its multifaceted horrors and devastations.

One important aspect of that development—a resistant response to it—has been the criminalization of rape as an act that can be genocidal. That step was far too long in coming because it can fairly easily be seen that rape may be an action intentionally used to "destroy, in whole or in part, a national, ethnical, racial or religious group, as such," especially when one recalls that the United Nations definition of genocidal acts is not restricted to direct or outright killing. Of course, rape can be tantamount to murder, for one can be raped to death, and various forms of social or psychological if not physical, death are often reported by the victims of genocidal rape. But raping and killing are not identical, at least not in every way. For that reason, it is highly significant that international law, late in the day though the decision may have been, now accepts that rape can indeed be a genocidal weapon. Rape can be such a weapon because genocidal acts include, in the words of the Genocide Convention, those that intend (a) to cause "serious bodily or mental harm to members of the group," (b) to inflict on the group "conditions of life calculated to bring about its physical destruction in whole or in part," (c) to impose "measures intended to prevent births within the group," or (d) to result in "forcibly transferring children of the group to another group." Rape, as we shall see in much more detail, can be a genocidal weapon in all of those ways.

The tipping point for international law came in the 1996-1998 case brought by the International Criminal Tribunal for Rwanda (ICTR) against Jean-Paul Akayesu (b. 1953), the Hutu mayor of the Taba commune in Gitarama prefecture. In the judgment against Akayesu, who was found guilty of committing genocide—and using rape to do so—rape for the first time was defined in international law, as follows: "The Chamber defines rape as a physical invasion of a sexual nature, committed on a person under circumstances which are coercive. Sexual violence which includes rape, is considered to be any act of a sexual nature which is committed on a person under circumstances which are coercive." In addition, the ICTR found that rape and sexual violence "constitute genocide in the same way as any other act as long as they were committed with the specific intent to destroy, in whole or in part, a particular group, targeted as such."[7] While the contributors to this book develop variations on themes related to the ICTR's findings in the Akayesu case, the authors' analyses are governed by understandings of rape, including the ways in which rape can be genocidal, that incorporate the ICTR's outlook.[8]

Contending with Loss of Trust in the World

No book could adequately cover all of the circumstances in the twentieth and twenty-first centuries where rape-as-policy has existed and where rape has been a weapon of war and genocide. That fact is supported by the events noted in the substantial chronology that follows this introduction. No chronology, however, can grasp the enormous magnitude of genocidal rape's atrocities. In a different way, the Jewish philosopher Jean Améry (1912-1978), who survived the Holocaust but eventually took his own life, offers a perspective that can help to reveal what is so fundamentally crushed and ruined when rape-as-policy is embedded in war and genocide.

Prior to his deportation to Auschwitz, Améry was interrogated and tortured in Belgium by his German captors. Torture left marks that went deep down. Likening its first blows to "rape, a sexual act without the consent of one of the two partners," Améry depicted how "he is on me and thereby destroys me," not necessarily by killing but definitely by demolishing what Améry called "trust in the world."[9] Significantly, and with similar effects in mind, the ICTR likened rape to torture: "Like torture, rape is used for such purposes as intimidation, degradation, humiliation, discrimination, punishment, control or destruction of a person. Like torture, rape is a violation of personal dignity, and rape in fact constitutes torture when inflicted by or at the instigation of or with the consent or acquiescence of a public official or other person acting in an official capacity."[10]

Améry noted that "trust in the world" is grounded in the conviction that "by reason of written or unwritten social contracts the other person will spare me—more precisely stated, that he will respect my physical, and with it also my metaphysical being." Trust in the world, he affirmed, is also rooted in "the expectation of help, the certainty of help, [which] is indeed one of the fundamental experiences of human beings." Améry added his belief that "the boundaries of my body are also the boundaries of my self. My skin surface shields me against the external world. If I am to have trust, I must feel on it only what I *want* to feel." Thus, the first blows of torture and rape are likely to dash those precious convictions and expectations. Once such violence strikes, as Améry put it, "a part of our life ends and it can never again be revived."[11]

Rape, especially rape-as-policy and in its genocidal forms, involves gender, sex, and violence but so much more because its wreckage extends beyond the meaning of such terms and the reach of those realities. As the ICTR stated, "the crime of rape cannot be captured in a mechanical description of objects and body parts." In Rwanda, the ICTR went on to say, rape's genocidal forms produced "physical and psychological destruction of Tutsi women, their families and their communities. Sexual violence was an integral part of the process of destruction, specifically targeting Tutsi women and specifically contributing to their destruction and to the destruction of the Tutsi group as a whole." Sadly, *Tutsi* is but one of many group names that could fit the ICTR's description of the disastrous toll that is taken by rape-as-policy and whenever rape becomes a weapon of war and genocide.

The Chapters That Follow

Using the question "Are women human?" as its point of departure, Carol Rittner's opening chapter provides not only a compact overview of major catastrophes unleashed in the twentieth and twenty-first centuries by rape as a weapon of war and genocide but also a challenging reflection on the contradiction and collision between the response, "Of course, women are human" and the stubborn persistence of and frequent indifference to genocidal rape. Rittner's orienting document comes from an essay by the feminist philosopher Catharine MacKinnon. As Rittner contextualizes that document, she sets a tone found repeatedly in this book by pressing her readers to take steps against the injustice that creates the contradiction noted above and the carnage of the collision that takes place when the affirmation, "Of course, women are human," is trampled by rape-as-policy.

In contrasting but complementary ways, the Holocaust scholars Eva Fogelman and Dagmar Herzog direct attention to issues about rape and other forms of sexual violence during the Nazi genocide against the Jews. Using survivor testimony as well as Holocaust scholarship to focus her reflections, Fogelman shows that while rape was not intentionally and systematically used as a weapon of genocide by the Nazis, the rape of Jewish women at the hands of German men—and others, too—was more widespread than interpreters of the Holocaust used to think. Also relying on survivor testimony, Herzog concentrates on the punishment inflicted on male homosexuals in German concentration camps. Frequently that punishment took forms that only the word *rape* could denote. Herzog's chapter is a reminder that while women and girls typically are the targets when rape is a weapon of war and genocide, men and boys also can have genocidal sexual abuse inflicted upon them.

Christina Morus highlights testimony from Selma, a Bosniak woman, to focus attention on the ethnic cleansing and genocide that took place in the former Yugoslavia between 1992 and 1995. As the nationalistic ambitions of Serbian, Croatian, and Bosnian Muslim (Bosniak) ethnic groups intensified and collided, rape-as-policy—intentional and systematic uses of rape as a weapon of war and genocide—became one of the hallmarks of those particularly vicious conflicts. Serbs were not alone in using rape as a weapon of ethnic cleansing and genocide, but reliable research indicates that Serb forces raped between 20,000 and 50,000 women and girls, the majority of whom were of Bosniak ethnicity. Morus's account, however, does not dwell entirely on the devastation. She also concentrates on the resilience of women who were sexually abused during war in the former Yugoslavia, encouraging her readers to consider how to stand in solidarity with them.

Tazreena Sajjad keeps the focus on the former Yugoslavia by using excerpts from a trial transcript as her orienting document. We learn that Witness 50, as she is identified in the proceedings of the International Criminal Tribunal for the Former Yugoslavia (ICTY), is a Bosniak woman who, in Sajjad's words, was "raped so often that she lost count of how many times and how many men." At least one of her assailants was tried and convicted by the ICTY. What interests Sajjad even more, however, are questions about the possibility of justice in the wake of genocidal rape, the ability of international tribunals to deliver justice, and the jeopardy faced by abused women when they testify in court. These concerns lead Sajjad to consider Rwanda as well as the former Yugoslavia as she wrestles with "the culture of impunity" that must be overturned to curb if not eliminate rape as a weapon of war and genocide.

Well known for his studies about the perpetrators of mass murder, James Waller features testimony by Pascasie Mukasakindi, one of many Tutsi women raped during the Rwandan genocide. Taking Mukasakindi's testimony as his point of departure, Waller develops what he calls "a psychological analysis of rape as a tool of 'othering' in genocide." His analysis emphasizes that a process of "othering," which appears in one way or another wherever rape becomes genocidal, provides a context in which massive and systematic sexual abuse becomes a likely outcome of and driving force in warring conflicts. Waller's analysis is particularly helpful because it provides early warning signals about conditions that could generate rape-as-policy if they are left unchecked.

Jessica Hubbard's chapter also uses testimony from sexually abused Tutsi women. The testimonies become Hubbard's points of departure for probing "crucial issues about how, or even whether, justice can be obtained in the aftermath of genocidal rape." Concentrating on the ICTR's case against Jean-Paul Akayesu, which produced the world's first conviction for the defined crime of genocide after trial before an international tribunal, Hubbard details the dilemmas that continue to affect the women who survived genocidal rape in Rwanda. Their testimony is vital if "the culture of impunity" identified by Sajjed is to be broken and if steps are to be taken to check the process of "othering" identified by Waller. Hubbard argues not only that support for those women must be maximized but also that such support depends considerably on international and individual resistance in circumstances that are likely to make rape a weapon of war and genocide.

By shifting the focus to Guatemala, Roselyn Costantino suggests that the use of rape as a weapon of war and genocide ranges far and wide around the world. Using the testimony of Guatemalan women as her points of departure, Costantino shows the widespread nature of sexual abuse in Guatemalan civil conflict that has been aided and abetted by international interests, including those of American economics and politics. She points out that genocide and *femicide*, the destruction—often systematic—of women as women, are often inseparable, for the destruction of a group, in whole or in part, depends on destroying women and girls as real or potential mothers. Like Morus, Costantino calls attention to the resilience of women who have survived genocidal rape. As she pays tribute to them, Costantino asks us, her readers, to consider what we can do to stand with those women, and then she helpfully offers a list of suggestions, each one of them within our reach, if we have the will to act.

Lee Ann De Reus describes herself as "an activist scholar," stating that "my research and advocacy are reciprocally motivated by a quest for social justice." Her research and advocacy keep her in close contact with the Democratic Republic of Congo (DRC) and, in particular, with Panzi Hospital in Bukavu, South Kivu province, where she has interviewed and worked with Congolese women who are coping with the aftereffects of rape that has taken place in the midst of war that swirls around control of valuable "conflict minerals": tantalum, tin, tungsten, and gold. Often mined by exploited children, these elements are especially needed for contemporary technology and electronics. In addition to her perceptive overview of the current situation in the DRC, where the typical person makes about $280 annually and dies at the age of 48, De Reus, like Costantino, concludes her chapter with concrete suggestions for action that can make a positive difference for the DRC and specifically for its women and girls.

Julie Kuhlken's chapter is called "Weapon of Sadness," an apt way to identify rape as a weapon of war and genocide. The sadness and grief spread wide by such atrocity were part of what led to a 2007 report by the United Nations' Secretary-General Ban Ki-moon, which deals with the protection of civilians in armed conflict. Kuhlken uses excerpts from that document—especially portions that address sexual violence—to focus her chapter. One of those excerpts contains a sad observation about our world: "In no other area is our collective failure to ensure effective protection for civilians more apparent—and by its very nature more shameful—than in terms of the masses of women and girls, but also boys and men, whose lives are destroyed each year by sexual violence perpetrated in conflict." Detailing how rape as a weapon of war and genocide attacks simultaneously the economic and moral basis of a community, Kuhlken argues that sidelining the "weapon of sadness" is unlikely to take place without ongoing social action to increase recognition of the value of women and their economic activities.

The process of "othering" identified by James Waller often involves media—radio, television, film, and now even "social networking"—that can spread propaganda, cultivate negative stereotypes, and incite people to attack "others" who are deemed threatening. Paul Bartrop realizes the importance of media as far as rape as a weapon of war and genocide is concerned, but his chapter focuses on ways in which film might be used to combat such atrocity. While rape scenes in films about war and genocide have been relatively rare, Bartrop catalogs and analyzes a number of significant cinematic responses to rape as weapon of war and genocide. His account supports the chapter's conclusion that the work of daring filmmakers, actors, and actresses may make an invaluable ethical and political contribution, one that perhaps can be made in no other way.

Carl Wilkens, the only American to remain in Rwanda throughout the 1994 genocide, devotes his life to promote education about and resistance to human rights abuses and genocide in particular. His chapter, "The Power of Presence," begins with a letter Wilkens received from a young woman named Gillian after he visited her school. She sincerely thanks Wilkens for "flying across the country to tell us what we were all supposed to learn in kindergarten but never really figured out—people are decent—start small—do what you think is right—what you think is kind." Wilkens helps us to see the wisdom in Gillian's summation, for the use of rape as a weapon of war and genocide is the very antithesis of what we ought to learn but have never really figured out. Nevertheless, the power of *our* presence, contends Wilkens, is not negligible. It could be enough to make for good all the difference in the world.

John Roth's closing chapter echoes Wilkens by urging attention to a fragile but emerging norm called the Responsibility to Protect. R2P, as it is sometimes called, became more than an idealistic concept in September 2005, when heads of state and government agreed to paragraphs 138 and 139 in the Outcome Document of the United Nations World Summit. Those paragraphs underscore not only that each individual state has the primary responsibility to protect its populations from genocide, war crimes, crimes against humanity, and ethnic cleansing but also that international responsibility should ensure that the world's populations are protected from those atrocities, which certainly include uses of rape as a weapon of war and genocide. A key issue, however, is how to motivate support for this objective. Roth concludes the book by calling attention to voices among the dead as well as the living that might help to move us in that direction.

Jeanette Uwimana, the raped Tutsi woman whose words began this introduction, is one of many. In our own ways, that description fits us all. The world's vast population, now seven billion and growing, drives home how large "many" can be. Being among so many can make "one" seem utterly insignificant, especially when war and genocide, exacerbated by torture and rape, wreak their havoc so widely and persistently as to destroy trust in the world. In spite of those realities, Jeanette Uwimana, one of many, believes that her testimony could make a difference, could help perhaps to rebuild hopes and dreams. Each and all, the contributors to this book ask you, please, to share her conviction, to let it grow, as much as you are able, as you work your way through the chapters that follow.

Notes

1. Jeanette Uwimana's testimony can be found in *The Men Who Killed Me: Rwandan Survivors of Sexual Violence*, ed. Anne-Marie Brouwer and Sandra Ka Hon Chu (Vancouver, Canada: Douglas & McIntyre, 2009), 49-56. See 51 for the quotation. This introduction's epigraph appears on 56.

2. Since the time of the assassination, disputes have raged regarding whether Habyarimana's plane was downed by Hutus or Tutsis. With the issuing of a January 2012 report from an expert investigation headed by the French judges Marc Trévedic and Nathalie Poux, the most reliable evidence indicates that the responsibility belongs to as yet unnamed Hutu extremists. Linda Melvern, a leading scholar of the Rwandan genocide, has provided a good overview of the controversy in her article, "Rwanda: At Last We Know the Truth," which appeared in *The Guardian* (January 10, 2012) and is available at: http://www.guardian.co.uk/commentisfree/2012/jan/10/rwanda-at-last-we-know-truth?INTCMP=SRCH. Accessed January 17, 2012.

3. *The Men Who Killed Me* contains a helpful, compact overview of the context and details of the Rwandan genocide, the sexual violence that pervaded it, and comparative data regarding other conflict situations in the twentieth and twenty-first centuries where sexual violence has been widespread. See 11-26.

4. Ibid., 54.

5. For documentation of these data, see the website for the Survivors Fund (SURF), which provides support for survivors of the Rwanda genocide, who number between 300,000–400,000. Available at: http://survivors-fund.org.uk/resources/rwandan-history/statistics/. Accessed December 2, 2011.

6. The full text of the United Nations Convention on the Prevention and Punishment of the Crime of Genocide is available at: http://www.hrweb.org/legal/genocide.html. Accessed December 3, 2011.

7. See Prosecutor v. Akayesu, Judgment (paragraphs 598 and 731), International Criminal Tribunal for Rwanda, Case No. ICTR-96-4-T (1998). The entire Judgment is available at: http://www.unictr.org/Portals/0/Case%5CEnglish%5CAkayesu%5Cjudgement%5Cakay001.pdf. Accessed December 2, 2011.

8. Subsequent to the Akayesu case, definitions of rape pertaining to crimes against humanity and genocide have been elaborated and amplified. In particular, some prosecutions carried out after the Akayesu case by the International Criminal Tribunal for the former Yugoslavia, went beyond the ICTR in their

detailed attention to the ways in which sexual penetration, coercion, and lack of consent should be understood. Helpful discussion of these developments can be found in Patricia Viseur Sellars's article, "Rape," in *Genocide and Crimes Against Humanity*, ed. Dinah L. Shelton (Farmington Hills, MI: Gale Cengage, 2005). Available at: http://www.enotes.com/rape-reference/rape. Accessed December 11, 2011. Among other things, this article describes how rape of men and boys is being interpreted as a crime against humanity. See also "Rape May Be an Act of Genocide in International Law," which is available at: http://clg.portalxm.com/library/keytext.cfm?keytext_id=201. Accessed December 11, 2011. This site is provided by the Center on Law & Globalization. The article includes links to other texts that are instructive.

9.   Jean Améry, *At the Mind's Limits: Contemplations by a Survivor on Auschwitz and Its Realities*, trans. Sidney Rosenfeld and Stella P. Rosenfeld (Bloomington, IN: Indiana University Press, 1980), 28.

10. See Prosecutor v. Akayesu, Judgment (paragraph 597), International Criminal Tribunal for Rwanda, Case No. ICTR-96-4-T (1998). For access information regarding this document, see note 7 above.

11. Améry, *At the Mind's Limits*, 28-29.

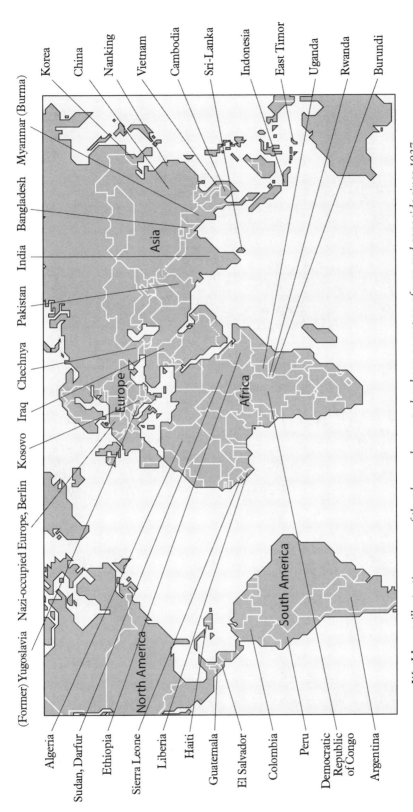

(Former) Yugoslavia Nazi-occupied Europe, Berlin Kosovo Iraq Chechnya Pakistan India Bangladesh Myanmar (Burma)

Korea China Nanking Vietnam Cambodia Sri-Lanka Indonesia East Timor Uganda Rwanda Burundi

Algeria Sudan, Darfur Ethiopia Sierra Leone Liberia Haiti Guatemala El Salvador Colombia Peru Democratic Republic of Congo Argentina

Europe Asia Africa North America South America

World map illustrating many of the places where rape has been a weapon of war and genocide since 1937. Although names and boundaries may have changed, the map refers to the locations as they were typically known when the atrocities took place.

CHRONOLOGY, 1937-2011

Carol Rittner and John K. Roth

Where does one begin a chronology highlighting events and documents related to armed conflict and sexual violence? Any century could be the starting point because there has never been a time when women and girls, and sometimes men and boys as well, were safe from sexual violence during war and genocide. But, because this book primarily focuses on rape as a weapon of war and genocide from the mid-1930s to the time of its publication early in the second decade of the twenty-first century, the chronology begins with events that took place shortly before the outbreak of World War II, a catastrophe that affected women and men alike in unspeakable ways. The chronology, incomplete as it may be, tries to provide readers with a broad context for the essays that follow. We thank Deirdre Mullan, RSM, for her assistance, especially in identifying relevant United Nations documents.

1937–1938

December 1937–
January 1938   During the Sino-Japanese war (1937-1945), the Imperial Japanese Army overruns Nanking, China's capital city. For seven weeks (December 1937-January 1938), Japanese soldiers sack the city, execute thousands of soldiers, slaughter and rape tens of thousands of civilians, all in contravention of the rules of war. This incident becomes known as "the Rape of Nanking." One bizarre result is that the Imperial Japanese military institutes a system of so-called "comfort houses"–brothels–where kidnapped women and girls from throughout the Japanese-conquered Asia-Pacific are forced into sexual slavery for the pleasure of Japanese military officers and

enlisted men. The first "comfort house" is opened near Nanking in 1938.

1938

November 9–10   Following the assassination of a minor German diplomat in Paris by a young Jewish man, the *Kristallnacht* pogrom—instigated by Nazi minister of propaganda, Josef Goebbels (1897–1945)—erupts in Germany and Austria. Jewish establishments are looted and burned; 30,000 Jewish men are interned in concentration camps. The first major reports of Nazi mob rape directed against Jewish women occurred during *Kristallnacht*.

1939

September 1   Nazi Germany invades Poland; two days later, Britain and France declare war on Germany; World War II begins. During World War II, the Nazis marched into Polish and Russian villages, looted homes, especially Jewish homes, and singled out Jewish women and girls for rape, often in front of their parents, spouses, and siblings. During World War II and the Holocaust, thousands of Jewish and non-Jewish women and girls—in hiding, ghettos, prisons, brothels, concentration camps, and elsewhere— were sexually abused by German soldiers, guards, and SS members and by Germany's allies and collaborators as well as by fellow prisoners.

1945

May 8   Nazi Germany surrenders; World War II ends in Europe. Between March and November, 1945, as the war in Europe draws to a close, Nazi Germany surrenders, and the Allies' occupy Germany, approximately 1.9 million cases of rape are perpetrated on women and girls in the territories of the devastated Third Reich by soldiers of the Allied forces, primarily by soldiers of the Red Army, but also by American and French troops in considerable numbers. Between April 24 and May 3, in and around Berlin, an estimated 100,000 women are raped.

June 26   At a meeting in San Francisco, representatives of 44 countries sign the Charter establishing the United Nations (UN). The charter comes into force on October 24.

August 6   An American B-29 airplane drops an atom bomb on Hiroshima, Japan. Between 70,000 and 80,000 people are killed; an additional 70,000 are injured.

August 9   An American B-29 airplane drops a second atom bomb, this time on Nagasaki, Japan, killing between 35,000 and 40,000 people.

September 2   Japan surrenders; World War II ends.

November 20   The Nuremberg War Crimes Trials begin. Suspects are charged with and tried for crimes against peace, crimes against humanity, and war crimes. At Nuremberg, sexual forms of torture, including rape, are documented but not prosecuted as independent crimes. Rape arises only as a peripheral issue.

1946

January 10   The UN General Assembly meets for the first time in London.

January 17   The UN Security Council holds its first meeting.

May 3   The International Military Tribunal for the Far East (aka

Tokyo War Crimes Tribunal) convenes in Tokyo to prosecute Class A war criminals. They are charged with and tried for crimes against peace, crimes against humanity, and war crimes. Based partly on evidence of mass rapes that occurred under their authority, the Tokyo Tribunal convicts several Japanese military and political leaders. It is the first time rape is specifically identified as a war crime and commanders held responsible for rapes committed by soldiers under their command.

June 21   The UN establishes the Commission on the Status of Women, a mechanism to promote, report on, and monitor issues relating to the political, economic, civil, social and educational rights of women.

1948

March   The only military tribunal convened to investigate the sexual abuse of "comfort women" by Japanese soldiers is convened in Batavia (Jakarta), the Indonesian capital. The tribunal convicts several Japanese military officers in cases involving 35 Dutch women.

December 9   The UN General Assembly adopts the Convention on the Prevention and Punishment of the Crime of Genocide.

December 10   The UN General Assembly adopts the Universal Declaration of Human Rights.

1949

August 12   Written in response to the atrocities committed during World War II, the Geneva Conventions are adopted. The Conventions extend protection to women civilians, stating that they must be "especially protected against any attack on their honor, in particular against rape, enforced prostitution, or any form of indecent assault." Rape, however, is not listed as a "grave breach," even though the Fourth Convention for the Protection of Civilian Persons (Article 27) views rape, enforced prostitution, and all forms of indecent assault as crimes under national and international rules of war.

1950–1953   On the Korean peninsula, a bloody war is fought between North and South Korea. The UN, with the United States as the principal participant, comes to the aid of South Korea; the People's Republic of China comes to the aid of North Korea.

1952

December 20   The UN General Assembly adopts the Convention on the Political Rights of Women.

1954–1962   French-Algerian war, a conflict during which military authorities considered rape a banal form of torture, useful for making prisoners (male or female) talk, or to terrorize them.

1954–1975   Second Indo-China war (aka Vietnam war), which grew out of a long-standing conflict between France and Vietnam. In late 1961, President John Kennedy sends military advisors, which began America's long involvement in Vietnam. The last American combat soldier left in March 1973. Both Vietnamese and American soldiers are guilty of rape, but few are prosecuted for such crimes. Unofficially, but with full knowledge of military commanders, there are "bang bang parlors" in and around military camps. Thousands of Amerasian children are left behind by American troops when the U.S. leaves Vietnam.

1956   Sudan, geographically Africa's largest country, declares its independence from Egypt and Great Britain. Sudan has experienced civil war with only a ten-year pause since independence in 1956. More than 2 million people have been killed and twice that many displaced in the long-running war between successive governments of the north and peoples of the south.

1960–1996   In Guatemala, during a protracted civil war, more than 200,000 people lose their lives; most are Maya civilians. A UN-sponsored truth commission, The Commission for Historical Clarification (CEH), created after the war ended in 1996, documented unspeakable atrocities: murder, mutilation, rape, and torture, and held the Guatemalan state responsible for acts of genocide against Maya communities. In one incident in 1982, soldiers killed more than 160 civilians in the village of Las Dos Erres and for three days straight raped the young women of the village.

1964–present According to the UN Human Rights Council, the South American country of Colombia "has endured decades of armed conflict and gross human rights violations that have caused a protracted humanitarian crisis." The UN Special Rapporteur on violence against women noted, "Sexual violence by armed groups has become a common practice." A 2010 survey of 407 municipalities in Columbia, in which there is an active presence of armed actors, found that between 2001 and 2009, 95,000 women have been raped.

October 1965–
March 1966   In Indonesia, conservative forces, including the army and Muslim militias, kill at least 100,000 people as part of a sustained campaign against left-wing forces. An overwhelming number of the victims are members of

the Indonesian Communist Party (PKI), or those suspected of supporting Communists. Members of the
Communist-aligned women's organization, *Gerwani*, are
abused, raped and murdered.

1968

March 16   In an infamous incident during the Vietnam War,
                Company C, 1ˢᵗ Battalion, 20ᵗʰ Infantry of the U.S. Army
                conducted a search and destroy mission on the South
                Vietnamese village of Son My, which included the sub-
                village of My Lai. U.S. soldiers murdered and raped vil-
                lagers, destroying everything they found there. The exact
                number of rapes committed is unknown (somewhere
                between 175-400 women, children, and elderly villagers
                were killed); however, multiple rapes occurred, includ-
                ing vaginal, anal, oral, and gang rape.

1971

March 25   The government of Pakistan initiates a genocidal cam-
                paign against Bengalis in the province of East Pakistan,
                ostensibly to suppress a Bengali nationalist movement.
                During a war lasting months, Pakistani troops kill 1-3
                million people and rape an estimated 250,000 girls and
                women.

December 4   India intervenes in the conflict in East Pakistan on the
                side of Bengali guerrillas and, after a two-week war,
                forces Pakistan to surrender. Shortly thereafter, East
                Pakistan is officially recognized as Bangladesh.

1971–1973   The new government of Bangladesh responds in various
                ways to the victims of sexual violence during the war
                for independence in East Pakistan, including declar-
                ing rape victims *birangonas* (war heroines), ostensibly

to acknowledge their "sacrifice" for the country and to facilitate their reintegration into society. By 1973, however, the issue is relegated to oblivion in government and journalistic consciousness, replaced by an overwhelming silence on the subject.

1971–1979   In Uganda, Idi Amin (1925-2003) overthrows Milton Obote (1925-2005) in a *coup*. He and his government are responsible for the deaths of an estimated 300,000 of their own people. During the Amin years, there are reports of rapes of women, beheadings of men, women, and children, and cannibalism.

1974

August 4   Based largely on the recommendations of the UN Commission on the Status of Women, the UN General Assembly declares 1975 International Women's Year. The UN declares the period between 1976 and 1985 the UN Decade for Women.

June 19-July 2 The first world conference on the status of women is convened in Mexico City to coincide with the 1975 International Women's Year. Of the 133 UN member state delegations gathered there, 113 are headed by women.

1975–1979   The war in Vietnam spills over into Cambodia. Pol Pot (1925-1998) and his Khmer Rouge forces overthrow the American-backed Lon Nol (1913-1985) government in Cambodia. The Khmer Rouge massacre, work, and starve to death an estimated 1.5 million of their own Cambodian people. The Khmer Rouge is dislodged only after Vietnam's army invades Cambodia.

1975–1999   Widespread violence against women erupts in Timor-Leste (commonly known as East Timor), including cases of sexual slavery, sexual violence as a means of intimidation, and sexual violence as a result of the climate of impunity created by the Indonesian security forces operating in the island.

1976–1983   Years of the "Dirty War" (*Guerra Sucia*) in Argentina, when a vicious military dictatorship rules the country and perpetrates state-sponsored violence. Victims include several thousand left-wing activists, including trade unionists, students, journalists, Marxists, Peronist guerrillas, and alleged communist sympathizers, either proved or suspected. The crimes committed by the military junta include taking hundreds of babies from their biological mothers and giving them to military officers and their families to raise.

1976

December   The United Nations Development Fund for Women (UNIFEM) is established to provide financial and technical assistance to innovative programs and strategies that promote women's human rights.

1977

June 8   Additional Protocols I and II are added to the Geneva Conventions. These protocols further extend legal protection against sexual violence, especially for female civilians and combatants, including sexual violence in civil conflicts. The protocols give attention to "outrages upon personal dignity, in particular humiliating and degrading treatment, rape, enforced prostitution and any form of indecent assault."

1979

December 18   The UN General Assembly adopts the Convention on the Elimination of all Forms of Discrimination Against Women. As an international treaty, the Convention contains two major provisions: (1) It establishes an international Bill of Rights for Women and specifies a set of actions to be undertaken by the nations of the world to ensure that these rights are enjoyed. (2) It mandates the establishment of the Committee on the Elimination of Discrimination Against Women (CEDAW), which is charged with ensuring that the provisions of the Convention are observed.

1980–1988   Iran–Iraq war; casualty figures are uncertain, but reliable estimates suggest more than 1.5 million casualties; an estimated 1 million are dead.

1980s–1990s   Rape-as-policy is employed in multiple ways–including as a weapon of terror, war, ethnic cleansing, and genocide in numerous places: Liberia, Uganda, Ethiopia, Rwanda, Myanmar (Burma), and the former Yugoslavia. In Uganda, between 1980 and 1986, 70 percent of women in the Luwero District report being raped by soldiers, with a large portion of them indicating that they were gang-raped by as many as ten soldiers in a single episode. In Peru, according to Human Rights Watch, the Peruvian military ordered mass rapes of civilians. According to numerous human rights organizations, sexual violence also occurred during conflicts in El Salvador and Columbia.

1980–1992   During twelve years of civil war in El Salvador, approximately 70,000 people lose their lives in killing and bombing raids waged against civilians throughout the Salvadoran countryside.

1980

July 14-30   The Second UN Global Conference on Women is held in Copenhagen, Denmark.

1981

March   Amnesty International publishes *Women in the Front Line*, the first of its numerous reports outlining the abuse of the human rights of women throughout the world.

December 11   The village of El Mozote in El Salvador comes under attack by the forces of the government, resulting in the massacre of some 900 civilians, one of the worst atrocities in modern Latin American history.

1983–present In Sudan, an estimated 2 million people, mostly civilians, have died as the result of civil war. The present government, which seized power in 1989, has used famine and rape as weapons of war, causing untold suffering and death.

1984

December 10   The UN General Assembly adopts the Convention against Torture and Other Cruel, Inhuman or Degrading Treatment or Punishment.

1985

July 15-26   The Third UN International Conference on Women is held in Nairobi, Kenya, at the end of the UN Decade for Women (1976-1985). The delegates underscore the importance of addressing gender-based violence as an international human rights issue.

1989   General Omar al-Bashir (b. 1944) takes control of Sudan
                      by military coup, which allows the National Islamic
                      Front government to inflame regional tensions. In a
                      struggle for political control of the area, weapons pour
                      into Darfur. Conflicts increase between African farmers
                      and many nomadic Arab tribes.

1989–1994   During conflict in Liberia, many women suffer sexual
                      violence, including rape. A World Health Organization
                      (WHO) study finds 33 percent of Liberian women report
                      rapes. In over half of these assaults, more than one per-
                      petrator is involved, and weapons are used in a great
                      majority (90 percent).

1990

August   Iraq invades and seizes Kuwait but is expelled by US-led,
                      UN coalition forces during the Gulf War of January–
                      February 1991.

1991

November 25   Women's organizations around the world launch the first
                      16 Days of Activism Against Gender Violence campaign.
                      The launch begins on the anniversary of the 1960 assas-
                      sination of the three Mirabal sisters in the Dominican
                      Republic and ends on December 10, International
                      Human Rights Day, the anniversary of the signing of the
                      UN's Universal Declaration of Human Rights.

1991–1999   Focused on a decade-long war in Sierra Leone, a
                      Physicians for Human Rights (PHR) survey published
                      in 2002 reports that some form of war-related sexual
                      violence took place in 13 percent of the nation's house-
                      holds. More than half of the PHR's respondents (53 per-
                      cent) who had "face to face" contact with the rebel forces

experienced some form of sexual violence. The rape victims included 33 percent who were gang raped.

1992   The UN Committee on the Elimination of Discrimination Against Women (CEDAW) moves to rectify the omission of gender-based violence in the 1979 Convention on the Elimination of All Forms of Discrimination Against Women.

March 26   The issue of the *birangonas* (war heroines) receives renewed attention in Bangladesh as a result of the "Peoples' Tribunal." Held in Dhaka, this mock trial of local collaborators features testimonies of victims of sexual violence. Official attention to these assaults, however, is short-lived, with Bangladesh making little effort to address sexual crimes committed against women.

December   Jan Ruff-O'Herne (b. 1923), an Australian national born in Dutch colonial Indonesia and a former "comfort woman" (Japanese sex slave), breaks nearly fifty years of silence about her sexual enslavement by the Japanese military during World War II. She helps to spark an international movement seeking accountability and reparations from the Japanese government for its wartime sexual enslavement of thousands of Asian women and girls.

1992-1995   Yugoslavia disintegrates in a vicious civil war. Backed by Yugoslav President Slobodan Milošević (1941-2006), Serbian military and paramilitary forces expel Muslims from territory under their control, set up concentration camps, rape thousands of women and girls, and kill tens of thousands of civilians. An estimated 20,000 to 60,000 women and girls were subjected to sexual violence in "rape camps." According to an American CIA report, Croats, Muslims, and Serbs all commit atrocities against each other, but those of the Croats and Muslims lacked "the sustained intensity, orchestration, and scale of the Bosnian Serbs' efforts."

1993

January   The UN sends a team, headed by former Polish Prime Minister Tadeusz Mazowiecki (b. 1927), to former Yugoslavia to investigate human rights abuses, including reports of widespread systematic use of rape for the goal of ethnic cleansing, especially in Bosnia-Herzegovina. The UN Human Rights Commission passes a resolution identifying rape as a war crime for the first time and calls for an international tribunal to prosecute these crimes.

January 21   Amnesty International issues a report on abuses against women, *Bosnia-Herzegovina: Rape and Sexual Abuse by Armed Forces*.

May 25   With Resolution 827, the UN Security Council establishes "an international tribunal for the sole purpose of prosecuting persons responsible for serious violations of international humanitarian law committed in the territory of the former Yugoslavia" since 1991. The tribunal's official name is the International Criminal Tribunal for the former Yugoslavia (ICTY). The ICTY Statute explicitly includes rape within its definition of crimes against humanity. The convictions eventually secured at the ICTY entrench sexual violence, rape, and sexual enslavement as international crimes and confirm that they can amount to torture and genocide. As of mid-2011, the ICTY had indicted 161 individuals and 28 of them had been convicted for responsibility in crimes of sexual violence.

August 15   Japan's Prime Minister Morihiro Hosokawa (b. 1938)
                 formally recognizes that the Japanese government kid-
                 napped and confined 70,000-200,000 Korean, Chinese,
                 Filipina, and Indonesian women to serve its military
                 forces as sexual slaves or "comfort women" during World
                 War II.

December 20   At its 48th session, the UN General Assembly adopts
                 the Declaration on the Elimination of Violence Against
                 Women.

1993–1996   In Burundi on October 31, 1993, a group of Tutsi army
                 officers kidnap and kill Burundi's first Hutu president.
                 Over the next three years, mass violence, instigated
                 by both Tutsi and Hutu extremists leaves an estimated
                 200,000 civilians dead.

1994

March   The UN/Organization of American States International
                 Civilian Mission in Haiti condemns the use of rape
                 against Haitian women and implicates armed civil-
                 ian auxiliaries, attachés, members of the Front for the
                 Advancement and Progress of Haiti, and Haiti's armed
                 forces in a political campaign of violence and terror that
                 targeted women.

March 4   The UN Commission on Human Rights adopts
                 Resolution 1994/45 in which it decides to appoint a UN
                 Special Rapporteur on Violence Against Women, includ-
                 ing its causes and consequences.

April 6–July   After a plane carrying the presidents of Rwanda and
                 Burundi is shot down over Kigali the night of April 6,
                 1994, supporters of the extremist Hutu-dominated
                 Rwandan government slaughter an estimated 800,000

Tutsi and moderate Hutu over a period of three months. An estimated 250,000–500,000 women and girls are raped and sexually mutilated by soldiers of the Hutu-dominated Rwandan army and by members of the Hutu *Interahamwe* (militias). The UN Commission on Human Rights says that during the genocide, "Rape was systematic and used as a 'weapon' by the perpetrators of the massacres . . . rape was the rule and its absence the exception." In 2000, a survey of 1,125 women who survived rape during the 1994 genocide found that 67 percent were HIV positive.

November 8   The UN Security Council adopts Resolution 955, establishing the International Criminal Tribunal for Rwanda (ICTR). It is empowered to try individuals for genocide, crimes against humanity, and war crimes. Following the precedent set by the ICTY, the ICTR includes sexual violence within its Statute. As of 2011, there have been 11 ICTR convictions for sexual violence, beginning with the 1998 conviction of Jean-Paul Akayesu (b. 1953), a Hutu and former government official in Rwanda convicted of using rape as an instrument of genocide and as a crime against humanity.

1994–1999   On December 11, 1994, Russian troops invade Chechnya, a breakaway Russian republic located in the Northern Caucasus Mountains in the southeastern part of Europe. Augmented Russian forces take Grozny, Chechnya's capital, in March 1995, but at the cost of heavy civilian casualties. Chechen guerrilla resistance continues in other areas of the republic. Both sides commit atrocities, although the far larger Russian military is guilty of the worse excesses. A peace treaty is signed in 1997. Russian troops withdraw but return in late 1999, after which heavy fighting resumes. An estimated 100,000 people die and more than 600,000 people are forced to flee their homes during the 1990s. There are reports and evidence of widespread torture and rape.

1995   The Fourth World Conference on Women is held in Beijing, China, with delegates from 189 countries. Delegates adopt the Beijing Platform for Action. It declares that rape in armed conflict is a war crime, and, under certain circumstances, could be considered an act of genocide.

June 10   Signatories of the Madrid Declaration condemn all forms of violence against women and establish values, behavior, and commitments that could lead to the eradication of violence against women. Specific emphasis is placed on the involvement and awareness of men.

1996   The United Nations Development Fund for Women (UNIFEM) establishes a Trust Fund in Support of Actions to Eliminate Violence Against Women, the first global mechanism devoted exclusively to providing resources and expanding visibility on this issue.

1997   Secular women are targeted by Muslim revolutionaries in Algeria and reduced to sex slaves.

1998

May   With food shortages and mass unemployment as the pretext, Indonesian security forces allegedly rape ethnic Chinese women during a spate of rioting in several major cities, including Jakarta.

July 17   A diplomatic conference in Rome adopts the Statute of the International Criminal Court (ICC), which paves the way for a permanent international forum to prosecute genocide, crimes against humanity, and serious war crimes. Rape, sexual slavery, enforced prostitution, forced pregnancy, enforced sterilization, and sexual violence are codified as war crimes and crimes against humanity. The ICC will be located at The Hague, Netherlands.

September 2   Jean-Paul Akayesu, a Hutu and former government official in Rwanda, is convicted in the first genocide case prosecuted before an international tribunal (ICTR). The conviction is historic because it establishes that rape, when committed with intent to destroy a group, in whole or in part, can be an act of genocide.

December   The International Criminal Tribunal for the former Yugoslavia (ICTY) sentences the local commander of the Croatian defense council, a Bosnian Croat named Anto Furundžija, to ten years imprisonment for the confinement and repeated rape of a Muslim woman by his subordinates. Furundžija is found guilty as a co-perpetrator of torture and of aiding and abetting the perpetration of an outrage on personal dignity, including rape against the victim.

From the perspective of women's rights, the conviction of Furundžija, in particular his conviction for rape as a form of torture is a positive step. According to critics, it sets a troublesome procedural precedent for the treatment of victims of sexual violence during the criminal trial process.

1998 - 1999   During the war in Kosovo, Serbian soldiers rape between 30 and 50 percent of the women of child-bearing age in some Kosovar villages.

1999

December 17   The UN General Assembly designates November 25 as the International Day for the Elimination of Violence Against Women.

2000

March 20   The first International Criminal Tribunal for the former Yugoslavia (ICTY) trial dealing exclusively with charges of sexual violence against women commences. Radomir Kovac, Dragolub Kunarac, and Zoran Vukovic, all members of the Bosnian Serb military and paramilitary forces are charged with crimes committed against Bosnian Muslim women in Foča, Bosnia and Herzegovina, in 1992 and 1993. On February 22, 2001, the three defendants are found guilty of rape as a crime against humanity.

June 5-9   A special session of the UN General Assembly, Beijing + 5, makes violence against women a priority concern and reviews the implementation of the 1995 Beijing Platform for Action.

October 31   UN Security Council unanimously adopts Resolution 1325 on Women, Peace and Security. It is the first formal and legal document from the UN Security Council that addresses the impact of war on women. Resolution 1325 requires parties in a conflict to respect women's rights and to support their participation in peace negotiations and in post-conflict reconstruction.

December   The Women's International War Crimes Tribunal on Japan's Military Sexual Slavery during World War II is held in Tokyo. The Tribunal intends to highlight the systematic sexual enslavement of tens of thousands of Asian women, the "comfort women" of World War II. More than a thousand people take part in the Tribunal, which hears testimony from 64 survivors from nine countries, as well as from two Japanese veterans who were themselves perpetrators of sexual violence.

2001

September 11   Al Qaeda terrorists carry out a series of four coordinated suicide attacks after hijacking four American commercial passenger jet airliners. They crash two of the airliners into the Twin Towers of the World Trade Center in New York City, one into the Pentagon in Arlington, Virginia, and another into a field near Shanksville in rural Pennsylvania after some of its passengers and flight crew attempt to retake control of the plane, which the hijackers had redirected toward Washington, DC. Thousands are killed. Following the September 11 terrorist attacks, a U.S., Allied, and anti-Taliban Northern Alliance military action in Afghanistan topples the Taliban for sheltering Osama bin Ladin, head of Al Qaeda.

2003–present   U.S.-led invasion of Iraq and the ouster of the Saddam Hussein (1937-2006) regime. US forces remain in Iraq under a UN Security Council mandate through 2009 and under a bilateral security agreement thereafter.

2003   Two Darfuri rebel movements–the Sudan Liberation Army (SLA) and the Justice and Equality Movement (JEM)–take up arms against the Sudanese government, complaining about the marginalization of the area and the failure to protect sedentary people from attacks by nomads. The government of Sudan responds by unleashing Arab militias known as *Janjaweed* ("devils on horseback"). Sudanese forces and *Janjaweed* militia attack hundreds of villages throughout Darfur. More than 400 villages are completely destroyed and millions of civilians are forced to flee their homes. The UN International Commission of Inquiry on Darfur finds that "rape and sexual violence have been used by the Janjaweed and Government soldiers . . . as a deliberate strategy with a view to . . . terrorizing the population, ensuring control over the IDP [Internally Displaced Persons] population and perpetrating displacement."

2004   Beginning in 2004, accounts of physical, psychological, and sexual abuse, including torture, rape, sodomy, and homicide of prisoners held in the Abu Ghraib prison in Iraq (also known as Baghdad Correctional Facility), administered and managed by the American military forces, come to public attention.

January 28   In Stockholm, Sweden, at the first major intergovernmental international conference on genocide since the adoption of the 1948 UN Convention on Genocide, delegates from 58 nations adopt The Stockholm Declaration on Genocide. It calls for collective efforts of the international community to prevent genocide, ethnic cleansing, and mass killings.

April   In Rwanda, an organization called Widows of the [1994] Genocide, polls and tests 1,200 of its 25,000 members and finds that 80 percent had been raped and 66 percent are HIV-positive.

July 18   Amnesty International issues a major report, *Darfur: Rape as a Weapon of War; Sexual Violence and Its Consequences.* This report finds that rape and other forms of sexual violence in Darfur are being used as a weapon of war in order to humiliate, punish, control, inflict fear, and displace women and their communities.

July/August   The U.S. State Department, the Coalition of International Justice's Darfur Atrocities Documentation Project, and the U.S. Agency for International Aid (USAID) send a team of twenty-four investigators to Chad to interview black African refugees from the Darfur region of Sudan to ascertain whether genocide has been and is continuing to be perpetrated by the government of Sudan and the *Janjaweed* (Arab militia). During the course of their interviews, the investigators discover that many females–they only interview women 18 years of age and older–have been raped, gang-raped, and impregnated as the result of such rape.

September 9   Speaking before the U.S. Senate Foreign Relations Committee, Secretary of State Colin L. Powell (b. 1937) states that genocide has taken place in Sudan and that the government in Khartoum and government-sponsored *Janjaweed* "bear responsibility" for rapes, killings, and other abuses that have left 1.2 million black Africans homeless. The information is contained in an eight-page report, "Documenting Atrocities in Darfur."

2005

March 8   Médecins Sans Frontières (Doctors without Borders) issues a major report, "The Crushing Burden of Rape: Sexual Violence in Darfur." It states that the sexual violence carried out by Sudanese government troops and *Janjaweed* against black African women in Darfur "has been nothing short of ubiquitous."

July 29   A UN report accuses Sudanese authorities of taking no action against militiamen and soldiers who commit widespread rape in Sudan.

2006

June 21-23   An International Symposium on Sexual Violence in Conflict and Beyond is held in Brussels, Belgium. Representatives of governments, the European Commission, civil society, and the United Nations meet to strengthen their shared commitment and action to prevent and respond to sexual violence in conflict and post-conflict situations. They issue The Brussels Call to Action, which, among other things, calls for urgent and long-term action to prevent sexual and gender-based violence by promoting gender equity and equality and the economic, social, and political empowerment of women.

2007

July 30   The UN's Division for the Advancement of Women of the Department of Economic and Social Affairs (ECOSOC), on the basis of input provided by UN entities, as part of the activities of the Task Force on Violence Against Women of the Inter-Agency Network on Women and Gender Equality, issues a report that claims extreme violence against women is pervasive around the world and local authorities do little to stop it or to prosecute those responsible.

October   The first World Conference on Japanese Military Sexual Slavery is held at the Law School of the University of California, Los Angeles.

2008

February   UN Secretary-General Ban Ki-moon (b. 1944) launches his 2008-2015 campaign "UNITE to End Violence Against Women." Through this campaign, the Secretary-General spearheads the accelerated efforts of the UN system to address violence against women, specifically sexual violence in conflict.

June 19   The UN Security Council unanimously adopts Resolution 1820, which recognizes that sexual violence can be categorized as a war tactic, war crime, crime against humanity, and an act of genocide. Resolution 1820 is the first Security Council resolution to recognize conflict-related sexual violence as a matter of international peace and security. Resolution 1820 demands the "immediate and complete cessation by all parties to armed conflict of all acts of sexual violence against civilians."

July   The prosecutor of the International Criminal Court (ICC), Luis Moreno Ocampo (b. 1952), accuses Sudan's General Omar al-Bashir (b. 1944) of genocide, crimes against humanity, and war crimes in Darfur.

2009

March 4   Sudanese President Omar al-Bashir is the first sitting president to be indicted by the International Criminal Court. He is indicted for directing a campaign of mass killing, rape, and pillage against civilians in Darfur. The court issues an arrest warrant for al-Bashir but rules that there is insufficient evidence to prosecute him for genocide.

July   UN Secretary-General Ban Ki-moon tells the UN Security Council that sexual violence poses a threat to international peace and security when used as a tactic of war. "Like a grenade or a gun, sexual violence is part of their arsenal to pursue military, political, social and economic aims. The perpetrators generally operate with impunity."

August 4   The UN Security Council passes Resolution 1882, "Children and Armed Conflict," which condemns "all violations of applicable international law involving the recruitment and use of children by parties to armed conflict as well as their re-recruitment, killing and maiming, rape and other sexual violence … against children in situations of armed conflict."

September 30   U.S. Secretary of State Hillary Clinton (b. 1947) intro-
                duces Resolution 1888 at the UN Security Council. Like
                Resolution 1820 passed the previous year, 1888 condemns
                conflict-related sexual violence and aims to equip the UN
                with measures to prevent it and to address impunity.

October 5   The UN Security Council passes Resolution 1889,
                "Women and Peace and Security," which seeks to
                strengthen the implementation of Resolution 1325 and
                specifically addresses women's needs in post-conflict and
                peace building periods.

November 24   At UN headquarters in New York City during the official
                observance of the tenth anniversary of the International
                Day for the Elimination of Violence Against Women, UN
                Secretary General Ban Ki-moon launches his Network of
                Men Leaders as part of his UNITE campaign.

December 16   The UN Security Council passes Resolution 1960, which
                calls for a monitoring and reporting framework to track
                sexual violence in conflict.

2010

February 2   UN Secretary-General Ban Ki-moon appoints
                Margot Wallström (b. 1954) of Sweden as his Special
                Representative on Sexual Violence in Conflict.

March   Two women's tribunals take place. In New York, the
                Nobel Women's Initiative and the Women's League of
                Burma organize the International Tribunal on Crimes
                Against Women of Burma. At the Tribunal, 12 women
                testify about rape, torture, and murder in front of 200
                people, with a further 2,000 watching by webcast. The
                four judges, who included human rights experts and
                Nobel laureates, find both the Government of Burma

[Myanmar] and the military responsible for the crimes.

In Guatemala, indigenous women recount their experiences in the Tribunal of Conscience against Sexual Violence during Internal Armed Conflict, organized by various Guatemalan groups, with support from UN partners, including UN Women. The Commission for Historical Clarification (CEH), set up in the aftermath of the war in Guatemala, found that sexual violence was widespread during more than three decades of conflict in the country. It estimates that military personnel committed about 90 percent of these crimes. Some women waited thirty years to talk about their horrific experiences, including rape, forced pregnancy, sterilization, and sexual slavery.

July 2   The UN General Assembly creates UN Women, the United Nations Entity for Gender Equality and the Empowerment of Women. Former President of Chile, Michelle Bachelet (b. 1951) is appointed as a UN Under-Secretary General and Executive Director of UN Women.

November 22   The war crimes trial of Congolese former rebel leader, Jean-Pierre Bemba (b. 1962) begins at the International Criminal Court (ICC) in The Hague, Netherlands. The former Vice President of the Democratic Republic of Congo is accused of two counts of crimes against humanity and three counts of war crimes for his alleged role in the conflict in the Central African Republic (CAR). Chief ICC prosecutor Luis Moreno Ocampo tells the court that the militiamen who raped and killed hundreds of civilians in the CAR in 2002-2003 were under Bemba's "effective authority and control." Describing the rapes as "crimes of domination and humiliation," Ocampo argues that Bemba turned a blind eye to such attacks and was "even more responsible than his subordinates." It is the first ICC case tried primarily on sexual violence charges.

Almost half of the witnesses are women. Ocampo tells the court that its decision will "influence the behavior of thousands of military commanders around the world."

December 16   The UN Security Council adopts Resolution 1960, reiterating the demand for the complete and immediate cessation of sexual violence by all parties to armed conflict.

2011

January   The United Nations Development Fund for Women (UNIFEM) is merged into UN Women, the corporate entity of the UN dedicated to gender equality and the empowerment of women.

February   Eleven Congolese soldiers, including Lt. Colonel Kibibi Mutware, are indicted by a military court for crimes against humanity for their part in the mass rape of more than 40 women and girls in the town of Fizi, Eastern Democratic Republic of Congo, on New Year's Day, 2011. Mutware and three fellow officers are found guilty and sentenced to twenty years imprisonment; five other soldiers receive sentences of between ten and fifteen years. The soldiers also are ordered to pay the women reparations.

March 11   After a trial lasting nearly four years, judges in the Special Court for Sierra Leone at The Hague begin deliberations for a final judgment in the case against Charles Taylor (b. 1948), the former president of Liberia, who stands accused of war crimes and crimes against humanity committed during his involvement in Sierra Leone's horrifying civil war (1991-2002). On April 26, 2012, the judges found Taylor guilty on eleven counts of aiding and abetting such crimes, including rape and sexual slavery. He was sentenced to fifty years in prison.

April 28   Susan Rice (b. 1964), U.S. Ambassador to the United Nations, tells the UN Security Council that Libyan leader, Muammar Gaddafi (1942-2011) is dispensing viagra to his forces to encourage them to rape women. (There is a belief that the drug increases and improves sexual performance.) Libyan postgraduate law student Eman al-Obeidy (b. 1982) tells foreign journalists that Gaddafi's forces gang-raped her. Earlier in April, Margot Wallström, UN Special Representative on Sexual Violence during Conflict, issued a statement alleging that reports of rape in the Libyan war have been "brutally silenced."

May 26   After remaining at large for years, the Bosnian Serb military leader Ratko Mladic (b. 1943) is arrested. As a result of his involvement in the 1990s in the siege of Sarajevo and the July 1995 Srebrenica massacre of Muslim men and boys in the former Yugoslavia, Mladic is accused, by the ICTY at The Hague, of war crimes, crimes against humanity, and genocide.

June 24   The International Criminal Tribunal for Rwanda finds Pauline Nyiramasuhuko (b. 1946), former Minister for Family and Women's Affairs in the Hutu-controlled government of Rwanda during the 1994 genocide, and her son, Arsene Ntahobali, a former militia leader, both guilty of genocide, war crimes, and crimes against humanity, including rape. Nyiramasuhuko is the only woman to be charged before the special genocide court and the first to be convicted.

October 7   The Nobel Peace Prize 2011 is awarded jointly to Ellen Johnson Sirleaf (Liberia, b. 1938), Leymah Gbowee (Liberia, b. 1972) and Tawakkol Karman (Yemen, b. 1979) "for their non-violent struggle for the safety of women and for women's rights to full participation in peace-building work."

October 21   President Barack Obama (b. 1961) announces the complete withdrawal of U.S. forces from Iraq by the end of 2011.

Sources Used to Compile the Chronology

Books

Barstow, Anne Llewellyn, ed. *War's Dirty Secret: Rape, Prostitution, and Other Crimes Against Women*. Cleveland, OH: The Pilgrim Press, 2000.

Bloxham, Donald, and A. Dirk Moses, eds. *The Oxford Handbook of Genocide Studies*. Oxford: Oxford University Press, 2010.

Brownmiller, Susan. *Against Our Will: Men, Women and Rape*. New York: Fawcett Columbine, 1975.

Chang, Iris. *The Rape of Nanking*. New York: Basic Books, 1997.

Charny, Israel, ed. *Encyclopedia of Genocide*. 2 vols. Santa Barbara, CA: ABC-Clio, 1999.

Hedgepeth, Sonja M., and Rochelle G. Saidel, eds. *Sexual Violence Against Women During the Holocaust*. Waltham, MA: Brandeis University Press, 2010.

Herzog, Dagmar, ed. *Brutality and Desire: War and Sexuality in Europe's Twentieth Century*. New York: Palgrave McMillan, 2009.

Horvitz, Leslie Alan, and Christopher Catherwood. *Enclyclopedia of War Crimes and Genocide*. 2 vols. New York: Facts on File, Inc., 2011.

Neuffer, Elizabeth. *The Key to My Neighbor's House: Seeking Justice in Bosnia and Rwanda*. New York: Picador, 2001.

Rittner, Carol, and John K. Roth, eds. *Different Voices: Women and the Holocaust*. New York: Paragon House, 1993.

Rittner, Carol, John K. Roth, and James Smith, eds. *Will Genocide Ever End?* St. Paul, MN: Paragon House, 2002.

Ruff-O'Herne, Jan. *50 Years of Silence*. Sydney, Australia: Tom Thompsons Editions, 1994.

Smith, Merril D., ed. *Encyclopedia of Rape*. Westport, CT: Greenwood Press, 2004.

Totten, Samuel, ed. *Plight and Fate of Women During and Following Genocide*. New Brunswick, NJ: Transaction Publishers, 2009.

United Nations Women. *In Pursuit of Justice: 2011-2012 Progress of the World's Women*. New York: UN Women, 2011.

Websites

Amnesty International	www.amnesty.org
BBC	www.bbc.co.uk
Doctors without Borders	www.doctorswithoutborders.org
Human Rights Watch	www.hrw.org
The Huffington Post	www.huffingtonpost.com
Physicians for Human Rights	www.physiciansforhumanrights.org
US Holocaust Memorial Museum	www.ushmm.org
United Nations	www.un.org

1

"Are Women Human?"

Carol Rittner

"Are women human?" I ask. "Of course they are," the students always say. "Why would you even ask such a question?"
—*Carol Rittner*

In my view, when thinking, studying, or teaching about rape as a weapon of war and genocide, no question is more important than "Are women human?" For that reason, I have chosen to orient this chapter by calling attention to a short essay that uses that question as its title. "Are Women Human?" is by Catharine A. MacKinnon, the well-known scholar and professor of law at the University of Michigan.[1]

The Universal Declaration of Human Rights defines what a human being is. In 1948, it told the world what a person, as a person, is entitled to. It has been fifty years. Are women human yet?

If women were human, would we be a cash crop shipped from Thailand in containers into New York's brothels? Would we be sexual and reproductive slaves? Would we be bred, worked without pay our whole lives, burned when our dowry money wasn't enough or when men tired of us, starved as widows when our husbands died (if we survived his funeral pyre), sold for sex because we are not valued for anything else? Would we be sold into marriage to priests to atone for our family's sins or to improve our family's earthly prospects? Would we, when allowed to work for pay, be made to work at the most menial jobs and exploited at barely starvation level? Would our genitals be sliced out to "cleanse" us (our body parts are dirt?), to control us, to mark us

1

and define our cultures? Would we be trafficked as things for sexual use and entertainment worldwide in whatever form current technology makes possible? Would we be kept from learning to read and write?

If women were human, would we have so little voice in public deliberations and in government in the countries where we live? Would we be hidden behind veils and imprisoned in houses and stoned and shot for refusing? Would we be beaten nearly to death, and to death, by men with whom we are close? Would we be sexually molested in our families? Would we be raped in genocide to terrorize and eject and destroy our ethnic communities, and raped again in that undeclared war that goes on every day in every country in the world in what is called peacetime? If women were human, would our violation be *enjoyed* by our violators? And, if we were human, when these things happened, would virtually nothing be done about it?

It takes a lot of imagination—and a determinedly blinkered focus on exceptions at the privileged margins—to see a real woman in the Universal Declaration's majestic guarantees of what "everyone is entitled to." After over half a century, just what part of "everyone" doesn't mean us?

The ringing language in Article 1 encourages us to "act towards one another in a spirit of brotherhood." Must we be men before its spirit includes us? Lest this be seen as too literal, if we were all enjoined to "act towards one another in a spirit of sisterhood," would men know it meant them, too? Article 23 encouragingly provides for just pay to "everyone who works." It goes on to say that this ensures a life of human dignity for "himself and his family." Are women nowhere paid for the work we do in our own families because we are not "everyone," or because what we do there is not "work," or just because we are not "him"? Don't women have families, or is what women have not a family without a "himself"? If the someone who is not paid at all, far less the "just and favorable remuneration" guaranteed, is also the same someone who in real life is often responsible for her family's sustenance, when she is deprived of providing for her family "an existence worthy of human dignity," is she not human? And now that "everyone" has had a right "to take part in the government of his country" since the Universal Declaration was promulgated, why are most governments still run mostly by men? Are women silent in the halls of state because we do not have a human voice?

A document that could provide specifically for the formation of trade unions and "periodic holiday with pay" might have mustered the specificity to mention women sometime, other than through "motherhood," which is more bowed to than provided for. If women were human in this document, would domestic violence, sexual violation from birth to death, including in prostitution and pornography, and systematic sexual objectification and denigration of women and girls simply be left out of the explicit language?

Granted, sex discrimination is prohibited. But how can it have been prohibited for all this time, even aspirationally, and the end of all these conditions still not be concretely imagined as part of what a human being, as human, is entitled to? Why is women's entitlement to an end of these conditions still openly debated based on cultural rights, speech rights, religious rights, sexual freedom, free markets—as if women are social signifiers, pimps' speech, sacred, or sexual fetishes, natural resources, chattel, everything but human beings?

The omissions in the Universal Declaration are not merely semantic. Being a woman is "not yet a name for a way of being human," not even in this most visionary of human rights documents. If we measure the reality of women's situation in all its variety against the guarantees of the Universal Declaration, not only do women not have the rights it guarantees—most of the world's men don't either—but it is hard to see, in its vision of humanity, a woman's face.

Women need full human status in social reality. For this, the Universal Declaration of Human Rights must see the ways women distinctively are deprived of human rights as a deprivation of humanity. For the glorious dream of the Universal Declaration to come true, for human rights to be universal, both the reality it challenges and the standard it sets need to change.

When will women be human? When?

I teach courses about the Holocaust and other genocides of the twentieth and twenty-first centuries. Among the books we read is Iris Chang's *The Rape of Nanking*.[2] One of the issues I always discuss with students is the fact that Japan was—perhaps still is—a "male-dominated society."[3] I draw attention to what Chang has to say about how "the molding of young men to serve in the Japanese military began early in life,"[4] and how, in the years prior to the beginning of the second Sino-Japanese War (1937), "The Japanese soldier was not simply hardened for battle in China; he was hardened for the task of murdering Chinese combatants and non-combatants alike."[5] We look at documentary films about the orgy of cruelty perpetrated on Chinese men, women, and children by the Imperial Japanese military when they invaded Nanking, the capital of China at the time, in December 1937. The battle for Nanking had followed a particularly tough fight at Shanghai where Chinese forces had put up stiff resistance against the Japanese Army, which overall had expected an easy victory in China. We read about how "an estimated 20,000-80,000 Chinese women were raped" in Nanking and its surrounding area, and we discuss how many soldiers of the Imperial Japanese Army "went beyond rape to disembowel women, slice off their breasts, [and] nail them alive to walls."[6]

"Are women human?" I ask. "What a crazy question!" students answer.

When we study World War II and the Holocaust, I sometimes have students read Ka-Tzetnik's nightmare novel, *House of Dolls*. It describes a day's routine in a nameless brothel in which young Jewish women under threat of death are forced to prepare their cots for the arrival of German soldiers who do "Enjoyment Duty" and, then, after raping the women, write reports about the performance of their "dolls."[7] Other times, I use sections of *A Woman in Berlin*, the journal kept by an anonymous German gentile woman who lived through the Russian conquest of Berlin as World War II was drawing to an end in Europe, and hordes of Soviet soldiers raped German women—old, young, even barely pubescent girls—with wild abandon.[8] As Antony Beevor points out in his introduction to this remarkable narrative:

> For obvious reasons it has never been possible to calculate the exact number of rape victims in 1945. A general estimate given is two million German women; this figure excludes Polish women and even Soviet women and girls brought to Germany for slave labor by the Wehrmacht. But the figures for Berlin are probably the most reliable of all of Germany—between 95,000 and 130,000 according to the two leading hospitals. These can hardly be inflated figures if one takes into

account that at least a dozen women and girls were raped in the single medium-sized apartment block where the author lived.[9]

"Are women human?" I ask. "What a stupid question!" students say. "Of course women are human."

I draw their attention to Bangladesh—most of them do not even know where in the world Bangladesh is—so I have to use lots of maps to help them locate it in South Central Asia.[10] Even less do they know about "the extreme and systematic violence that precipitated the creation of Bangladesh," an event "largely neglected by genocide scholars."[11] In 1971, during a period of about nine months, Pakistani soldiers raped between 200,000 and 400,000 women; no one knows exactly how many, but thousands of these raped women became pregnant. Pakistani soldiers, however, were not the only ones who raped. Moslem Biharis—hireling *Razakars*[12] who collaborated with the Pakistani Army during the war of independence—also were "most enthusiastic rapists."[13]

Even though recently independent, Bangladesh, a largely Muslim country, had its practices and traditions. "And by tradition, no Muslim husband would take back a wife who had been touched by another man, even if she had been subdued by force."[14] In an effort to break that tradition and because of the particular suffering women and girls endured during the war against Pakistan, the Bangladesh government of Sheik Mujibur Rahman (1920-1975) declared Bengali women "heroines" of the 1971 war of independence. The government told "husbands the women were victims and must be considered national heroines. Some men [took] their spouses back home, but these are very, very few."[15]

From Bangladesh, I move back to Europe, to the former Yugoslavia in the 1990s, although there could have been many stops along the way—Indonesia, Cambodia, Burundi, Guatemala, Sierra Leone, Liberia, East Timor, among other places—but there is only so much time and all too few classes in a semester to cover the ever growing problem of rape used as a weapon of war and genocide in our fractured and fragile world.

Of course, we know that since time immemorial, in times of conflict and violence, women have been raped as an act of violence and a demonstration of power. In the former Yugoslavia, particularly in Croatia and Bosnia between 1992 and 1995, sexual violence against women was rampant. (Men and boys were also sexually violated, but never as extensively or systematically as were women and girls.) While all sides raped, Serb soldiers and paramilitary groups raped women and girls on a massive scale.[16] They raped and sodomized women and girls in an effort aimed at "ethnically cleansing" non-Serbs from territory Serbs claimed or had "conquered" during the ensuing conflict.

Students read about the rape camps the Serbs established in "hotels, schools, restaurants, factories, peacetime brothels, or even animal stalls in barns, fenced pens, and auditoriums. The purpose of these camps was to punish women through sexual assault . . . No one was exempt . . . Serb captors told women that they would impregnate them" so as to create "'Chetnik babies' who would kill Muslims when they grew up."[17] The students read testimonies of women such as twenty-year-old Emina, who told how the Serb Chetniks came into her village, killed the men, then dragged her, her fourteen-year old neighbor, and a girl from a neighboring village into a cellar where they raped them.[18] They read about mayhem in Miljevina, a small working class town in the area of Foca, Bosnia-Herzegovina, where Serb troops killed many people and assaulted many women, including a 45-year-old Muslim woman who, along with four younger women, including her daughter-in-law, was beaten, tortured, and raped. "[W]hat didn't they do with us there! . . . they did whatever came into their heads."[19] Sometimes I have them read Slavenka Drakulić's grim and horrific novel about women held in a Serb rape camp, *S.: A Novel about the Balkans*.[20] It is a work of fiction, but devastatingly true. Drakulić's book, as one reviewer wrote, "puts a human face on the abstraction of wartime atrocities and ethnic cleansing."[21]

A fact-finding team sent to the former Yugoslavia by the European Community (EC) in the early 1990s estimated that during the conflict there, Serb forces, military and paramilitary, raped more than 20,000 Muslim women in Bosnia alone.[22] The Bosnian Ministry of the Interior estimated the number of rape victims, including Serbian and Croatian women as well, to be higher—50,000.[23] Whatever the number, and we shall never know it exactly, what we do know is that thousands upon thousands of women of all ages, shapes, and locations were raped, sodomized, and destroyed.

"Are women human?" I ask. "Of course they are," the students always say. "Why would you even ask such a question?"

After the former Yugoslavia, I turn to Rwanda, that tiny Central African country that many of us probably had never heard of before the 1994 genocide there. As the genocide scholar Adam Jones observes, the violence in Rwanda was so horrific that

> In just twelve weeks, at least one million people—overwhelmingly Tutsi, but also tens of thousands of Hutus opposed to the genocidal government—were murdered, primarily by machetes, clubs, and small arms. About 80 percent of victims died in a "hurricane of death . . . between the second week of April and the third week of May," noted Gérard Prunier. "If we consider that probably around 800,000 people were slaughtered during that short period . . . the daily killing rate was at least five times that of the Nazi death camps."[24]

As for what happened specifically to women during that genocide, one can only echo Myrna Goldenberg, writing about women vis-à-vis men during the Holocaust: "Different horrors, same hell."[25] Men and women alike suffered and died at the hands of the *genocidaires*. Men and women alike were mutilated and hacked to death, were burned and shot in schools and churches, in fields and forests, in homes and on the streets, but women—women were overwhelmingly targeted for sexual violence.

In the Rwandan genocide, thousands of Tutsi women as well as some moderate Hutu women were sexually violated in the most sadistic and brutal manner imaginable.[26] *Genocidaires* raped and sodomized women, sexually mutilating them with objects such as sharpened sticks or gun barrels, holding them in sexual slavery for days and weeks.[27] René Degni-Segui, the United Nations Special *Rapporteur* on Rwanda, in a report to the UN after the genocide, said that "calculating backward from the number of pregnancies caused by rape . . . at least 250,000 women—and as many as 500,000 [were] raped in Rwanda in 1994."[28] Again, we shall never know the exact number of women raped by *genocidaires* during the 1994 genocide, but human rights observers and medical workers testify that during the 100 days of genocide in Rwanda, rape was the rule and its absence the exception. The Hutu-controlled Rwandan government urged, even ordered, Hutu men to rape, sodomize, and impregnate Tutsi women during the genocide. Sexual violence was not incidental but central to the genocidal intent of the extremist government.

In cultures that see woman as the property of a man, as was the case in Rwanda and in former Yugoslavia too—both solidly traditional, patriarchal societies—violating women was an indirect yet potent way of attacking and violating male enemies.[29] As Elizabeth Neuffer writes, "Rape as part of warfare is not just about having sex, it is also about having someone else's property."[30]

"Are women human?" I ask. "What kind of a question is that?" responds one young man. "Of course, women are human. It's self evident," he says. "Indeed," I say, "but Catharine MacKinnon thinks that answer is too easy, too problematic, and so do I." I remind him, as well as the entire class, what MacKinnon says:

> If women were human, would we be a cash crop shipped from Thailand in containers into New York brothels? Would we be sexual and reproductive slaves? . . . Would our genitals be sliced out to "cleanse" us . . . to control us, to mark us out and define out cultures? Would we be trafficked as things for sexual use and entertainment worldwide in whatever form current technology makes possible? . . . Would we be raped in genocide to terrorize and eject and destroy our ethnic communities . . . If women were human, would our violation be *enjoyed* by our violators? And, if we were human, when these things happen, would virtually nothing be done about it?[31]

MacKinnon's list of outrages, past and present, goes on and on. Her rhetoric is grim but effective. Inequality on the basis of gender is a pervasive reality of women's lives all over the world. So is sex-related violence. Rape by strangers and acquaintances, rape within marriage, domestic violence, trafficking into sex work, the abuse of women and girls in the pornography industry—in all of these ways, argues MacKinnon, women suffer aggression and exploitation, because women are women and for no other reason. The risk of violence and violation within the household is one thing women share in common, irrespective of their social position, creed, color, or culture. So, too, is vulnerability to rape in times of war and genocide—the well-documented mass rapes of Bosnian women in the former Yugoslavia and Rwanda, not to mention the more recent widespread sexual violence perpetrated on women in the Democratic

Republic of Congo and Darfur,[32] being just a few examples of an appalling reality that increasingly characterizes most armed conflicts.

The reason rape is so widespread in war and genocide is because it is so effective in helping to destroy, in whole or in part, an ethnic, religious, national or racial group. For most people, the answer to the question, "Are women human?" is "Yes, of course women are human," but the *reality for women* in too many parts of the world, given their experience, is "We may be human, but we are not treated as equally human to men." The simple question "Are women human?" can lead us to see more clearly a male-dominated world that long has tolerated, condoned, and even encouraged gender-based violence and abuse.

There is a long history of male predominance supported by culture, tradition, religion, legislation, living conditions, and socio-economic structures. Dominant and violent masculinities are packaged in ways that especially appeal to young male minds. Through the print media, films, advertisements, toys, video games, and the internet, young boys and men are taught at an early age that this is "a man's world" and that violence is the norm. War is normalized in many hot spots around the world, from Africa to Europe, from the Americas to the Middle East, from Asia to the Pacific islands. A large gap persists between the principles of equality in documents such as the United Nations Declaration of Human Rights, or even in speeches politicians give for public consumption in world forums such as the UN or the European Parliament, and the reality on the ground for women and girls, particularly but not only in conflict zones. The day to day reality is that gender injustice is widespread, and when there is conflict and war, those who suffer most are women and children. "War," writes Rhonda Copelon, "tends to intensify brutality, repetitiveness, public spectacle, and likelihood of rape. War diminishes sensitivity to human suffering and intensifies men's sense of entitlement, superiority, avidity, and social license to rape."[33] In war there is no victory for women, no matter which side wins.[34]

When we consider the use of rape as a weapon of war and genocide, no question is more important than "Are women human?" How we encourage and enable each other to develop, or at least to begin to develop, genuine and real attitudes of humane equality toward and about women and girls during peacetime will have an impact on the attitudes and behavior exhibited by men and boys toward women and girls during times of extreme violence, because the extreme violence that they suffer during war and genocide does not arise solely out of the conditions of conflict. It is directly related to the attitudes men—the young and the not so young—have toward women and girls in peacetime. All forms of violence against women are related. We must challenge the political and ideological structures that still legalize any form of violence against women and girls anywhere in the world, that demean and dehumanize them in any way whatsoever. If we hope to eradicate violence against women in the twenty-first century, all of us, women and men alike, must be able to see in our "vision of humanity, a woman's face."[35]

Notes

1.   Catharine A. MacKinnon, "Are Women Human?" in *Are Women Human? And Other International Dialogues* (Cambridge, MA: Harvard University Press, 2006), 41-43. The essay is reprinted with permission from Catharine A. MacKinnon and Harvard University Press.

2.   Iris Chang, *The Rape of Nanking* (New York: Penguin Books, 1997).

3.   Ibid., 24.

4.   Ibid., 29.

5.   Ibid., 55.

6.   Ibid., 6.

7.   Ka-Tzetnik 135633, *House of Dolls* (London: Grafton Books, 1956). Yehiel Dinur (1909-2001), an Israeli writer whose nom de plume was Ka-Tzetnik 135633, was a survivor of Auschwitz who wrote several books about the Holocaust. Miryam Sivan's essay, "'Stoning the Messenger': Yehiel Dinur's *House of Dolls* and *Piepel*" in *Sexual Violence Against Women During the Holocaust*, ed. Sonja M. Hedgepeth and Rochelle G. Saidel (Waltham, MA: Brandeis University Press, 2010), 200-216, details the controversies surrounding Dinur and his *House of Dolls*.

8.   Anonymous, *A Woman in Berlin: Eight Weeks in the Conquered City*, trans. Philip Boehm (New York: Picador, 2005).

9.   Ibid., xx.

10. Formerly East Pakistan, Bangladesh came into being only in 1971, when the two parts of Pakistan split after a bitter war that drew in neighboring India.

11. The scholar Bina D'Costa, as quoted in Angela Debnath, "The Bangladesh Genocide: The Plight of Women," in *Plight and Fate of Women During and Following Genocide*, ed. Samuel Totten (New Brunswick, NJ: Transaction Publishers, 2009), 47, writes that the war of 1971 is "one of the most under-researched conflicts in the world."

12. "In the context of Islamic history Razakars were volunteers to defend or support Islam. But in Bangladeshi context, Razakar means traitors or collaborators of the Paki army who helped them, in our liberation war in 1971, in identifying and killing millions of Bangalees involved in or even supporting the liberation war. The Razakars were mainly the members of Muslim league, Jamat-e-Islam and other Islamic groups and factions." See "War Criminals II: Collaborators (Razakars)," (May 9, 2001), which is available at: http://muktadhara.net/page42.html. Accessed September 25, 2011.

13. Susan Brownmiller, *Against Our Will: Men, Women and Rape* (New York: Fawcett Columbine Books, 1975), 79-80, 81.

14. See further, ibid., 81.

15. Ibid., 80.

16. See further, Beverly Allen, *Rape Warfare: The Hidden Genocide in Bosnia-Herzegovina* (Minneapolis: University of Minnesota Press, 1996); Roy Gutman, *A Witness to Genocide* (New York: Simon and Schuster, 1993); and, Alexandra Stiglmayer, ed., *Mass Rape: The War against Women in Bosnia-Herzegovina* (Lincoln: University of Nebraska Press, 1994).

17. Todd Salzman, "'Rape Camps,' Forced Impregnation, and Ethnic Cleansing," in *War's Dirty Secret: Rape, Prostitution, and Other Crimes against Women*, ed. Anne Llewellyn Barstow (Cleveland: The Pilgrim Press, 2000), 73.

18. Alexandra Stiglmayer, "The Rapes in Bosnia-Herzegovina," in *Mass Rape*, ed. Stiglmayer, 97-98.

19. Ibid., 104.

20. Slavenka Drakulic, *S.: A Novel about the Balkans*, trans. Marko Ivić (New York: Penguin Books, 2001).

21. This comment is from the excerpt of a review in the *St. Petersburg Times* reprinted in the 2001 paperback edition of *S.: A Novel About the Balkans*.

22. European Council Investigative Mission into the Treatment of Muslim Women in the Former Yugoslavia, *Report to the European Council Foreign Ministers,* January 8, 1993, paragraph 14.

23. Stiglmayer, "The Rapes in Bosnia-Herzegovina," in *Mass Rape,* ed. Stiglmayer, 85.

24. Adam Jones, *Genocide: A Comprehensive Introduction,* 2d ed. (New York: Routledge, 2006), 346.

25. See Myrna Goldenberg, "Different Horrors, Same Hell: Women Remembering the Holocaust," in *Thinking the Unthinkable: Meanings of the Holocaust,* ed. Roger S. Gottlieb (New York: Paulist Press, 1991), 150-66.

26. Elizabeth Neuffer, *The Key to My Neighbor's House: Seeking Justice in Bosnia and Rwanda* (New York: Picador, 2002), 271-92.

27. Human Rights Watch, *Shattered Lives: Sexual Violence during the Rwandan Genocide* (New York: Human Rights Watch, 1996), 39.

28. Quoted in Neuffer, *The Key to My Neighbor's House,* 276.

29. Salzman, "'Rape Camps,' Forced Impregnation, and Ethnic Cleansing" in *War's Dirty Secret,* ed., Barstow, 79.

30. Neuffer, *The Key to My Neighbor's House,* 272.

31. MacKinnon, "Are Women Human?", 41-42.

32. For information about rape in eastern Congo and in Darfur, see further various reports issued by Amnesty International (www.amnesty.org), Doctors without Borders (www.doctorswithoutborders.org), Human Rights Watch (www.hrw.org), and the website of the United Nations (www.un.org).

33. Rhonda Copelon, "Resurfacing Gender: Reconceptualizing Crimes against Women in Time of War," in *Mass Rape,* ed., Stiglmayer, 213.

34. Comment by Noeleen Heyzer, former Director of UNIFEM, at a March 2006 Advisory Board meeting of Mercy Global Concern, New York, NY.

35. MacKinnon, "Are Women Human?", 43.

Further Suggested Reading

MacKinnon, Catherine A. *Are Women Human? And Other International Dialogues.* Cambridge, MA: Harvard University Press, 2006.

Moser, Caroline O.N. and Fiona C. Clark, eds. *Victims, Perpetrators or Actors? Gender, Armed Conflict and Political Violence.* London: Zed Books, 2001.

Not a Minute More: Ending Violence Against Women. New York: UNIFEM, 2003.

Salbi, Zainab. *The Other Side of War: Women's Stories of Survival & Hope.* Washington, DC: National Geographic, 2006.

The Shame of War: Sexual Violence Against Women and Girls in Conflict. New York: United Nations OCHA/IRIN, 2007.

Ward, Jeanne. *Broken Bodies, Broken Dreams: Violence Against Women Exposed.* New York: United Nations OCHA/IRIN, 2005.

Questions for Discussion

1. What does it mean to be "human"? Are there certain criteria against which one can measure "humanness"? Explain.

2. Are human rights "universal"? What are "women's rights"? Are "women's rights" "human rights"? Explain.

3. How is language "gendered"? Explain.

4. What is meant by a "gendered power relationship"? How are women and girls affected by gendered power relationships on individual, family, and societal levels?

5. What psychological processes of men and boys affect the ability of women and girls to be accepted by them as full, equal, and effective participants in society?

6. Are women human? Explain.

2

Rape during the Nazi Holocaust:
Vulnerabilities and Motivations

Eva Fogelman

Why, if they were going to kill them [the Jews] anyway, what
was the point of all the humiliation, why the cruelty?
—*Gitta Sereny to Franz Stangl*[1]

Of the 52,000 interviews conducted by the University of Southern
California Shoah Foundation Institute of Visual History and
Education, more than 48,000 are with Jewish survivors of the Holocaust.
These interviews include more than a thousand testimonies, mostly from
women, that reference rape and sexual molestation.[2]

Two documents orient this chapter on rape during the Holocaust,
Nazi Germany's genocidal onslaught against Europe's Jews. The first is a
short excerpt from one of the Shoah Foundation's testimonies.

We never knew what kind of work we will be assigned and if we would
return. Girls were disappearing and we heard they were raped and shot.
. . . [One day] while sitting on the floor, and not offered food or water,
a guard was watching us. Then guards picked out girls including me.
They were drunk and all had pistols in their hand. The officer facing
me said, '"You, upstairs." I did go upstairs. In his office he raped me. He
humiliated me. He tortured me sexually. I thought that was the end of
me. When I was crying and weeping and asking for mercy, he said: "You
bitch. Don't you know who I am? I am Viktors Arājs, the boss of this
place." I was taken downstairs. We were all sitting weeping, looking at
each other. Some had torn clothes."[3]

At the time she gave the testimony above, Zelda-Rivka Hait (b. 1920) was a young Jewish woman from Kuldiga, Latvia.[4] She hoped to finish her education and immigrate to Palestine. Unfortunately, when World War II began in September 1939, she lived in the Latvian city of Riga under Russian occupation. When the Germans invaded on June 22, 1941, the Jews of Riga were soon ghettoized and forced to do hard labor. Viktors Arājs (1910-1988), the man who raped Hait, was a Latvian who collaborated with the Nazis. He became the commander of the Latvian Auxiliary Security Police, which was established in early July 1941. Also known as the Arājs Commando, it carried out mass murder of Jews in Latvia and Belarus. Meanwhile, the morning after Arājs raped her, the door opened and Hait saw a German officer who had befriended her earlier on. He saved her life. Hait was sick for several days. She never saw the other girls again. She heard from their families that all of them were killed.

The second orienting document for this chapter comes from an essay by Myrna Goldenberg. A pioneering Holocaust scholar, she is one of the first to concentrate on the Holocaust's impact on Jewish women and to explore, in particular, the sexual violence inflicted upon them during that genocide. Only in relatively recent times—primarily since the early 1990s—has the topic of women and the Holocaust received much scholarly attention. Emphasis on rape during the Holocaust came even later, and research on this topic is still work in progress. The following excerpt compactly adds historical contextualization for points this chapter makes about rape during the Holocaust.

> According to Nazi race theory, intimate contact between Jews and Germans would contaminate the German bloodline and subvert racial purity, a key principle of Nazism. Thus, sexual violence against Jewish women involved breaking laws so fundamental that they defined the Nazi regime's ideology. Indeed, to an extent often unacknowledged, the Nazi regime fostered a preoccupation with sexuality, sometimes to express its ideals, such as the prohibition of race-defilement (*Rassenschande*) and the monitoring of cases relating to that crime, and sometimes to use sex as a reward for officers and even privileged prisoners who went to the brothels that were established in some of the concentration camps.

Despite the prohibitions against race-defilement, rape of Jewish women by German men occurred on several levels of social and commercial interaction. Although these acts showed the power of German men, the fact is that under the swastika Jews, both women and men, *were made powerless and targeted for elimination*. Thus, rape of Jewish women, unlike rape in the former Yugoslavia, Rwanda, Darfur, and the Democratic Republic of Congo, was not an instrument of genocide or ethnic cleansing. During the Holocaust, rape *was eclipsed by the "Final Solution,"* the state-sponsored plan to annihilate all European Jews, which was the Nazi instrument of choice by which to achieve its genocidal goal. In the face of systematic total elimination of Jews, rape and other forms of sexual violence were redundant but still very real tools of terror and racial dominance. The Nazis' death camps, forced labor squads, planned starvation and overcrowding, psychological and physical torture, and inhuman medical experiments were effective and nearly successful means of achieving what the Nazis set out to do in the Holocaust.

In Nazi Germany, rape and other forms of sexual abuse against Jewish women were scarcely primary issues, but *Rassenschande* was. It was a crime and a serious one. Indeed, any sexual involvement with a Jew could involve the crime of race defilement as it was defined in the 1935 Nuremberg Law for the Protection of German Blood and German Honor, which outlawed marriage and extramarital intercourse "between Jews and subjects of German or kindred blood." Violation of this Law for the Protection of German Blood and German Honor was interpreted to include not only extramarital intercourse between Jews and Germans but also "touching or even looking" because even such mild or passive acts might threaten German honor.[5]

Vulnerabilities to Rape

As Goldenberg emphasizes, unlike other genocides—Cambodia is also an exception—rape was not a policy component of the "Final Solution of the Jewish problem" during World War II. In most genocides (excluding Cambodia and the Holocaust), rape is a weapon, part of the policy of the perpetrators. During the Holocaust, as Goldenberg and Kirsty

Chatwood suggest, rape evolved, as Chatwood puts it, into a "by-product of the dehumanization process of genocide."[6] Although Nazi law against *Rassenschande*, "race-defilement," forbade Germans from having sexual relations with Jews and punishment for those who were caught could be severe, these measures did not eliminate sexual relations between Germans and Jews, including German-inflicted sexual violence against Jewish women, at least not completely.[7] As for non-German collaborators such as Victors Arājs, German law against *Rassenschande* made little difference.

Jewish women, men, and children were vulnerable to rape not only by the Germans but also by a variety of collaborators and local people in German-occupied European countries, as well as by military personnel of the Axis and Allies—particularly the Russian liberators, who were notorious for raping women at liberation. It should also be noted that the rapists were not just men, but also women SS guards and other female officials. Arguably the most notorious and sadistic was Irma Grese (1923-1945), a high-ranking SS woman in Auschwitz, an especially cruel and "imaginative" sexual pervert, who often tortured her victims before killing them.[8] Although their stories are beyond the scope of this chapter, it is important to note that non-Jewish victims of Nazi persecution—among them political resisters, Communists, Socialists, homosexuals, Seventh-day Adventists, Jehovah's Witnesses, Sinti and Roma ("Gypsies"), and the mentally and physically handicapped—were also vulnerable to rape.

It is difficult to estimate the prevalence of rape of Jewish women because several factors have inhibited survivors from revealing such dehumanization. For instance, the psychological dynamics of personal shame and survivor guilt, and religious and cultural norms, tarred a raped woman as tainted, and thus not a good prospect as a partner.[9] Also, women who were sexually violated on repeat occasions over extended periods of time were often killed after serving their rapists' purpose.

There is a myth that only pretty women were raped. Over the course of the war, oppressed Jewish women became more undesirable as sexual objects, but even though rape may have become less prevalent, the Germans and other perpetrators were not deterred from committing acts of sexual violence. Early on, the motivation for rape may have been more related to enhancing masculine gender identity, and therefore women who were more attractive were more desirable as sexual prey to satisfy rapists' masculine insecurities. The psychology of rape teaches us that the purpose of rape is not the satisfaction of sexual urges, but it is often a perverse means to prove one's masculinity.

The Holocaust data that we do have need to be considered in this context. In the 1,040 Shoah Foundation interviews that refer to rape and sexual molestation, most of the reported rapes were perpetrated by liberators—508 incidents. In the camps, there were 262 reported incidents and 272 in the ghettos. In other situations, rape was less prevalent, and includes rape by aid-givers, 39; in hiding, 33 (it is not clear whether this includes hiding with partisans); in prisons, 24; during deportation, 21; during forced marches, 12; during transfers and in refugee camps, 7; and in forced labor battalions, 1. Jewish women were not necessarily safe with Jewish men. In partisan groups, women who were alone feared Jewish men who might rape them. In order to avoid this fate, a woman might attach herself to a particular man who would then protect her. The relationship with a protector sometimes began with a man who initially raped her.

Founded in the early 1980s, the Fortunoff Video Archives at Yale University contains more than 4,400 Holocaust survivor testimonies. Only about ten of them recount sexual assault perpetrated against those female survivors or against women known to them. One reason for this relatively small number of candid testimonies about sexual assault may be that these tapes were geared for sharing with family members and school children. There is shame in knowing that a son or daughter or grandchild would hear about a parent or grandparent being raped or sexually abused by a German, a fellow partisan fighter, or a liberator. Another possible reason for the dearth of information may be that the subject was not broached at the time that the interviews housed at Yale were taped, ten to twenty years before the USC Shoah Foundation interviews were conducted. With a changing cultural climate and growing knowledge of how Jews were victimized in the Holocaust, it is possible that in the later interviews for the USC Shoah Foundation, some Holocaust survivors decided to be more candid in order to validate their experiences.

It is interesting to note that some of the early memoirs and novels written immediately after the liberation of the German concentration camps vividly describe the sadistic nature of both men and women in the camp hierarchy. Often the sadism expressed itself in sexual violence. Na'ama Shik explains that this early openness about rape and sexual violence was not yet contaminated by the reaction of the external world, which often engaged in "blaming the victim."[10]

Motivations for Rape

Research shows that "rape is not an aggressive manifestation of sexuality, but rather a sexual manifestation of aggression. In the perpetrator's psyche it serves no sexual purpose but is an expression of rage, violence, and dominance over a woman."[11] However, in order to understand a more specific meaning of rape during the Third Reich, this behavior needs to be examined within its social, political, and cultural contexts.

In the Third Reich, the motivation to rape was not monolithic. Rapists were motivated, at least, by entitlement, sadism, or masculine ego gratification. These motivations were neither exclusive to the Third Reich nor mutually exclusive; often one or the other is more prevalent. As with all rapes, these were not acts that were motivated by sexual gratification. Rape also provided an opportunity to humiliate and dehumanize the victim. Some acts were committed clandestinely, while others were public displays to enhance this humiliation and dehumanization of the victim.

In cases of "entitlement rape," the perpetrator can feel entitled to rape a woman because he has done or will do a favor for her, or has projected his feelings of interest on to her. When she does not reciprocate, the frustration of this unrequited interest drives the perpetrator to take what he feels he is entitled to, the woman herself. In the process, he objectifies her and dehumanizes her. Take, for example, Flora Singer's mother, a Jew who disguised herself as a Belgian woman during World War II. While Flora and her mother were eating in a café, a group of German officers joined them, ordered food and wine, moved over to their table and started talking to Flora's mother with the assistance of an interpreter. She described how she was alone and had to feed three young children because her husband was a Belgian prisoner of war. One of the German officers volunteered to help them smuggle food the next day. As Flora and her mother were getting ready for bed, there was a knock on the door, and the German officer got angry that he was not let in. So, he pushed his way into the room, picked up Flora off the bed, and put her in a corner outside the room. When her mother tried to protect her, he forcefully moved her away again. Flora sat outside the room and waited for what seemed like an eternity, hoping that the angry officer would not harm her mother. When he finally walked out of the room, he had a bloody scratch on his face, and Flora walked back into the room to find her mother sobbing.[12]

We assume the German officer did not know that Flora and her mother were Jewish. The sense of entitlement would have been even greater with Jewish women, who should have been doubly grateful that they were not being killed. Indeed, the typical German assumption was that a Jewess would be willing to pay with her body for any act of kindness. As Olga Lengyel (1908-2001) writes in her memoir about Auschwitz, "food was the coin that paid for sexual privileges."[13] Since Jewish women had no power during the Third Reich, any resistance against a male sexual overture was totally unacceptable to German men, who felt entitled to any favors they wanted from Jewish women. In the words of the Polish writer Tadeusz Borowski (1922-1951), a former Auschwitz prisoner, "Never [had] there been such an easy market for female flesh."[14] One example cited by Borowski involves repairs in the women's block of Auschwitz, known as the Persian Market "because of its exotic character."[15] For such repairs, the block Elder "had to pay . . . she could pay in various ways: with gold, food, the women of her block, or with her own body. It depended."[16]

In Auschwitz, the latrine was an area where women subjected themselves to sexual abuse from male prisoners to get basic necessities for survival. Gisella Perl (1907-1988) describes these exchanges in her memoir, *I Was a Doctor in Auschwitz*:

> Their full pockets made them the Don Juans of Camp C. They chose their women among the youngest, the prettiest, the least emaciated prisoners and in a few seconds the deal was closed. Openly, shamelessly, the dirty, diseased bodies clung together for a minute or two in the fetid atmosphere of the latrine—and the piece of bread, the comb, the little knife wandered from the pocket of the man into the greedy hands of the woman. At first I was deeply shocked at these practices. My

pride, my integrity as a woman revolted against the very idea. I begged and preached and, when I had my first cases of venereal disease, I even threatened to refuse treatment if they didn't stop prostitution. But later, when I saw that the pieces of bread thus earned saved lives, when I met a young girl whom a pair of shoes, earned in a week of prostitution, saved from being thrown into the crematory, I began to understand—and to forgive.[17]

It is interesting to note that what I call "entitlement rape" has often been known as "sex in exchange for food"[18] or "prostitution" in exchange for food.[19] Such interpretations place blame on the victim for whom an extra piece of bread or even a spoon was a matter of life or death. For the women, these choices were choiceless.

Sometimes the act of rape is a sadistically motivated behavior, not part of a real or implied reciprocal nonverbal agreement. "Sadistic rape" could enable the German perpetrator, for example, to have "omnipotent control over the life and death of prisoners and the seemingly opposite sense of impotence, of being a powerless cog in a vast machine controlled by unseen others."[20] These "polarized feelings" experienced by those working for the Nazi bureaucracy are explained by psychohistorian Robert J. Lifton, who interviewed Nazi physicians and wrote an important book called *The Nazi Doctors*. "Sadism," argues Lifton, "is an aspect of omnipotence, an effort to eradicate one's own vulnerability and susceptibility to pain and death."[21] Therefore, the more one degrades a victim the greater potential for omnipotence.

A telling example of a "sadistic rape" is described by Leah Finkel from Przytyk, Poland, who was taken out of her house and, like other young girls in her town, put to work cleaning the offices of the German occupiers.[22] She sensed that the Germans intended to rape these girls. Finkel escaped once by opening the window of the office she was cleaning and jumping out. When the Germans caught her making a second escape attempt, she was sent to clean the street and shovel snow. As Leah tried to escape from a German rampage to capture women, she fled to the woods and was protected by a Polish man, only to be discovered later. This time, and subsequent times, she was not so lucky and was brutally assaulted and raped by the German soldiers. She recalls, "He kicked me. I was bleeding for months in all kinds of parts. They took us back and forth every day. From rectum, stomach, vagina all over kicking with pointy boots." This kind of sexual perversion is best explained by psychoanalyst Louise J. Kaplan, who states that "every perversion is an effort to give some expression to, while yet controlling, the full strength of potentially murderous impulses to chew up, tear apart, explode, hack to pieces, burn to ashes, rip through to create one hole out of mouth, belly, anus, and vagina."[23]

After liberation, a German officer who had assaulted Leah was seen on a train by some of the survivors, and he was killed. Leah feels that at least she got some satisfaction knowing that he did not get away like so many of the other perpetrators.

A third motivating factor for rape is masculine ego gratification, which often entails gang or mass rape. For example, as Holocaust survivor Eta Wrobel was writing her memoir *My Life My Way* with Jeanette Friedman, she described to her co-author how Poles grabbed a pretty Jewish girl, raped her, stripped her naked, and ran her through a gauntlet on the main street of a village until she was beaten to death.[24] Some of the men who acquired notoriety during the Holocaust were individuals who were not professional successes in civilian life, and this new regime gave them an opportunity to advance in a career, get recognition, and thereby enhance their masculine self-esteem. The act of rape adds to the already-increased bravado of being an officer, having power and privileges, and the positive self-image gained from aggressive ideals such as the Nazis' "Aryan" ideal. The ego-gratification of a gang rape is derived from validation by one's peers. It offers acceptance and enhances status within the social group.

The "masculine ego-gratification rape" can be understood as an individual psychological phenomenon, but also as the product of situational factors that contribute to such barbaric behavior. What most offers an explanation for this gang rape is the prisoner dilemma experiment of Stanford University social psychologist Philip Zimbardo. In the prisoner-guard situation, losing control is not an uncommon reaction, even under normal circumstances. Zimbardo created an experiment involving twenty-four prisoners and guards who were divided randomly and placed in circumstances where each person was to play the assigned role for two weeks. The "prisoners" and "guards" were selected from a group of college students who answered a newspaper advertisement calling for volunteers for a psychological study of "prison life." The volunteers were tested to rule out anyone who showed tendencies towards rigid adherence to conventional values and a submissive, uncritical attitude toward authority.[25] The simulation began with wailing police sirens as nine young men were picked up at their homes, frisked, handcuffed, taken to a police station, fingerprinted and booked before being blindfolded and driven to a "prison" in the basement of the Stanford psychology building. There, three young men dressed as guards supervised their activities in a prison-like cell with cots, a small yard, and a solitary confinement "hole." The "guards" were instructed not to use physical punishment or aggression but to simulate dehumanizing conditions of prison life, such as fitting the "prisoners" with a chain and lock around one ankle, dressing them in a loosely fitted smock with no underclothes, and spraying them with a "delousing" liquid. The guards, who served eight-hour shifts, were given uniforms, whistles, and nightsticks. Videotapes and audio-recordings quickly showed that the guard's involvement went far beyond the role-playing. They started to enjoy their power by refusing to let the prisoners go to the toilet, insulting and humiliating them. By the end of day six, the study had to be terminated because the prisoners were getting extremely depressed, anxious, and angry, and the guards were out of control. One third of the guards were extremely cruel and rough.

Group influences are also a factor in individuals' engaging in more sadistic behavior than they would engage in alone. Sigmund Freud (1856-1939) explained that when people are part of a group, an individual gives up his power in the group and feels to be in harmony with them rather than in opposition to them. The support of the group provides a sense of increased power to its members, and a herd mentality induces suggestive influences that stimulate behavior that an individual would not be likely to enact alone.[26] Individuals in groups are also subject to greater conformity as distinguished from obedience. Conformity regulates the behavior among those of equal status, whereas obedience occurs within a hierarchical structure. Some of these insights have been augmented by Solomon Asch's long-important conformity studies, which show how a person under social pressure comes to adopt perceptions held by peers.[27]

Conclusion

The paradox of obedience, conformity, role-playing, and group pressure is that in every situation there will be individuals who will not conform to the requirements imposed by authority, peers, or the situation. During the years of the Holocaust, some Germans assisted Jews, which made them subject to arrest, imprisonment, or worse, but physical contact between Germans and Jews that inflicted dehumanization on Jewish women, children, and men was applauded and rewarded. Despite the Nuremberg Law against *Rassenschande*, despite the fact that rape was not an official weapon of genocide during the Holocaust, rape was a devastating aspect of the German degradation of Jews as human beings.

When the writer Gitta Sereny interviewed Franz Stangl (1908-1971), the former commandant of Sobibor and Treblinka, she asked him, "Why, if they were going to kill them [the Jews] anyway, what was the point of all the humiliation, why the cruelty?" Stangl answered her: "To condition those who actually had to carry out the policies. To make it possible for them to do what they did."[28] The Auschwitz survivor Primo Levi (1919-1987) gave his own interpretation of what Stangl meant: "Before dying the victim must be degraded, so that the murderer will be less burdened by guilt. This is an explanation not devoid of logic but it shouts to heaven: it is the sole usefulness of useless violence."[29]

Notes

1.   Gitta Sereny, *Into That Darkness: An Examination of Conscience* (New York: Vintage Books, 1983), 101.

2.   For help with this information, special thanks go to Crispin Brooks of the University of Southern California (USC) Shoah Foundation Institute for Visual History and Education. The Foundation's web site is: http://dornsife.usc.edu/vhi. Accessed September 26, 2011.

3.   Shoah Foundation interview, Zelda-Rivka Hait.

4.   Ibid.

5. This excerpt is adapted from Goldenberg's essay, "Sex-based Violence and the Politics and Ethics of Survival," which is forthcoming in *Different Horrors/ Same Hell: Gender and the Holocaust*, ed. Myrna Goldenberg and Amy Shapiro (Seattle, WA: University of Washington Press, 2013). In addition to her many articles, Goldenberg's books include: *Experience and Expression: Women, the Nazis, and the Holocaust*, ed. Elizabeth R. Baer and Myrna Goldenberg (Detroit, MI: Wayne State University Press, 2003) and *Testimony, Tensions, and Tikkun: Teaching the Holocaust in Colleges and Universities*, ed. Myrna Goldenberg and Rochelle T. Millen (Seattle, WA: University of Washington Press, 2007). For further information about the interpretation of the Law for the Protection of German Blood and German Honor, see Raul Hilberg, *Perpetrators Victims Bystanders: The Jewish Catastrophe 1933-1945* (New York: HarperCollins, 1992), 72. Also relevant for the issues in this chapter are Helene J. Sinnreich, "The Rape of Jewish Women during the Holocaust" as well as my essay on "Sexual Abuse of Jewish Women during and after the Holocaust: A Psychological Perspective." These two articles appear in Sonja M. Hedgepeth and Rochelle G. Saidel, eds., *Sexual Violence against Jewish Women during the Holocaust* (Waltham, MA: Brandeis University Press, 2010), 108-23, and 255-74, respectively.

6. Kirsty Chatwood, "(Re)-Interpreting Stories of Sexual Violence: The Multiple Testimonies of Lucille Eichengreen," in *Life, Death and Sacrifice: Women and Family in the Holocaust*, ed. Esther Hertzog (Jerusalem: Gefen Publishing House, 2008), 162.

7. For a concise overview of the debate that swirls about the degree to which the Nazi race defilement laws prevented German men from inflicting sexual violence against Jewish women, see Lenore J. Weitzman, "Women," in *The Oxford Handbook of Holocaust Studies*, ed. Peter Hayes and John K. Roth (Oxford: Oxford University Press, 2010), 209-11.

8. See, for example, the account of Grese provided by the former Auschwitz prisoner Gisella Perl in her memoir, *I Was a Doctor in Auschwitz* (New York: International Universities Press, 1948).

9. Na'ama Shik, "Sexual Abuse of Jewish Women in Auschwitz-Birkenau," in *Brutality and Desire: War and Sexuality in Europe's Twentieth Century*, ed. Dagmar Herzog (New York: Palgrave Macmillam, 2009), 221-46.

10. Ibid., 238.

11. Ruth Seifert, "War and Rape: A Preliminary Analysis," in *Mass Rape: The War against Women in Bosnia-Herzegovina*, ed. Alexandra Stiglmayer (Lincoln, NE: University of Nebraska Press, 1994), 55.

12. Flora M. Singer, *Flora: I Was but a Child* (Jerusalem: Yad Vashem, 2007), 33-35.

13. Olga Lengyel, *Five Chimneys: The Story of Auschwitz* (New York: Howard Fertig, 1983), 182.

14. Tadeusz Borowski, *This Way for the Gas, Ladies and Gentlemen*, trans. Barbara Vedder (New York: Penguin Books, 1976), 93.

15. Ibid., 86.

16. Ibid., 86. A block Elder was the prisoner in charge of order and compliance within a prison block. They were usually camp veterans.

17. Perl, *I Was a Doctor in Auschwitz*, 78-79.

18. Shik, "Sexual Abuse of Jewish Women in Auschwitz-Birkenau," 235.

19. Dagmar Herzog, "Introduction," in *Brutality and Desire*, 10.

20. Robert J. Lifton, *The Nazi Doctors: Medical Killing and the Psychology of Genocide* (New York: Basic Books, 1986), 447.

21. Ibid., 449.

22. Shoah Foundation interview, Leah Finkel.

23. Louise J. Kaplan, *Female Perversions: The Temptations of Emma Bovary* (New York: Doubleday, 1991), 127.

24. Eta Wrobel, with Jeanette Friedman, *My Life My Way: The Extraordinary Memoir of a Jewish Partisan in World War II Poland* (New York: YIVO Institute for Jewish Research, 2006). Wrobel did not include the rape scene in the final version of the book. (Author's conversation with Jeanette Friedman.)

25. Craig Haney, Curtis Banks, and Philip Zimbardo, "Interpersonal Dynamics in a Simulated Prison," in *International Journal of Criminology and Penology* 1 (1973): 69-97.

26. See Sigmund Freud, *Group Psychology and the Analysis of the Ego*, trans. and ed. James Strachey (New York: Norton, 1975).

27. See Solomon E. Asch, "Effects of Group Pressure upon Modification and Distortion of Judgment," in *Groups, Leadership, and Men: Research in Human Relations*, ed. Harold Guetzkow (Pittsburgh, PA: Carnegie Press, 1951).

28. Sereny, *Into That Darkness*, 101.

29. Primo Levi, *The Drowned and the Saved*, trans. Raymond Rosenthal (New York: Summit Books, 1988), 126.

Further Suggested Reading

Anonymous. *A Woman in Berlin: Eight Weeks in the Conquered City*. Translated by Philip Boehm. New York: Henry Holt, 2005.

Kaufmann, Paulus, Hannes Kuch, and Christian Neuhauser, eds., *Humiliation, Degradation, Dehumanization: Human Dignity Violated*. New York: Springer, 2011.

Ofer, Dalia, and Lenore J. Weitzman, eds., *Women in the Holocaust*. New Haven, CT: Yale University Press. 1998.

Rittner, Carol, and John K. Roth, eds. *Different Voices: Women and the Holocaust*. St. Paul, MN: Paragon House, 1993.

Vetlesen, Arne Johan. *Evil and Human Agency: Understanding Collective Evildoing*. Cambridge: Cambridge University Press, 2005.

Questions for Discussion

1. Why is rape so likely to occur in times of war and genocide?

2. Does it make sense to speak of rape during the Holocaust as a "by-product of the dehumanization process of genocide" rather than as a direct instrument of genocide during that catastrophe?

3. Do you agree with Franz Stangl, the former commandant of Sobibor and Treblinka, that cruelty, humiliation, and dehumanization are inflicted on people so that the perpetrators of mass atrocities can do their "work" more easily?

4. Zelda-Rivka Hait testifies that after she was raped a German officer saved her life. Why do you suppose he did so?

5. If you met Viktors Arājs, the man who raped Zelda-Rivka Hait, what would you say—or do—to him? Why?

3

Sexual Violence against Men: Torture at Flossenbürg

Dagmar Herzog

> . . . now he was really dead.
> —*Heinz Heger, The Men with the Pink Triangle*

"Torture at Flossenbürg," the text I have chosen as a focal point for this chapter, is taken from Heinz Heger's *The Men with the Pink Triangle*. This book was first published in German in 1972 and in English in 1980. Heinz Heger was a pseudonym for Josef Kohout (1917-1994), a homosexual man from Austria who was imprisoned in the Nazi concentration camps of Sachsenhausen and Flossenbürg during World War II.[1] The pink triangle was the badge that men imprisoned for homosexuality were forced to wear.

In several ways, the excerpt from Kohout's book is pertinent to the topic of rape and sexual violence in war and genocide. One point has to do with the importance of *historically contextualizing* instances of sexual violence in the cultural attitudes about sexuality specific to a time and place. Another involves the particular nature of sexual violence *within camp settings* as opposed to battlefields. And a third has to do with the manifest *pleasure in brutality* demonstrated by the perpetrators in this as in so many other wartime and genocidal settings. In addition, focusing on *sexual violence against men* helps us to gain a fresh vantage point and to think more deeply about what dynamics are at work in the more frequent phenomenon of sexual violence against women.[2] Here, then, is Kohout's account of what he witnessed one day at Flossenbürg.

My cell door had some thin cracks in it, through which it was possible to see very well and observe the main corridor. It was in this corridor, as I soon learned, that the torture of prisoners sent to the bunker took place.

While I was there, a prisoner with a pink triangle, from Innsbruck in Austria, was tortured to death in the bunker. He was stripped naked and his hands tied to a hook in the wall so that his body hung in the air, and he couldn't touch the ground with his feet. Two or three SS men who were assigned to the cell block, as the bunker was officially known, stood around and waited for the "performance" to start, i.e. the torture of the Tirol lad.

The first "game" that the SS sergeant and his men played was to tickle their victim with goose feathers, on the soles of his feet, between the legs, in the armpits, and on other parts of his naked body. At first the prisoner forced himself to keep silent, while his eyes twitched in fear and torment from one SS man to the other. Then he could not restrain himself and finally he broke out in a high-pitched laughter that very soon turned into a cry of pain, while the tears ran down his face, and his body twisted against his chains. After this tickling torture, they let the lad hang there for a little, while a flood of tears ran down his cheeks and he cried and sobbed uncontrollably.

But the depraved SS men were set on having a lot more fun with this poor creature. The bunker Capo had to bring two metal bowls, one filled with cold water and the other with hot. "Now we're going to boil your eggs for you, you filthy queer, you'll soon feel warm enough," the bunker officer said gleefully, raising the bowl with hot water between the victim's thighs so that his balls hung down into it. The prisoner let out a shattering scream for help, the pain hurt him so much. He tried to struggle free or roll to one side, but the ties on his hands and feet held him tight.

"Give him the cold water, then, he's already hot, the filthy swine," one of the SS men laughed brutally, whereupon the SS butchers took up the cold water and placed this bowl between their victim's thighs. Again he screamed in agony, for the cold water must have been excruciating after the extreme heat. Time and again he tried to break free from his chains, but he just exhausted himself fruitlessly.

This procedure was repeated several times, until the tormented victim lost consciousness, after he had screamed himself hoarse and could now only emit a kind of gurgle. A bucket of cold water was thrown over him to bring him round, then the torture was started again, with bits of skin now hanging visibly down from the victim's scalded scrotum.

While carrying out these tortures, the SS monsters got through a bottle or two of spirits that they passed around. They were already quite drunk when they hit upon a new torture that could only have been thought up in the brain of someone totally perverted.

"He's a bum-fucker, isn't he, let him have what he wants," growled one of the SS men, taking up a broom that stood in the corner and shoving the handle deep into the prisoner's anus. He was already incapable of screaming any more, his voice had simply seized up with pain, but his body jerked and tore at the chains; there was still a lot of life left in the lad. But the SS men only laughed the louder at the "filthy queer," who moved his lips as if to cry out without any sound emerging.

Finally they cut the fainting man down and let him fall to the floor, where he lay in a heap without stirring, his limbs bent under him. The drunken SS men staggered out into the open, but the last of them stumbled over the martyred prisoner who was still lying on the ground. Angrily he kicked the victim with the toe of his boot, and he began to stir again.

"The filthy queer's still alive," he burbled, taking up the wooden stool that was standing next to the wall and bringing it down with all his force on the victim's head. This finally freed the poor martyr from his pains, for now he was really dead.[3]

Male homosexuality continued to be illegal in post-Nazi West Germany and Austria. It was not until the early 1970s that Kohout could publish his account even under a pseudonym. It is no coincidence that he could do so only in the context of the gay rights movement that was growing at that time. In 1969, homosexuality was decriminalized in West Germany (female homosexuality had never been a crime there), and that decriminalization made possible the emergence of a broad-based gay rights movement. In 1971, homosexuality (both male and female) was finally decriminalized in Austria.

By the end of the World War II, approximately 100,000 German and Austrian men had been prosecuted by the Nazi government for same-sex activities. Close to half (more than 46,000) had been convicted and usually sent to prisons or penitentiaries. Between 10,000 and 15,000 were sent to concentration camps. There they were made to do impossibly hard labor, especially in rock quarries, and often tortured. At Buchenwald, men accused of homosexuality were subjected to medical experiments (for example, implantation of testosterone capsules in the testicles). Several hundred men were also castrated. Although the majority—perhaps 70 percent—survived these diverse torments, only often to be drafted into the Nazi armed forces, an estimated 7,000 died. The killing fields included not only concentration camps and prisons but also mental institutions and the cannon-fodder units deliberately sent into suicide missions on the Eastern front in the last desperate months of the war. Intensified prosecution of men caught in same-sex acts was also extended to lands occupied by the Nazis in the course of World War II, including Luxemburg, parts of Belgium, and the regions of France under direct German occupation, as well as both annexed and occupied Poland, and annexed portions of Czechoslovakia.

The Sexual Politics of Nazism

Considerable numbers of homosexual men were involved in the Nazi Party early on and attracted to its right-wing ideology, but once Adolf Hitler (1889-1945) came to power in January 1933, he moved quickly to try to please conservative forces, particularly the Christian churches. This action included a "battle against public immorality" in March 1933. Catholic and Protestant leaders alike were thrilled by the campaign to rid kiosks of pornography, sweep the streets of prostitutes, and shut down many gay and lesbian bars.

In the post-World War I Weimar Republic, Jewish medical doctors and sex rights activists in Germany had been strongly associated with efforts to promote a sexual morality based on consent, mutuality, satisfying experiences for women as well as for men, and the use of contraception. They also were involved in efforts to decriminalize homosexuality. Many church leaders, both Protestant and Catholic, were deeply threatened by what they perceived as the secularization within their own flocks; they shared the view that Jews were responsible for the sexual immorality that purportedly pervaded Weimar culture, and they hoped fervently that the Nazis would help in cracking down on this immorality.

Clergymen who were fully aware of the Nazis' anti-Jewish venom rushed to praise Hitler as a "marvelous gift from God" and a "through and through decent, clean character." They openly stated that the "immense power of international Jewry" was a "frightening" threat, while Hitler was providential: "It is absolutely certain that God sent us this man and through him protected us from a great danger."[4] Church leaders especially were enthusiastic about "the new government's level-headed yet firm approach toward filth wherever it is visible . . . therefore *Siegheil!*"[5]

After gaining endorsement from the churches, Hitler also needed the backing of the military leadership. In 1934, eighteen months into his rule, in his eagerness to win the support of the army, Hitler orchestrated the murder of his friend and close associate, Ernst Röhm (1887-1934), the openly homosexual head of the brown-shirt *Sturmabteilung* (SA, Stormtroopers). A number of other political rivals were murdered as well. Although Röhm had been killed above all because his overweening ambitions conflicted with Hitler's desire to curry the army leadership's favor, Röhm's homosexuality, which had not bothered Hitler before, became a convenient justification for the killings. In his pronouncements in the aftermath of the murders, Hitler played openly to popular homophobia.

As the vehemently homophobic Heinrich Himmler (1900-1945), head of the black-clad *Schutzstaffel* (SS, Protection Squad) increasingly gained power in the Third Reich, the government's policies changed. Already in 1935, the Nazis sharpened the existing law, Paragraph 175, which criminalized male homosexual activity, not only by expanding it to include Paragraph 175a, with its special provisions against seduction of minors and abuse of relations of dependency (such as teacher-student, boss-employee, officer-soldier), but also by widening the law's application. Previously, only "intercourse-like" actions had been criminalized (anal sex or rubbing the penis between the thighs); as of 1935 not only mutual masturbation but parallel individual masturbation and even "erotic" glances could fall under the law's purview. The populace was encouraged to participate in denunciations of neighbors and coworkers. By 1937, prosecutions of men for homosexual acts escalated considerably.

Significantly, all of this happened in a context that was *not* generally sexually repressive. Nazi doctors put themselves in the place of the Jewish doctors and sex rights activists who had been driven into exile, imprisoned, or killed. Nazi advice literature was filled with recommendations—often blatantly taken from Jewish-authored texts—on how to intensify orgasms or on how to use condoms (which remained legal throughout the Third Reich). Within two to three years of Nazi rule, by 1935-1936, Christian leaders realized that the Nazis actually had no intention of cleaning up Germany's sexual culture, but rather were constantly encouraging pre- and extramarital sex and mocking the churches for their prudery. "Fleshly lust" and a "spirit of uncleanness" were at work in the Third Reich, one evangelical Protestant commentator noted. "At first we believed that morality would improve in the Third Reich, today this hope reveals itself more and more as false."[6] And a Catholic clergyman warned that "the era has succumbed to a horrifying barbarism and overstimulation of the sexual drive." The "entirety of public and private life has today been gripped" by an "insane overvaluation of the sexual-sensual."[7] What church leaders had once blamed on Jews, they now—remarkably and fearlessly—blamed on Nazis.

However, despite their outrage over the Nazis' encouragements to heterosexual activity outside of marriage, the churches shared the Nazis' hostility to homosexuality. Thus, once the Nazis had been militarily and ideologically defeated in 1945, and the Christian churches had reacquired considerable political and cultural influence with the support of the Western occupiers, and while other Nazi-era laws were revoked, the law against male homosexuality remained in force in West Germany—including the Nazi addendum of Paragraph 175a. Although Nazi abuse and murder of homosexuals were well known in the immediate postwar era, the support given by the churches to anti-decriminalization efforts was a major factor in keeping the law on the books until 1969. A culture of intimidation shut down all efforts to bring justice to the victims; many men who had been imprisoned under Nazism were rearrested and imprisoned again in the postwar period.

Intimate Violence in the Name of Science

Although the Nazis rejected Christian sexual conservatism, several things about homosexuals bothered Nazi homophobes. One was homosexuals' purported refusal to live up to Nazi ideals of manliness; a second was their purported refusal to reproduce. But thirdly, the Nazi leadership was tremendously anxious that *it* not be perceived as "queer," internationally or domestically. Precisely because there had initially been a strong association in the public mind between Nazism and homosexuality due to the number of homosexual members in the SA, and in addition because the Nazi leadership was acutely aware that the many Nazi single-sex organizations like the Hitler Youth and the SS—and indeed the armed forces themselves—provided worryingly conducive environments in which homoerotic activity was a distinct and frequent possibility, the regime sought violently to prove Nazism's straightness.

Fourthly, and crucially, the Nazis were extremely interested in understanding and theorizing sexual orientation—and sex more generally. One consequence was an extraordinary amount of obscene intimate violence in the name of scientific inquiry. Nazism was not only a massive experiment in reproductive engineering but also very much preoccupied with the control of pleasure. Nazism involved a strong impulse to break through the mysteries of the human organism, a ferocious "will to know" about the functioning of bodies and psyches that, over and over, crossed the border into violence. Some of the patients in their regular practices, but above all the inmates of prisons and camps, provided medical doctors with human "guinea pigs" for an array of invasive investigations into sexual variability, desire and response, drive and dysfunction. The Nazis wanted to understand sex, to make sense of it, to be able to shape it.

In describing the sterilization experiments carried out in Auschwitz on Jewish and other prisoners, both women and men—with X-rays and short-wave rays, surgeries, or caustic substances injected into the genitals—medical professional Olga Lengyel (1908-2001), a Jewish prisoner, noted that they were "cruel games rather than serious quests for truth. Everyone has heard of heartless children who amuse themselves by tearing off the legs and wings of insects. Here there was one difference: the insects were human beings." At times, Lengyel reports, women sterilized with short-wave rays ("which caused unbearable pains in the lower part of the abdomen") would be cut open so doctors could observe the lesions. But also included in the "cruel games" was the demand that women whose bodies were already burned from the extreme levels of X-ray radiation applied to sterilize them should be tested to see if they still could copulate, and that boys who had been sterilized should be forced to masturbate after attempts to provoke an erection by invasive massaging of the prostate gland.[8] These "games" were undertaken in the name of delving into the mysteries of sex.

With respect to homosexuality, there was under Nazism intense competition among academic "theoreticians" eager to win the government's favor and—however ironic this may seem in view of the regime's wider obsession with biology—biological paradigms of sexual orientation turned out *not* to be the winning models. Both hormonal and genetic-hereditary explanations for sexual orientation were largely shunted aside in favor of developmental theories and the belief that sexual conversion back to heterosexuality was possible for the majority of men who engaged in same-sex sex. This view was presented not least as a vigorous refutation of the well-known (and, as it happens, Jewish, leftist, and homosexual) Weimar sex rights activist Magnus Hirschfeld's (1896-1935) insistence that homosexuality was constitutionally determined and that sexual orientation was largely unchangeable.

The eventually predominant Nazi model of homosexuality involved an assertion that heterosexuality was extraordinarily fragile. The punitive intensification of homophobic persecution from 1937 on was fueled by the idea that homosexuality was very much a possibility lurking within the majority of men, and that for many men it was a phase they literally went through in their youth. The key idea, as one expert put it, was that "with respect to homosexuality there is no stark either-or, no incurable fateful naturalness, but rather many transitional stages and in-between forms."[9]

The idea that sexual orientation was fluid and variable also informed the work of Nazi psychotherapists such as Dr. Johannes H. Schultz (1884-1970), author of the widely circulated, regime-endorsed advice manual *Geschlecht-Liebe-Ehe* (Sex-Love-Marriage, 1940). Schultz exemplified the combination of cheerful advancement of pleasurable heterosexual sex and noxious homophobia that was distinctive for Nazism. Through both his deep-breathing techniques and his reassuring, affirmative sex advice, Schultz could fairly portray himself as a man committed to and succeeding in enhancing heterosexuals' sex lives. But Schultz also openly advocated the murder of the handicapped and, behind closed doors, he choreographed torture. At the German Institute for Psychological Research and Psychotherapy in Berlin, Schultz and a commission of co-workers forced accused homosexuals to perform coitus with a female prostitute while the commission watched. Whoever performed heterosexually to their satisfaction under these conditions was set free; whoever did not, and hence had revealed his likely incurability, was sent to a concentration camp.

The idea to force men imprisoned for homosexuality to have heterosexual intercourse within the camps was an enlarged part of this same research agenda, which was sponsored by Himmler. Eventually, brothels were established in ten of the major Nazi concentration camps, including Flossenbürg in July 1943.[10] Initially, the brothels were designed to "reward" privileged prisoners (never Jews) for their labor contributions to the concentration camp enterprise. In these places, selected women were forced to provide sexual slave labor for other inmates, generally for six months, before they were murdered themselves. For those men who visited the brothels doing so was sometimes less an expression of sexuality than an attempt to maintain their sense of being alive in the midst of all-surrounding and ever-looming death—even as in this way they inevitably became participants in the victimization of the female prisoners. For the women prisoners forced into this labor must definitely be understood as victims of sexual violence. They were being raped repeatedly, by other prisoners, at the behest of the guards, in the course of their enslavement. *The Men with the Pink Triangle* discusses the "experiments" conducted there in forcing homosexual men to perform coitus with female prostitutes to see if they could be "cured" of their homosexuality—replete with the voyeurism of the guards who through peepholes watched prisoners during these acts and then discussed the details of what they had seen.

Camps as Laboratories of Domination

Every instance of sexual violence in war and genocide displays some combination of motives and functions in an ever-shifting, ugly kaleidoscope of human possibilities. For one thing, when perpetrators share in horrific violence, they reaffirm their bonds with one another. In addition, however, what especially requires explanation are those forms of "excess cruelty" or "gratuitous cruelty" that—as historian Doris Bergen puts it—are "unnecessary and even counterproductive in some cold, industrial form of killing." Citing the example of gangs of ethnic German thugs brandishing buckets full of the testicles they had cut off their male victims, Bergen suggests that sexual dismemberment of both men and women certainly works to intimidate the enemy populace. But she points out that specifically the deliberate dehumanization of the victim produced by "horrific, taboo-breaking sexual violence" is also about the assertion of power hierarchies between perpetrator and victim. Atrocity functions to "destroy the dignity and claim to humanity of those targeted for destruction in order to make the perpetrators' job easier."[11]

Inside the Nazi camps, such dynamics and others were at work, and here it is important to note the differences between camp situations and battle situations. While battlefields are dangerous territories where soldiers are deeply dependent on each other and continually afraid for their own lives, in the camps, perpetrators were safe and protected. In fact, guard duty in a concentration camp was an excellent way to avoid battlefront duty and death. The left-wing Catholic journalist Eugen Kogon, who was imprisoned in Buchenwald, commented after the war on how "fond of promiscuity" and of "drinking and whoremongering" were the SS officers and guards working in that "paradise of shirkers," the concentration camp system.[12] Along related lines, historian Henry Friedlander, one of the foremost experts on the mass murder of the disabled and its interconnections with the genocide of European Jewry, also remarked tersely about the perpetrators' "anything goes" attitude in the killing centers, which were rife with extensive alcohol consumption, "sexual licentiousness, . . . drunken orgies, numerous sexual liaisons, brawling and bullying, and stealing the property of victims." Such things took place, says Friedlander, among "staff members" who "worked day after day in a factory with only one product: corpses of murdered human beings."[13]

And there are yet further dynamics to consider in the Nazi camp situation. For in the perpetrators' sexual assaults, the innermost selfhood of the victims was targeted. In the camps, sexual humiliation of prisoners by the guards was constant. Thus, for instance, women entering Auschwitz—whether driven into "showers" and about to be killed by Zyklon B gas or spared from immediate death, stripped, shaved, and paraded for selections—were subjected to riding crops jabbed into breasts, menacing mocking commentary, and defloration with fingers. Whether intuitive or deliberate, the aim of these sexual violations was not only to rob the victims of their lives but also to destroy their dignity and their sense of their own worth and goodness. Beating and killing were not enough for the perpetrators. Through sexual violence, they intended to murder the soul of their victims before physical death took place.

It is also important to note that while the camps were places where the guards had total power over their prisoners, the guards often were thoroughly *bored*. This combination did much to turn the camps into laboratories of domination. As sociologist Wolfgang Sofsky has noted, there was at work within the camps "a form of military barracks harassment raised to a barbaric level, a brute and vicious hazing come unhinged." Among the examples cited by Sofsky was a day at Sachsenhausen when two Jewish men were seized and, "to the roaring laughter of the onlookers," had "a water hose placed in their mouths; the faucet was then turned on full blast, until their internal organs burst from the pressure." On another occasion, at Buchenwald, a rope was tied around a prisoner's genitals, and he was hung upside down.[14] Analyzing carnivalesque violence among American GIs in Vietnam, historian Joanna Bourke stresses not only the self-affirmation and group bonding that taboo-violation affords but also and especially the thrill of impunity and the gleefully exhilarating *enjoyment* that such outrageous violations apparently provide.[15] In sum, torture of the victims, particularly in the form of rape and sexual violence, was for perpetrators a major way to compete with and entertain each other. Outdoing each other in a spiral of ever greater grotesquerie was the goal.

Such dynamics are at work in "Torture in Flossenbürg," the excerpt from *The Men with the Pink Triangle* with which this chapter began. The torture inflicted on the young Austrian homosexual was not for the purpose of gaining information, but rather he is raped in multiple ways for the entertainment of the guards. From the start, the violence is specifically sexual: in the sense that tickling is used to torment, in the sense that the genitals are directly attacked, and in the sense that it is in his capacity as someone labeled homosexual that the victim is being violated. The entire event is accompanied by homophobic jokes. In German, "warm brother" is a slang term for queer man, and such references are made during the immersion of the victim's testicles in boiling water. Moreover, Kohout's testimony depicts not an individual perpetrator but a group dynamic through which the perpetrators amuse each other. Notably, alcohol adds to the party atmosphere and ramps up the competitive infliction of abuse, which culminates in the obviously homophobic violence of anal rape with a broomstick.

The Men with the Pink Triangle provides a concise and remarkable glimpse into the situation of homosexual men within the concentration camp universe. Kohout himself survived by sheer luck, accompanied by the occasional good fortune of being protected by fellow prisoners. His book covers a broad range of subjects, ranging from the daily camp atmosphere of backbreaking labor and utter terror to the intricacies of conflict and cooperation among the prisoners. As we have seen, its episodes also provide significant insights about the perpetrators. One more instance of that kind involves a Christmas Eve late in the war. Beside a festively decorated 10-meter-tall tree, eight dead men sway from a gallows while prisoners are forced to stand nearby and sing carols. The deliberately sacrilegious behavior of the perpetrators reveals a self-understanding—indeed an arrogance—that seems to put them above divine as well as human law. In another instance, the book describes a camp commander so obsessed with finding excuses to torment the homosexual prisoners that he crawled on his knees to check the barracks floors for dust—and if he found even the slightest speck, prisoners were forced to do knee bends and sit ups while the commander kicked them in the groin. Yet another glimpse provided by Kohout involves a camp commander who, "on more than thirty occasions," masturbated publicly while prisoners were being flogged.[16]

The end of the war meant the end of the concentration camps, but not the end of imprisonments, and certainly not the end of rape and sexual violence against men—homosexual or otherwise—during war and genocide. There would be more than 13,000 convictions for homosexuality in postwar Austria alone, and multi-year prison sentences were standard. The situation in West Germany was even worse: 100,000 men were prosecuted between 1945 and 1969 (as many as under Nazism), and approximately 50,000 were convicted and imprisoned; some committed suicide. Homosexual men lived in constant fear of being exposed. In the immediate aftermath of the war, a few short memoirs had appeared in journals, but *The Men with the Pink Triangle* was the first book-length, comprehensive treatment of the experiences of men imprisoned for homosexuality under Nazism, and—although at least two other memoirs have appeared since—it remains the best known.[17] Meanwhile, Kohout's pink triangle was given to the United States Holocaust Memorial Museum after his death in Vienna in 1994.[18]

Notes

1.   In the discussion that follows, I shall refer to Kohout as the author of *The Men with the Pink Triangle*. Kohout's book inspired Martin Sherman's 1979 play, *Bent*. A film version of the play appeared in 1997 under the direction of Sean Mathias.

2.   For further insight on this topic, see Patricia Viseur Sellars, "Rape," in *Genocide and Crimes Against Humanity*, ed. Dinah L. Shelton (Farmington Hills, MI: Gale Cengage, 2005). Available at: http://www.enotes.com/rape-reference/ rape . Accessed December 11, 2011.

3.   Heinz Heger, *The Men with the Pink Triangle*, trans. David Fernbach (Boston: Alyson, 1980), 82-84.

4.   Protestant pastors quoted in Hartmut Lehmann, *Protestantische Weltsichten: Transformationen seit dem 17. Jahrhundert* (Göttingen: Vandenhoeck und Ruprecht, 1998), 136-39.

5.   "Der frische Zug im neuen Staat," *Volkswart* 26 (1933): 170-71.

6.   Ernst Krupka's remarks in *Der Weg zum Ziel*, no. 18 (1935), quoted in "Pikanterien im Beichtstuhl," *Das schwarze Korps*, 26 June 1935, 5.

7.   Matthias Laros, *Die Beziehungen der Geschlechter* (Cologne: Staufen-Verlag, 1936), 11-12.

8.   Olga Lengyel, "Scientific Experiments," in *Different Voices: Women and the Holocaust*, ed. Carol Rittner and John K. Roth (New York: Paragon House, 1993), 120-26. This passage comes from Lengyel's book *Five Chimneys*, trans. Clifford Coch and Paul P. Weiss (Chicago: Ziff-Davis Publishing Company, 1947).

9. "Homosexualität—keine Erbkrankheit," *Deutsche Sonderschule* 5 (1938): 663. The author also argued that if the "mostly Jewish" sex experts in Weimar had had their way, the result would have been "appalling" and homosexuality could have become a "mass phenomenon."

10. See Robert Sommer, "Sexual Exploitation of Women in Nazi Concentration Camp Brothels," in *Sexual Violence against Jewish Women during the Holocaust*, ed. Sonja M. Hedgepeth and Rochelle G. Saidel (Waltham, MA: Brandeis University Press, 2010), 45-60, especially 47.

11. Doris Bergen, "Sexual Violence in the Holocaust: Unique and Typical?" *Lessons and Legacies VII: The Holocaust in International Context*, ed. Dagmar Herzog (Evanston, IL: Northwestern University Press, 2006), 188.

12. Eugen Kogon, *The Theory and Practice of Hell*, trans. Heinz Norden (New York: Berkley, 1968), 285-86.

13. Henry Friedlander, *The Origins of the Nazi Genocide: From Euthanasia to the Final Solution* (Chapel Hill, NC: University of North Carolina Press, 1995), 193-94, 237.

14. Wolfgang Sofsky, *The Order of the Terror: The Concentration Camp*, trans. William Templer (Princeton, NJ: Princeton University Press, 1997), 223-25.

15. Joanna Bourke, *An Intimate History of Killing* (New York: Basic Books, 1999), 3, 25-27.

16. Heger, *The Men with the Pink Triangle*, 55.

17. Pierre Seel, *I, Pierre Seel, Imprisoned Homosexual: A Memoir of Nazi Terror*, trans. Joachim Neugroschel (New York: Basic Books, 1995); Rudolf Brazda with Jean-Luc Schwab, *Itinéraire d'un triangle rose* (Paris: Florent Massot, 2010).

18. A distinctive collection of Josef Kohout's wartime belongings, including his pink triangle, was acquired by the United States Holocaust Memorial Museum after his death. For more about these holdings, Kohout's remarkable life, and the history of Nazi persecution of homosexuals, visit http://www.ushmm.org/research/collections/curatorscorner/detail.php?content=2011-07-28. Accessed September 26, 2011. At this link, the Museum's Klaus Müller underscores the significance of the Kohout collection.

Further Suggested Reading

Goldstein, Joshua S. *War and Gender: How Gender Shapes the War System and Vice Versa.* Cambridge: Cambridge University Press, 2001.

Grau, Günter, ed. *Hidden Holocaust? Gay and Lesbian Persecution in Germany 1933-45.* Trans. Patrick Camiller. Chicago: Fitzroy Dearborn, 1995.

Heineman, Elizabeth D., "Nazism and Sexuality: The Doubly Unspeakable?" In *Sexuality and German Fascism*, edited by Dagmar Herzog. New York: Berghahn Books, 2004.

Jones, Adam, ed. *Gendercide and Genocide.* Nashville, TN: Vanderbilt University Press, 2004.

Oosterhoff, Pauline, Prisca Zwanikken, and Evert Ketting. "Sexual Torture of Men in Croatia and Other Conflict Situations: An Open Secret," *Reproductive Health Matters* 12 (2004): 68-77. Available at: http://pramudithrupasinghe. weebly.com/uploads/4/2/1/8/4218922/sexual_torture_of_men_in_croatia_ and_other_conflict.pdf . Accessed September 26, 2011.

Russell, Wynne, "Sexual Violence against Men and Boys." *Forced Migration Review* 27 (2007): 22-23. Available at: http://www.fmreview.org/FMRpdfs/ FMR27/12.pdf . Accessed September 26, 2011.

Sommer, Robert, "Camp Brothels: Sexual Slavery in Nazi Concentration Camps." In *Brutality and Desire: War and Sexuality in Europe's Twentieth Century*, edited by Dagmar Herzog. New York: Palgrave Macmillan, 2009.

Stemple, Lara. "Male Rape and Human Rights." *Hastings Law Journal* 60 (2009): 605-47. Available at: http://uchastings.edu/hlj/archive/vol60/Stemple_60-HLJ-605.pdf . Accessed September 26, 2011.

Storr, Will. "The Rape of Men." *The Observer*, July 17, 2011. Available at: http:// www.guardian.co.uk/society/2011/jul/17/the-rape-of-men. Accessed September 26, 2011.

Questions for Discussion

1. What appears to motivate sexual violence against men? How are the motives similar in violence against women? How are they different?

2. What do you learn from the Kohout excerpt about the perpetrators' relationships to each other?

3. What role does alcohol play in the violence that Kohout describes?

4. Is there something timeless about the kinds of violence to which the SS guards subjected this man, or are the tortures they chose to inflict on him in some way specific to 1930s–1940s Europe?

4

War Rape and the Global Condition of Womanhood: Learning from the Bosnian War

Christina M. Morus

I am a person without an identity.
—*Selma, a Bosniak woman*

The document that orients this chapter contains testimony from a Bosniak (Bosnian Muslim) woman called Selma, a pseudonym used to protect her identity. Selma's story is about more than rape and war. It is about the life and death of a nation—about war and genocide's destructive power to strip away people's humanity and identity. Her story deals with dawning ethno-nationalism and intimate intra-fratricidal violence; it depicts people raped, tortured, and killed, often by friends and neighbors. But Selma's is also a complex story of gender oppression within which we begin to see a broader women's narrative about war and genocide. And in Selma's story there is hope about the possibility of maintaining humanity in the hysteria of war and about the prospect of transcending "us" and "them" thinking. To understand Selma's story, some historical contextualization is necessary.

On December 4, 1943, Josip Broz Tito (1892-1980) declared the existence of the Socialist Federation of Yugoslavia, which included six republics: Croatia, Montenegro, Serbia, Slovenia, Bosnia-Herzegovina (BiH), and Macedonia.[1] Tito envisioned a nation where "Brotherhood and Unity" would transcend ethno-national loyalties.[2] In some respects, Tito's vision materialized, particularly during the Cold War, given that Yugoslavia's Cold War neutrality, a comparatively open brand of socialism, and prominence in the Non-Aligned Movement allowed a relatively high standard of living, unrestricted international travel, and a flourishing cultural and intellectual scene. While some citizens were dissatisfied with Tito's rule, Yugoslavia was largely prosperous and stable under his control, and most citizens were generally content as Yugoslavs.

Tito's death in 1980 left a political vacuum. By the end of the Cold War a decade later, economic crises accompanied Yugoslavia's waning strategic importance, yet no leader capable of inspiring national confidence had emerged. The Federation's stability and prosperity deteriorated as opportunistic politicians, particularly in Croatia and Serbia, worked with idealistic intellectuals, ruthless media personalities, and power-hungry thugs to intensify and amplify common people's disparate discontent. Exploiting growing insecurities, Slobodan Milošević (1941-2006) ascended to power in Serbia, blaming problems on the "ethnic other" and advocating "Serbian unity" as the solution. This ideology fed rising Croatian ethno-nationalism, which increased instability and ramped up mistrust among people from diverse ethnicities, who continued to live— but more and more precariously—in integrated communities throughout Yugoslavia, particularly in BiH.[3] In this way, Tito's Pan-Slavic brotherhood gave way to xenophobic hysteria.

In June 1991, as Milošević's growing influence upset the balance among the republics, Slovenia declared independence and achieved freedom after a "Ten Day War."[4] Emboldened by Slovenia's secession, Croatia followed suit. An independent Croatia represented a host of perceived and actual threats to ethnic Serbs living in Croatia's Krajina region, and by September 1991, Croatia was at war. The war officially ended in 1992, but continued in Krajina until 1995.

Meanwhile, ethno-nationalism was also percolating in Bosnia-Herzegovina, the most multi-ethnic and religiously intermixed of the Yugoslav republics. With no clear ethnic majority, BiH was primarily populated by Bosniaks (Bosnian Muslims), Orthodox Christian Serbs, and Roman Catholic Croats. Convinced that it had no chance of survival within Serb-dominated Yugoslavia, a majority of BiH citizens voted in favor of secession, and although Bosnian-Serbs as a whole were staunchly against it, BiH declared its independence in March 1992. A tri-partite war broke out in April, lasting until December 1995. Pitting Bosnian Serbs (supported by Milošević and his regime), Bosnian Croats (with the support of Croatia's President Franjo Tudjman [1922-1999]) and Bosniak forces against one another, the conflict was further complicated by shifting Croatian alliances throughout. The most notorious atrocities of the nearly four-year conflict included the Serbian siege of Sarajevo, the mass murder of Bosniaks in Srebrenica, the proliferation of concentration camps, forced deportations, ethnic cleansing, genocide, and mass rape.

While combatants on all three sides are responsible for a range of war-time atrocities, the International Criminal Tribunal for the former Yugoslavia (ICTY) estimates that from 1992 to 1995, Serb forces raped between 20,000 and 50,000 women and girls, the majority of whom were of Bosniak ethnicity.[5] Dedicated rape camps were a common feature of the wartime landscape.[6] In schools, hospitals, homes, and barns, women and girls aged from six to seventy were raped repeatedly, some held captive as long as two years. The rape camps were predicated on intimate gendered indignities. Rapists, who often knew their victims before the war, peppered their misogynist taunts with familiarity. Sometimes brothers or fathers were forced to rape their own family members and were killed if they refused to do so. Many women were impregnated and held until termination of their pregnancy was impossible. Enforced domestic servitude, which included cooking and cleaning for their rapists, added to the abused women's humiliation. At their captor's will and whim, women were bought and sold, traded for goods, or given as rewards. While Serb soldiers committed the lion's share of atrocities early on, Croatian and Bosniak soldiers also perpetrated rape warfare. Survivor testimonies reveal an innumerable range of still unhealed physical, emotional, and social scars.

Now, here is Selma's testimony:[7]

> Around mid-1991, the Serbs I'd known seemed to change. I couldn't recognize people I'd been friends with for years. I'm not saying they were all war-mongers but they suddenly spoke of feeling threatened, saying we couldn't go on living together in the same community, and we should all go our separate ways. Some claimed that Muslims should leave Banja Luka. I tried to avoid disputes and went about my daily routine as if I didn't notice anything unusual, as if I couldn't hear the ominous, Muslim-threatening rhyme chanted day and night.[8]

In December that year, I took on a Serb woman, even though a Muslim applied for the same job. Two years earlier, I was given my shop in the divorce settlement. My ex-husband—we'd met on a school excursion—had remarried. I heard that just before the war he'd sold his property and returned to Serbia.

When the war began, I knew I also had to leave Banja Luka. The Serbs had seized complete power and started harassing Muslims, placing bombs in their houses, demolishing their shops, offices, and cafes. Muslims and Croats were being arrested and fired from their jobs.

I had saved about 15,000 Deutsch Marks, but happened to trust the wrong person who'd promised (for 3,000 DM) to connect me with a Yugoslav Army officer who'd make arrangements to fly me to Belgrade in a military plane and from there to any destination I chose. I planned to go to a friend in Munich. Some said my "contact" used the money to fly his family from Banja Luka, but others claimed he'd been arrested. I didn't have time to investigate further—I had to find another solution.

Sometime later, a Serbian woman—my school friend—promised that her brother would help me leave Banja Luka—otherwise impossible without a special permit. One afternoon, she visited my flat, which I hadn't left for days since I was prohibited from working. She promised that in two days, they'd come for me. She didn't ask for money in advance, telling me to pack my money, my documents and only my most necessary personal belongings. She kept her promise—two days later she turned up at my doorstep to find me no longer there. At that time, I was staying on the floor below, with my neighbors. I don't know what the new "tenants" told her, but she rushed out of the building to her brother's car which left immediately.

I watched through the curtain. I didn't dare show myself. No one could know I was there or alive. And alive I was: a battered, raped, disfigured heap of flesh and bones.

I'd been raped the day before, 21st August. It was early morning when they broke into my flat. They neither rang nor knocked on the door—simply forced it open. I don't know what time it was. I only remember a crushing noise woke me. I was about to jump out of bed when they burst into the bedroom. First I saw two men in uniforms without rank, wearing Serbian military caps. "On your feet, you whore!

Give us your money," one said calmly, grinning menacingly. I stood up. The other tore my nightdress. I reached for my dressing-gown but the first one said it wasn't a fashion show and to give him all my money, right away.

I said the money was in the living room and started for the door but he stepped in front of me, grabbing my breasts. His grip was so tight that I screamed. He slapped my face; the other one told him to be patient until I handed over the money. He let go and I went into the living room where I saw two others. I recognized one—he'd been a regular in the café opposite my shop. He'd worn plain clothes then. I didn't know his name, but remembered his face.

He found my purse with some Dinars and 3,000 DM that my friend had told me to prepare, my passport, and a few photographs. The other was searching through the wardrobe but he couldn't find any money since I had hid 5,000 DM in the lining of the dress I intended to wear on the trip, and the rest—4,000 DM was in my shoe. They went on searching, collecting my jewelry along the way (I didn't have much, but among other things there was a ring—a gift from my father—and a bracelet).

My "acquaintance" lost his patience and hit me, demanding more money and putting a gun to my temple. I told him about the money in the shoe, explaining I'd given the rest to a Yugoslav Army officer for the flight to Belgrade. "What Yugoslav Army? There's no Yugoslav Army anymore, we're Serbian troops now," he shouted, cursing.

He was the one to rape me afterwards. He did it on the floor, tying my wrists with a belt first. Actually, he tied them and fastened them to the table leg. The other one slouched in the armchair watching, shouting vulgar remarks. I tried to scream, but the rapist hit me in the mouth. I almost chocked from the blood dripping down my throat.

The two who'd burst into my bedroom raped me next. One of them beat me, but the other didn't. When the fourth's turn came—the one watching—he first whipped me with his belt and untied my hands, making me kneel in front of him. He unbuttoned his trousers and shouted, "Suck it, you whore!"

Afterwards, he kicked me several times with his boots; the others had already left. He stayed probably hoping to find more money. I remember this only vaguely—I lay in a pool of blood yet feel no pain.

The heavy boots echo in the hall. Then the thumping sound dies away and everything is quiet.

When I tried to get up, I felt the slight pressure of a hand on my shoulder. I gasped, fearing it was him, but it was the neighbor from the flat below. I couldn't believe my eyes—she was the most unlikely person to come to my aid! She hadn't spoken to me since they'd moved in three years earlier because, due to my negligence, her flat had been completely flooded. She'd been so persistent in avoiding me that she wouldn't even accept compensation for the damage or the help my husband offered to refurbish the flat. Her husband followed suit. When he couldn't avoid me in the hall, he averted his gaze.

So, that very neighbor was the only person to come to my rescue. "Please, hurry—they may return," she said, helping me to my feet. She led me to her flat—actually, dragged me, as I couldn't walk.

She crammed me into a wardrobe, airless and stuffy. The last thing I remember was the swishing of the mop on the floor (later she told me that to cover my tracks, they quickly cleaned the blood trail from my flat to theirs, as well as inside their flat.)

A painful, cold sensation on my face woke me. At first I couldn't see, but when my blurry sight cleared a little, I made-out the face of my neighbor kneeling beside me, wiping my face with a wet cloth. Everything became dark again. When I came round I was lying on the floor. My body was stiff but I felt no pain—only a mind-numbing buzz. I managed to touch my face on my third attempt, and felt the rough surface of a bandage. Raising my arm, I noticed a blue and grayish striped sleeve—someone had dressed me in men's pajamas.

I lay motionless, trying to move my toes. The fact that I wasn't paralyzed didn't mean much at the moment; I was completely indifferent—my mind was numb. After a while, the neighbor came. When she saw me awake, she bent down and whispered: "Don't be alarmed, I'll give you a painkiller." She brought a glass of white liquid and a straw. Drinking through the straw was a strenuous feat; it took what seemed like an eternity. The liquid tasted bitter, retched.

I don't know when I fell asleep, but that bitter taste is the last thing I remember. The next time I woke, the room was completely dark. My whole body ached, but the buzzing in my head was gone. I started remembering the previous day: my flat was broken into; I'd been raped and battered . . . For hours, I lay motionless in the dark. It was almost dawn when I fell asleep again. I'd slept for what seemed like only a moment when a baby-cry woke me.

I remembered she'd had a baby in March. Soon I heard a woman's and then a man's voice blending in with the baby-cry. I heard a woman say "Perhaps you could call in and say you won't be coming today. You'd better stay here in case those scumbags return."

It was already daylight when she came with a glass. I thought she'd brought that liquid again, but it was milk: the tastiest, most scrumptious milk I'd ever drunk, despite the pain of drinking. She asked if I could move and I mumbled in confirmation. "Look what they've done to you—the beasts," she said, leaving the room.

Later, as she removed the terribly stinky bandage from my face, I managed to ask the day and hour. She said it was August 22, almost noon. She put raw meat (a beef steak) on my face, explaining it would draw-out pain and swelling. She added she'd help me onto the bed as soon as her husband returned. (Fearing spinal injuries, they'd left me on the floor). While talking, she bandaged my face skillfully, like a real nurse.

Later, with her help, I managed to take a few steps: an achievement equal to a summit climb for me. She caught me looking at the pajamas and explained they were her husband's because she couldn't find hers. "I haven't had time to bring anything from your flat except this dress which I've already soaked, although I doubt these blood stains will come out," she said, recovering a bundle from under the bed. It was the dress I was to flee Banja Luka in. I remembered the 5,000 Deutsch Marks and the friend's promise to pick me up. But I couldn't recall whether I'd broke-down and admitted to the louts where I'd hidden money. I asked her, or rather mimed, to unfold the dress and pull out the seam. When she recovered the first banknote she smiled, saying it was a tiny bit of justice. When she'd removed all the notes, she asked if I'd planned to flee Banja Luka. I nodded and somehow explained about my friend and the plan. She eyed me for a few seconds, and then uttered her suspicion: "She may've had her fingers in this. If she doesn't show up today as planned, she's in it."

At half-past eight, actually a few moments earlier, my neighbor helped me to the window. She held me while I peered through the curtain. When my friend's brother's car pulled up looking for me, I felt enormously relieved. "I'm glad for you," she said.

I stayed in that flat for seventy-six days and no one found out. They concealed it even from their closest friends. All that time, my life depended on them. Had it leaked that they were hiding me, they could've been killed, even though they were Serbs. I hope you understand why I'm reluctant to reveal their names although they deserve (and have) all my gratitude. Rare are people who'd risk their own and their child's lives to save a person they'd been at odds with.

A fortnight later, I felt much better, though still bruised. I could walk. One day, the neighbor told me what happened after they'd dragged me into their flat. Those scumbags, the rapists, had returned an hour later. This had given my neighbor and her husband time to clean the blood from the hall and their flat. Expectedly, the louts asked around, searched a few flats, but luckily had trusted my neighbor completely when she said I was the last person she'd ever hide considering she hadn't spoken to me since she'd moved in.

The life of a fugitive was a difficult adjustment. I had to hide the smallest detail of my existence—even a bit of cigarette smoke would be tell-tale. Not only did I quit smoking, I learned to stay still for hours on end. When friends visited, I squeezed under the bed in "my" room, sweating until they left. When alone, I never moved, switched on the light, or used the toilet.

I never suspected anything when I missed my period: I reckoned it was a post-traumatic reaction. Pregnancy was impossible; I'd been a long-standing fertility patient at clinics in Sarajevo, Zagreb, Ljubljana, Lipik (I hear it was completely razed by Serbs) and Daruvar. I couldn't get pregnant. My husband left me because of that: his parents wanted a grandchild.

I began to realize something was amiss when morning sickness started occurring regularly, and I suddenly became queasy from smells. When I confided in my neighbor, she turned pale. That was the first time I saw her really frightened. She collected herself, admitting that her husband had already asked his brother—a Serbian army officer—to get me out, but he'd refused. I felt miserable, but worse than that helpless feeling was the knowledge that after all I'd done to get pregnant, I was now carrying an unwanted child.

At this point Selma fell silent. The tape first recorded faint sobs which gradually became louder until she wept desolately. I turned off the recorder at which point she reacted almost hysterically: "We have to finish," she cried and pressed the "record" button.

How could I have born it? The child would've been marked forever, only because I wished to be a mother. My neighbor suggested I give it up for adoption, but I wasn't brave enough. If I'd born a baby I would never be able to give it away. Did I have any other choice except that blasted abortion? If it could've been done in Banja Luka I would've without hesitation.

For the next few days, my neighbor was very reserved. I knew she was apprehensive—she didn't know how to help me. One day, her husband came to my room (it was unexpected since he hadn't done it before). "Don't be weary, please, don't despair, we'll find a solution. I'll get you out of Banja Luka even if it's the last thing I do," he said, trying to comfort me.

After a few days, she brought me the money I'd left with her, saying I'd need it soon. Then she brought me a pair of shoes—they weren't new, but they fit. She never gave me any details, but her cheerful mood suggested there was hope that things might go well after all.

My spirits lifted when she asked if I could sew a jacket and a skirt to look like a uniform. I replied that if I had a sewing machine I could whip something up for a whole unit. She left the room, returning a minute later with a bolt of grey fabric, saying it was for me.

That evening her husband brought a second-hand sewing machine which looked almost new. He bought it from a vendor in Gospodska Street for just 50 Deutsch Marks! He advised me to start immediately; I needed to be ready in two days. I was dumbfounded.

That evening I cut the shape of my latest design with blunt scissors. The next day, my hostess cut the buttons from her raincoat which perfectly matched the material. I had almost finished sewing when her husband returned. He couldn't believe his eyes: "You aren't just one of the best, but the very best seamstress I've ever seen," he said approvingly. He suggested his wife could find a matching blouse in her wardrobe, but she didn't have a light blue one. Finally he searched his shirts and found one. He explained that my transfer to Croatia was unofficially arranged with UNPROFOR—for a fee, of course.[9] I was supposed to look like a staff member.

I could hardly wait. That night and the next day I was elated, but apprehensive that something might go wrong. Luckily, as you can see, everything turned out. I left the flat—my hideout—at 2:45 a.m. on November 5, my neighbor, that dear friend, all in tears. I wept, too. Her husband drove me to a house in Nurije Pozderca Street where my liaison with UNPROFOR took over. While still in the car, my neighbor instructed me when and how to pay the UNPROFOR people (four sets of them: two in Bosnia, two in Croatia).

At three o'clock on the dot, we arrived at the meeting point. Attempting to make the parting less dramatic, my neighbor asked me to take good care of his shirt since it was his favorite. As I was about to open the car door, he thrust a piece of paper into my hand—a Vienna telephone number that I was to ring and say, "The Petrovics are in Zagreb and they're all well," meaning I'd arrived safely.

In an UNPROFOR jeep, wearing a blue helmet, I left Banja Luka at 7 a.m. The ride went smoothly, without a problem even when we drove through Serb-occupied territory and crossed into Croatia. The only complication was a two-hour delay when some UNPROFOR staff arrived late. I arrived in Zagreb early in the afternoon. I was lucky that the first person I met was Mrs. V.—she took care of everything. I'm forever indebted to this wonderful person.

Three weeks ago, she found me a job. I'm moonlighting in a designer boutique. I'll be paid less than my work is worth, but I'm not complaining. As soon as I recover completely I'll sit down to work. I'm still 1,800 DM short for an illegal transfer to Germany. Yes—illegal; how else could I go? I am a person without an identity.

—*Zagreb, 5 December 1992*

As Selma testifies, wartime and genocidal rape and its grotesque consequences force the victimized women to experience gender in the most primitive sense—as it is thrust upon them. But what about the men?

What did they think they were doing? Were the men who assaulted Selma "putting that bitch in her place"? Disciplining the unwieldy feminine form? Perhaps, but because rape is increasingly common as a systematic weapon in contemporary conflict, this phenomenon requires a wider lens. The continued proliferation of wartime and genocidal rape involves a variety of factors and motivations that are reflective of the global condition of womanhood during peacetime. Though gender inequality and oppression appear in different ways and degrees in every culture, they are entrenched and reinforced even in the most progressive circumstances. Are rapists such as those who attacked Selma encouraged by and relishing the benefits of global patriarchy? Let's think about that possibility.

Gender oppression, sexual violence, and war have a symbiotic relationship. Unfortunately, rape in war is commonplace, like looting, and has been treated as war's inevitable consequence, if not a victor's right—a spoil of war. In most accounts of war, rape is overlooked, downplayed, or regarded as a crime against the men to whom the "spoiled" women "belong"—a crime of (dis)honor or property damage. The latter perspective is rooted in the idea that wartime or genocidal rape, while assaulting women, primarily targets the men who cannot protect "their" women— their property. Sexual violence in the BiH War reflects these outlooks, suggesting that women's humanity is something afforded them by men, and women can be reduced to property at any point.

Significantly, men were also victims of sexual violence in the BiH War. Still, these acts were a symbolic subjugation, "feminizing" male victims through sexual domination, thereby symbolically relegating them to the "inferior" status of women. The rape of a man or boy is intended to emasculate and humiliate not only the specific victim but other males in the group who are helpless to prevent or stop the attacks. The powerlessness of femininity is imposed upon them all. Such developments underscore again the need to attend to globally entrenched assumptions about gender and how those assumptions influence our larger understanding of war.

Yet, let it not be said that no progress has taken place. In 2001, for example, a landmark ICTY verdict found three Bosnian Serb leaders guilty for their role in war rape.[10] This decision underscored that sexual torture, enslavement, and rape are crimes against humanity, a significant development in international law, in the recognition of women's war experiences, and, by extension, in the global consciousness of women's humanity. Unfortunately, these developments remain insufficient to end systematic rape in war and genocide. Criminalizing such rape is crucial but only a start. Criminalization does not address the prevalent mindset that makes systematic mass rape possible. Further, while the brutal campaigns of mass rape in Bosnia-Herzegovina, and then in Rwanda, drew human rights advocates' attention to wartime and genocidal rape, the proliferation of sexual violence continues virtually unabated in ravaged places such as Darfur and the Democratic Republic of Congo.

As one considers how to reveal and combat the cultural assumptions that make mass rape possible in war and genocide, it is important to note that narratives and analyses of conflicts such as the ones in Bosnia-Herzegovina and Rwanda typically focus on the ethnic differences that seem to govern them. Such frameworks, however, are usually gender-biased in the sense that they overlook, or at least do not highlight, gendered realities that are also decisive. Instead the conventional frameworks of analysis submerge women's gendered experience while ethnicity looms much larger. Ethnically-focused narratives typically are dominated by male experiences; women play supporting roles—the grieving mother or wife, for example, or the passive victim of the ethnic "other." In this context, women are useful as historical evidence of ethnic injustice, but their political utility is more relevant than their humanity. Moreover, as their testimony seems to have value only through these limited roles, women who have been assaulted and abused in mass sexual violence are left either to truncate their experiences and narratives to fit conventional expectations or to remain voiceless. Neither option allows women full human agency. Hence, even in circumstances where it is recognized that mass sexual atrocities have taken place, the usual frameworks of interpretation and analysis—and even for the indictment and prosecution of perpetrators—continue to emphasize ethnic conflict and to downplay, if not ignore, gender oppression.

What if war and genocide are narrated and analyzed from much more gendered perspectives? That issue played a key part in the response of Women in Black, the Serbian anti-militarist feminist group that published *Women's Side of War*, a collection of war testimonies from Serbian,

Croatian, Bosnian, and Kosovar-Albanian women. *Women's Side of War* shows that the experiences of women across ethnic lines are more similar then different. It shows, too, that attention to women's experiences may help to establish inter-ethnic solidarity by empowering women to find a public voice that can both create greater gender consciousness and transcend divisive ethnic frameworks.

Women's Side of War differs from many accounts of war and genocide because its narratives emphasize experiences that transcend ethnicity. Much more than a record of ethnically-driven victimization, the testimonies in *Women's Side of War* highlight a range of human experience: for example, being forced to flee at a moment's notice while pregnant; the helplessness of waiting for one's missing and perhaps murdered husband to return; the humiliations of refugee life compounded by the lasting wounds of sexual assault. That range of experience is not restricted to one group or another but cuts across and through those divisions. The narratives in *Women's Side of War*, moreover, are not only about suffering, loss, and grief; they extend to the necessity to "go on," to cope, for instance, with the loss of one's partner and breadwinner or with the frustration of submerging one's own trauma in order to be caregiver to a returning husband.

Also embedded in *Women's Side of War* are examples of people who reach across ethnic lines to help one another, which, among other things, reflects the book's intention to de-center and dislocate the assumptions that perpetuate ethnic conflict and the gender inequality that usually attends and helps to fuel it. *Women's Side of War* does not provide a solution for the issues it addresses—no book can do so—but wisely and credibly it does suggest that women can use the common threads of their gendered experiences as a creative foundation for senses of identity that enhance women's public presence, empowering women to advance global gender consciousness and political policy that can curb sexual violence in war and in peace.

Selma's testimony, which you have read above, comes from *Women's Side of War*. That testimony by a Bosniak woman who was raped by Serbian soldiers depicts hideous gendered violence, but it contains much more than that. Selma voices despair as her identity and nation dissolve. But we also see a person who, though brutalized by Serb soldiers, never expresses totalizing ethnic hatred. We become aware of people who, at great risk, reach across ethnic lines to aid and comfort one another. And perhaps most importantly, as we think about Selma's story, we may discover that we identify with her humanity. In addition to creating empathy for her, Selma's testimony can and should move us to strive for greater global gender equity, a key condition for saving others and even ourselves from the destructiveness of mass sexual violence in war and genocide, and in peacetime, too.

Notes

1.   Tito was of Croatian and Slovenian descent. He led the Yugoslav partisans in overthrowing the Axis powers in Yugoslavia before World War II ended in the rest of Europe in 1945. In the Socialist Federation of Yugoslavia, each republic had equal power and was named for its largest ethnic group. Only Bosnia-Herzegovina did not have a clear ethnic majority. Serbia, the largest republic, contained two autonomous provinces: Kosovo (ethnic-Albanian majority) and Vojvodina (ethnic-Hungarian majority).

2.   "Brotherhood and Unity" was a popular Titoist slogan that summarized Yugoslavia's ideal and its policy of inter-ethnic unity. The main groups in the former Yugoslavia—Serbs, Croats, and Bosniaks—have shared a common language, culture, and customs. These groups are descendants of Slavic European stock. Their ethnicity is physically indistinguishable—often even to one another. Religion provides the primary differentiation among these groups. "Serbian" and "Montenegrin" implies "Orthodox Christian" and "Croatian" implies "Roman Catholic." Persons formerly known primarily as "Bosnian-Muslim" are now more commonly called "Bosniak," a term that distances the religious association from the ethno-national affiliation. But the Muslim identity of these people remains a key factor in the ethnic differences and tensions within the region.

3.   Cindy S. Snyder, Wesley J. Gabbard, J. Dean May, and Nihada Zulćić, "On the Battleground of Women's Bodies: Mass Rape in Bosnia-Herzegovina," *Affilia* 21 (2006): 184-95. With no ethnic majority, people in BiH were truly intermixed. In a 1991 census, nearly 44 percent identified as Bosnian-Muslim, 30 percent as Serbian, 17 percent as Croatian, and the rest "other." About one-third of urban marriages were reported as "mixed."

4.   The ensuing war was brief, owing to Slovenia's largely homogeneous population and the fact that the multi-ethnic Yugoslav National Army (JNA) had little taste for killing Yugoslavs.

5.   Sabrina P. Ramet, *Balkan Babel: The Disintegration of Yugoslavia from the Death of Tito to the Fall of Milošević*, 4th ed. (Boulder: CO: Westview Press, 2002), 67.

6.   Karen Engle, "Feminism and Its (Dis)contents: Criminalizing Wartime Rape in Bosnia-Herzegovina," *The American Journal of International Law* 99 (2005): 778-816, see especially 784-85.

7.   Selma [pseudonym], in *Women's Side of War*, ed. Lina Vušković and Zorica Trifunović, trans. Mira Janković, Stanislava Lazarević, Dubravka Radanov, et al. (Belgrade, Serbia: Women in Black, 2008), 51-57. The testimony was originally published in Seada Vranić, *Pred Zidom Šutnje* (Zagreb, Croatia: Antibarbarus, 1996). *Women's Side of War* is available at: http://www.zeneucrnom.org/pdf/womens_side_of_war.pdf. Accessed September 27, 2011. Selma's testimony is reprinted with permission from Women in Black and Antibarbarus.

8.   The Serbian rhyme can loosely be translated as: "You devil Muslims, your days are numbered."

9.   The United Nations Protection Force (UNPROFOR) was the first UN peacekeeping force in Croatia and Bosnia-Herzegovina during the Yugoslav wars. UNPROFOR existed from the beginning of UN involvement in February 1992 until March 1995, when the Protection Force dissolved as a result of UN restructuring.

10.   Sarah L. Henderson and Alana S. Jeydel, "Women and Sexual Violence during War," in their book *Women and Politics in a Global World*, 2nd ed. (New York: Oxford University Press, 2009), 303-21, see especially 313.

Further Suggested Reading

Allen, Beverly. *Rape Warfare: The Hidden Genocide in Bosnia-Herzegovina and Croatia*. Minneapolis, MN: University of Minnesota Press, 1996.

Carpenter, R. Charli. *Forgetting Children Born of War*. New York: Columbia University Press, 2010.

————, ed. *Born of War: Protecting Children of Sexual Violence Survivors in Conflict Zones*. Bloomfield, CT: Kumarian Press, 2007.

Drakulić, Slavenka. *S.: A Novel about the Balkans*. Translated by Marko Ivić. New York: Penguin Books, 2001.

Leydesdorff, Selma. *Surviving the Bosnian Genocide: The Women of Srebrenica Speak*. Translated by Kay Richardson. Bloomington, IN: Indiana University Press, 2011.

Scholz, Sally J. "Human Rights, Radical Feminism and Rape in War." *Social Philosophy Today* 21 (2005): 207–20.

Stiglmayer, Alexandra, ed. *Mass Rape: The War against Women in Bosnia-Herzegovina*. Lincoln, NE: University of Nebraska Press, 1994.

Weitsman, Patricia A. "The Politics of Identity and Sexual Violence: A Review of Bosnia and Rwanda." *Human Rights Quarterly* 30, 3 (2008): 561-78.

Žarkov, Dubravka. *The Body of War: Media, Ethnicity and Gender in the Break-up of Yugoslavia*. Durham, NC: Duke University Press, 2007.

Questions for Discussion

1. How does Selma's story reflect some of the unique ways women are affected by war?

2. In what ways is the reaction of Selma's neighbor surprising, and how might this aspect of Selma's experience affect her outlook on the future?

3. Selma refers to herself as a "person without an identity." What could she mean?

4. How do we see evidence of global gender inequities in Selma's story?

5. Her story is filled with tragedy, but can parts of Selma's story be viewed as hopeful?

6. How could Selma's story be effective in raising gender consciousness?

5

Rape on Trial: Promises of International Jurisprudence, Perils of Retributive Justice, and the Realities of Impunity

Tazreena Sajjad

Can you—would you be able to recognize Zoran Vukovic today?

—Prosecutor Kuo to Witness 50

A trial transcript provides the document that I have chosen to orient this chapter. The transcript features testimony from a Bosnian Muslim woman identified in the court proceedings as Witness 50. In the summer of 1992, at the age of sixteen, Witness 50 was taken prisoner by soldiers near her village in Bosnia, held for two months, and raped so often that she lost count of how many times and how many men. She was raped vaginally, anally, and orally; she was gang raped by ten men at a time; she was raped by soldiers and paramilitary thugs; she was threatened with guns and knives while being raped; she was trapped in an apartment where she had to clean for the soldiers who raped her all night.[1]

Witness 50 was one of thousands of Bosnian Muslim women who were sexually enslaved and tortured by Bosnian Serbs, Serbs, and Montenegrins during the Bosnian War of 1992-1995. She was one of sixteen women from the town of Foča (pronounced **Fo**-cha) and its surrounding villages in southeastern Bosnia who agreed to testify in 2000 before the International Criminal Tribunal for the former Yugoslavia (ICTY), located in the Netherlands at The Hague. The following excerpt

61

is from testimony given by Witness 50 on March 29, 2000, in the Foča trial case named and numbered as Kunarac et al. (IT-96-23).[2]

Prosecutor Kuo: And when you arrived at Buk Bijela, where did you go, or where were you taken?

Witness: We were taken to one of the rooms in these barracks.

Prosecutor: Were you taken out separately from that room at some point?

Witness: Yes.

Prosecutor: Who took you out?

Witness: Am I supposed to say the name?

Prosecutor: If you know the name, please say it.

Witness: A man named Zoran Vukovic took me out.

Prosecutor: Did you know this man from before the war?

Witness: I might have seen him before the war. The face seemed very familiar to me. Whether I knew it from before, I don't know.

Prosecutor: Did you know his name before the war?

Witness: I don't remember.

Prosecutor: Did you learn his name during the war?

Witness: On several occasions, yes.

Prosecutor: At the time that he took you out at Buk Bijela, did you know his name?

Witness: I don't remember. . . .

Prosecutor: Do you remember the first time that you were taken out from [the] Partizan [Sports Hall]?

Witness:	Yes.
Prosecutor:	Do you remember when it was?
Witness:	Perhaps a day or two later, after our arrival in the Partizan.
Prosecutor:	Do you remember who took you out?
Witness:	Yes.
Prosecutor:	Who was it?
Witness:	It was what I talked about a moment ago, when I was in the WC. Two soldiers whom I did not know came, and among them was Zoran Vukovic again.
Prosecutor:	When you say again, do you mean the same person who raped you at Buk Bijela?
Witness:	Yes.
Prosecutor:	Do you remember if he was armed at that time?
Witness:	Yes, he was.
Prosecutor:	Where did he take you?
Witness:	He took me to an apartment. I assume that it had been abandoned, because I didn't see anybody there. When he brought me to that apartment, he took me into one of the rooms, which was to the left-hand side of the hallway. There was a big bed there for sleeping in. I don't remember exactly whether there was a cupboard or what there was there, but it was a bedroom. And then it happened once again; I was raped again.
Prosecutor:	Did Zoran Vukovic say anything to you?
Witness:	Well, yes. They would always say things. But once he

had done what he was about—I mean, once he had raped me, when he finished raping me, he sat down and lit a cigarette, and he said that he could perhaps do more, much more, but that I was about the same age as his daughter, and so he wouldn't do anything more for the moment.

Prosecutor: Can you—would you be able to recognize Zoran Vukovic today?

Witness: Yes, I could.

Prosecutor: I'm going to ask you to look around the courtroom, and please take your time. Let us know if you recognize somebody here who was the Zoran Vukovic you have described.

Witness: If I look from the door going down, the first person next to the guard with dark hair is Zoran Vukovic.

Prosecutor: To help clarify the record, could you just describe something he's wearing?

Witness: He is wearing a light blue shirt, a dark blue suit.

Prosecutor: Your Honour, may the record reflect that the witness has pointed out the accused, Zoran Vukovic.

The Foča trials convicted Zoran Vukovic, a member of the Bosnian Serb Army (VRS) and a member of the paramilitary in Foča, and sentenced him to twelve years' imprisonment for raping Witness 50. Also convicted of rape were Dragoljub Kunarac, leader of a VRS unit, and Radomir Kovac, sub-commander of the VRS military police and a paramilitary leader in Foča. The Tribunal sentenced them to 28 and 20 years' imprisonment, respectively.[3]

After the war ended, many of the women and girls who survived Foča made their way to Sarajevo. There they heard the news about the verdict and sentencing. Nezira Zolota, spokesperson for a Sarajevo-based association of female camp survivors, talked to some of the Foča women when the report came in. The leniency of the sentences left them "seriously shaken," she said. The "minimum punishment . . . actually minimized the suffering of the victims."[4]

Rape and Sexual Violence in International Law

The appearance and testimony of survivors of rape is a relatively recent phenomenon at international war crimes trials, marking a new era in which international humanitarian law recognizes wartime rape as a war crime,[5] a crime against humanity,[6] and, in some instances, an act of genocide.[7] This legal recognition of the systematic sexual attack on women and girls (and at times men and boys) as a strategy of warfare and even genocide is a significant paradigm shift. No longer is rape taken to be a by-product of armed conflict, perpetrated more or less with impunity, but it can be judged to be an act of war and genocide for which individuals are accountable. With the trial transcript from Foća as its point of departure, this chapter traces the development of international jurisprudence in recognizing rape as an act of war and genocide, the limitations of retributive justice, and the persistent realities of impunity, which deny justice for the vast majority of sexual violence survivors.

Sexual violence as a tool of war and genocide is not a new phenomenon. The large-scale systematic sexual abuse of women and girls during conflict is as old as the history of conflict itself. Contemporary history has recorded the large-scale rape of Chinese women and girls in Nanjing in the late 1930s, the exploitation of Korean "comfort women" by Japanese soldiers through the 1940s and 1950s, the campaign of gang rapes by the Red Army in Germany as World War II ended, the sexual abuse and exploitation of Vietnamese women by American soldiers during the Vietnam War in the 1960s and 1970s, the use of rape and sexual violence against the indigenous Mayan population by Guatemalan soldiers during the civil war (1960-1996). That list, however, is scarcely exhaustive. Sexual violence has been employed in armed conflict in places as diverse as Afghanistan, Bangladesh, Chechnya, Darfur, Iraq, Kashmir, Kuwait, Liberia, Sierra Leone, Sri Lanka, Sudan, and Uganda. In the early twenty-first century, pervasive and particularly brutal acts of sexual violence against young girls and women in the Democratic Republic of Congo defy imagination where acts of torture are concerned. Yet, until almost the end of the twentieth century, international legal proceedings rarely, if ever, addressed such sexual violence. Rape did not draw attention in the trials that took place in Europe after World War II. During the Tokyo tribunal (1946-1948), the Allies' prosecution of high-ranking Japanese officials for crimes committed in the Far East did include the mass rapes committed in Nanjing in 1937. But the indictment did not mention the sexual enslavement of approximately two hundred thousand "comfort women" in the countries occupied by the Japanese Imperial Army. This omission was conspicuous given that in 1948 a Dutch military court in Batavia (Indonesia) prosecuted and convicted twelve Japanese army officers for sexually enslaving thirty-five Dutch women.[8] After that, for almost fifty years, courts fell silent about the crime of rape and sexual violence during military conflict. These results meant that countless sexually abused women disappeared from the public sphere. With little access to psychological support but besieged by social stigma, they had to cope with trauma and shame as best they could. In some circumstances— Bangladesh is one example—political calculations led to amnesty for war criminals. Creating circumstances where perpetrators could consolidate their economic and political bases, such amnesty intensified the climate of fear and shame in which those who survived systematic sexual violence had to live. The absence of political will to bring the perpetrators to justice combined with cultural taboos to imprison the women in a world of silence and denial.

Given the pervasiveness of sexual violence in armed conflict, the need for substantive *legal* responses grew increasingly urgent. To a degree, some responses of that kind have been in place for decades, but the law that embodies them has not been adequately enforced. While similarities and differences exist between international human rights law and international humanitarian law, both forms of law provide specific provisions for women and girls.[9] The Universal Declaration of Human Rights (UDHR, 1948), the International Covenant on Civil and Political Rights (ICCPR, 1966), and the United Nations Protocol to Prevent, Suppress, and Punish Trafficking in Persons (2000), denounce all forms of torture, slavery, and degrading treatment.[10] The Convention on the Rights of the Child (CRC, 1989) and its Optional Protocol (2000) oblige states to protect children from sexual assault and torture. The Convention against Torture (CAT, 1984) prohibits torture at all times, stipulating that "no exceptional circumstances whatsoever, whether a state of war or a threat of war, internal political stability or any other public emergency, may be invoked as a justification for torture."[11] Other conventions that specifically mention the prohibition of sexual violence against women include the United Nations Declaration on the Elimination of Violence against Women (EVAW, 1993),[12] the Convention on the Elimination of all forms of Discrimination Against Women (CEDAW, 1979),[13] and the Inter-American Convention on Violence (1994). Further, the Optional Protocol to the Women's Convention (1999) provides measures to monitor and ensure compliance with the Women's Convention.[14] The rights enshrined in these conventions are to be respected regardless of the presence of an armed conflict or public emergency. That understanding is deeply rooted in international law. The Martens Clause of the Hague Conventions (1899, 1907), for example, supported the principle that fundamental human rights norms do not cease to be applicable during armed conflict. In that same tradition, Common Article 2 to the 1949 Geneva Conventions indicates that basic human rights must be respected in times of war. War provides no excuse for setting aside "the provisions which shall be implemented in peacetime."[15]

Within the framework of international humanitarian law that explicitly protects women and girls, the first specific reference to rape and other forms of sexual mistreatment is found in Article 27 of the Fourth Geneva Convention.[16] It states: "women shall be especially protected against any attack on their honour, in particular against rape, enforced prostitution or any form of indecent assault."[17] Furthermore, because rape and sexual violence qualify as "inhuman treatment" under Article 147 of the Fourth Geneva Convention, those acts would also constitute "grave breaches" of the Geneva Conventions. The International Red Cross confirmed such an interpretation when it found that rape constitutes a grave breach of the Geneva Conventions since it is "willfully causing great suffering or serious injury to the body or health."[18]

Well and good though these developments in international law have been, they fell short when it came to enforcement. However, when war broke out in the former Yugoslavia in the early 1990s, human rights mobilization, often sparked by feminist scholarship and initiatives, coalesced into significant international pressure for action to curb and prosecute wartime sexual violence against women. The developments within the International Criminal Tribunal for Former Yugoslavia (ICTY) and later the International Criminal Tribunal for Rwanda (ICTR) have advanced the legal reconceptualization of and response to sexual violence in internal and international conflicts.

The 1993 United Nations statute establishing the ICTY included rape and enslavement as crimes against humanity, a charge second only to that of genocide.[19] Importantly, this provision constituted the first time that cases of rape and sexual violence were identified as crimes against humanity and subject to prosecution within an international court.[20] The ICTY eventually brought numerous indictments that included charges for rape and sexual violence. The Foča trials in particular were groundbreaking for the ICTY. Three Bosnian Serb veterans—the previously mentioned Dragoljub Kunarac, Radomir Kovac, and Zoran Vukovic—were accused of systematic sexual violence against Muslim women in Foča. They were found guilty on multiple counts including systematic and savage rape, torture, and enslavement. More than that, the ICTY interpreted their acts as crimes against humanity. Thus, for the first time in the ICTY's deliberations, individuals were convicted of crimes against humanity for acts of rape, and for the first time in any international court, enslavement was found to be a crime against humanity.

As the presiding judge, Florence Mumba of Zambia, summed up the proceedings, "The three accused are not ordinary soldiers whose morals were merely loosened by the hardships of war. They thrived in the dark atmosphere of the dehumanization of those believed to be enemies. . . . Rape was used by members of the Bosnia Serb armed forces as an instrument of terror." Mumba added that the actions of the three defendants showed "the most glaring disrespect for the women's dignity and their fundamental human rights on a scale that far surpasses even what one might call the average seriousness of rapes during wartime."[21]

In July 1998, a treaty creating a permanent International Criminal Court (ICC) expressly named crimes based on sexual violence as part of that court's jurisdiction. Two months later, on September 2, 1998, before cases of that kind reached the jurisdiction of the ICC or even the ICTY's Foča trials, the International Criminal Tribunal for Rwanda (ICTR) found former Rwandan mayor, Jean-Paul Akayesu, guilty of nine counts of genocide, crimes against humanity, and war crimes. During the Akayesu trial, Tutsi women testified that they had been subjected to repeated collective rape by Hutu militia, including assaults that Akayesu viewed.[22] They spoke of witnessing other women being gang-raped and murdered while Akayesu stood by, reportedly saying to the rapists at one point "don't complain to me now that you don't know what a Tutsi woman tastes like."[23] The verdict in the Akayesu case produced the first conviction in an international court for rape as a crime against humanity; the first conviction of genocide by an international court, a decision that, for the first time, included rape as an act of genocide; and the first time an international court punished sexual violence in a civil war. The ICTR broke further ground in providing the widest definition of rape in international law to that point, recognizing that rape consists of a physical invasion of a sexual nature, committed on a person under coercive circumstances and that sexual violence, including rape, is not limited to physical invasion of the human body and may include acts that do not involve penetration or even physical contact.

The ICTY and ICTR decisions, plus the establishment of the ICC, did much to advance recognition of sexual violence in international humanitarian law and other UN Resolutions. Subsequently, the definition of a crime against humanity has continued to expand, taking further into account the specific indignities forced upon women during conflict. The definition of rape has also expanded since the ICTR's work—from being considered a war crime and a crime against humanity and an act of genocide, it is now also legally seen as a form of torture and a weapon of enslavement. Consider the following cases. On February 25, 2009, after a four-year trial, the Special Courts of Sierra Leone found former Revolutionary United Front (RUF) interim leader Issa Hassan Sesay and RUF commander Morris Kallon guilty on sixteen of eighteen counts of war crimes and crimes against humanity, and former RUF chief of security Augustine Gbao guilty on fourteen counts. Among the charges was that of forced marriage, marking the first time a court has convicted on the charge of forced marriage, which the prosecution argued should be considered a crime against humanity distinct from other forms of sexual violence such as sexual slavery. Meanwhile, Joseph Kony, head of the notorious Lord's Resistance Army in central Africa, has been indicted on more than thirty charges of war crimes and crimes against humanity, including the charge of recruiting and using child soldiers, which takes into account the use of girl soldiers for sexual enslavement.[24]

The Limitations of Law

Certainly, significant legal progress has been made in recognizing the specific sexual indignities women and girls are subjected to during war and genocide. The criminalization of rape and sexual violence focuses analysis on issues of command, control and execution, and individual culpability, and, as Nicola Henry argues, the prosecution of rape and sexual violence under international law is significant for at least four reasons: It contributes to the preservation of post-conflict collective memory by establishing a historical record of rape as a war crime; signals the acknowledgement of rape as a deplorable, condemnable, and punishable act of war; ensures that perpetrators are held accountable for their crimes; and includes victims who otherwise may have been deprived of ways to speak about the atrocities committed against them.[25] Henry's catalog could apply as well to rape and sexual violence when they are interpreted to be crimes against humanity and/or genocidal acts. Despite the strides made in international law, however, the complexity of indicting and prosecuting individuals for sexual crimes means that most women and girls never see their perpetrators in court. When it comes to curbing sexual violence as a war crime, crime against humanity, or an act of genocide, the law faces considerable difficulties, and those difficulties leave wide latitude for perpetrators to act with impunity.

Conviction rates: The international conviction rates for gender-based crimes are low. Taking into account the ICTY, the ICTR, and other United Nations special courts, such as the one in Sierra Leone, successful prosecutions for sexual violence number less than forty at the time of this writing. The majority of them come from the ICTY, which had the benefit of a gender advisor to focus attention on cases involving rape and other forms of sexual violence. The ICTR, in particular, has been criticized for failing to include rape charges on initial indictments—even in the case of Akayesu, who was not originally accused of gender-related crimes.[26] More recently, at the Special Courts for Sierra Leone, the case against members of the pro-government militia, the Civil Defense Forces (CDF), did not include rape or other sexual offenses.[27] Although the prosecutors tried to amend the CDF indictment to include allegations of crimes of sexual violence, the judges refused, arguing that the accused would have insufficient time to prepare a defense against the allegations.[28] The number of convictions for wartime rape and sexual violence in national courts is negligible, almost absent.

Challenges of investigation: Legal recourse tends to be extremely stringent and the burden of proof does not always hold up to the realities on the ground. First, for rape and sexual violence to be tried as a *jus cogens* (compelling law) crime, one that violates a norm internationally accepted as so fundamental that it may not be disregarded, those actions must be found to be part of a systematic, organized pattern to cause the destruction of the other. In the case of genocidal rape, specifications of the UN's Genocide Convention demand the need to prove intent. In reality, while wartime rape is very much a part of the strategy of war, its often hit-and-run nature makes it difficult, indeed improbable, to establish a pattern in a way that will be acceptable in a court of law. Consider, for example, the types of sexual violence perpetrated against Congolese women, which have been defined by Human Rights Watch researcher Juliane Kippenberg as a "ceremony of violence" in which thousands of women have been raped by members of the many warring militias and infected by HIV. Despite the pervasive and systematic quality of these assaults, much of the sexual violence is also conducted in ways that make it seem much more random and uncoordinated—such as women being grabbed in their houses and attacked on the streets or being forced to "sell sex for survival." In such contexts, beyond the challenge of proving cases of rape legally, there are other obstacles such as collecting sufficient documentation to try cases in court. Obviously, assaulted women who die in the onslaughts against them are unable to testify in court, but those who survive often are reluctant or afraid to do so.

Security: When courts are hybrid or local in nature, and when the general rule of law in the country is weak, the security of survivors and witnesses is a source of serious concern because of threats made against their personal safety. Further, the adversarial nature of the legal system implies that defense lawyers grill witnesses to create reasonable doubt in the minds of judges. In many countries, the burden of responsibility to prove rape and sexual violence falls on the women. This nature of traditional defense lawyering and a public admission of being raped mean that there is great reluctance to share the experiences endured during conflict.

Additional resources: Experiences in the ICTY went a long way to establish the provisions for a gender advisor for court procedures. The ICC now has a Gender Unit to tend to the special needs of survivors of sexual crimes. However, these provisions demand additional resources that local courts may not be able to provide.

Legal capacity: Tribunals involve slow, daunting, and expensive processes. International courts have neither the capacity nor the time to prosecute large numbers of people, so local courts, if and when established, have to take up much of the caseload. These circumstances raise additional concerns because local legal systems may be ill-equipped, in terms of both capacity and inclination, to deal with crimes of mass sexual violence. Further, confidence in the local judiciary can be low, determined by the levels of corruption among law enforcement agents, including judges. Local justice also makes many victims reluctant to speak, especially when it is easy to identify who has been subjected to gender-based crimes.

Sentencing: As seen in the Foča trials, survivors and human rights organizations are not always satisfied with the sentences that are handed down to rapists. Consider, for example, the case of Radovan Stankovic, a member of a Serb paramilitary unit. Originally, Stankovic was indicted by the ICTY, but that tribunal turned him over to a Bosnian court for prosecution. In part, the hope was that his trial in a national court would send a signal that such courts could effectively prosecute cases of mass sexual violence. The Bosnian court convicted Stankovic on charges of detaining Muslim women, subjecting them to forced labor, beatings, and rape, and turning them into sex slaves for fellow soldiers. He personally raped at least three women. Stankovic was given a sixteen-year prison sentence. Although the evidence against him was strong, he was acquitted on some of the sexual assault charges. The results in this case produced little satisfaction. Bakira Hasecic, a spokesperson for women victimized by sexual assault, spoke for many when she said, "It seems that in this country it is better to be a war criminal than a victim."[29]

It should be noted, however, that national courts may take action that supports the hope the ICTY expressed in sending the Stankovic case to a Bosnian court. In December 2006, for instance, a Bosnian court's appeals chamber sentenced Bosnian Serb Nedjo Samardzic, one of Stankovic's associates, to twenty-four years in jail. His original sentence of thirteen years and four months for aiding and abetting persecution, rape, and torture of Muslims in Foča was overturned because of procedural errors. A new trial was ordered, and it produced much stiffer results.[30] A few wartime rape trials have also successfully taken place in Serbian, Croatian, and even Congolese courts, albeit with difficulties.

The Continuing Search for Justice

The limitations of the juridical system have exposed the multidimensional questions of justice raised by rape and sexual violence during war and genocide. First, not much evidence exists to support the claim that such trials have a deterrent effect or that they provide satisfactory societal retribution or victim vindication in the aftermath of armed conflict and genocide.[31] Eric Stover argues that a "preliminary weakness of writings on justice in the aftermath of war and political violence is the paucity of empirical evidence to substantiate claims about how well criminal trials achieve the goals ascribed to them."[32] Further, the pursuit of justice is not a panacea for healing victims. As Vanessa Pupavac argues, "the international therapeutic paradigm and the increased popularity of war trauma studies obscures the material needs of survivors, pathologizes war-affected nations, authenticates the political, social and moral claims of the powerful and cultivates victims as vulnerable, infantile and in need of rescue."[33] Still others have argued that the hypothesized "therapeutic" nature of criminal trials is overly simplistic and the short-term catharsis and the re-opening of wounds within this context may be counterproductive.[34] Indeed, the Zambian justice Florence Mumba, who served on the ICTY and ICTR, recognized that "legal justice is too dry especially for the victims, and in a context where people have been hurt so much, international courts with their limited statutes, limitations in procedural law, constraints in sentencing, cannot meet the high expectations of survivors."[35]

These arguments capture a critical point—rape and sexual violence are attacks on a woman's body and dignity; such assaults have profound psychological, medical, economic, and social ramifications that plague survivors and their families for the rest of their lives. Responses in courts of law are simply inadequate to cope with the trauma inflicted when rape becomes a war crime, a crime against humanity, or an act of genocide.

One response to this shortfall has been to explore alternative mechanisms of justice, independent of or complimenting the juridical system, which are more restorative and victim-centered and allow for community-based support and focus on survivors and their narratives. The Rwandan *gacaca* and the Ugandan *Mato Oput* processes, for example, were embraced because of their focus on exploring local and traditional communal ways of achieving truth and reconciliation. Tried within their communities, by people who knew them and their deeds, the accused might find acceptance through confession and community service. If full justice still eluded the survivors of their assaults, the perpetrators' confessions may have contributed something to the coping process.

Still, there are several reasons why the promise of such mechanisms should not be overestimated. First, pressing questions remain about whether community-based justice mechanisms are appropriate for handling rapists and dealing with violations of *criminal* law. Second, the gender element in many traditional justice mechanisms is largely missing. Women often are not among the key leaders and arbitrators in these local processes. Third, it is important to question the rationale behind a state's decision to utilize these supposedly reconciliatory measures, especially if the local and communal structures are politically employed to circumvent the legal obligations of the state to prosecute and if they do not resonate with the survivors of sexual violence. Finally, it is important to remember that despite the recognition of rape and sexual violence as a *jus cogens* crime, the role of socio-cultural norms may minimize the wrongdoing and the harm it causes, leaving many victims invisible. The social standing of women during "peace" time and their positions within local legal systems can determine how societies treat survivors of rape and sexual violence. For example, in countries such as Sierra Leone, where women do not have the right to refuse sex within marriage, rape is still not considered a serious legal crime. In the context of wartime, this type of rationalization translates to the right to rape women who were captured and kept during the period of conflict. In conservative societies, such as Afghanistan and Iraq, where a woman's standing is defined by her social relationships, and the stigma of sexual attack is carried not only by the survivor but also by her whole family, the need to testify in court or in public that such violence took place, even if perpetrators would be held culpable as a result, collides with the need to protect family honor and prevent social humiliation.

Ultimately, seeking justice in courts of law does not overcome many of the socio-political circumstances that define the realities of survivors of wartime and genocidal sexual violence. Nevertheless, the pursuit of justice in courts, which signifies political commitment from the state and the international community to name, blame, and shame perpetrators, to remove them from power, and to provide some measure of justice, if not restitution, resonates with many survivors. Unfortunately, the vast majority of survivors of wartime and genocidal rape and sexual violence live outside the promises of such courts. Beyond socio-cultural restraints, political calculations in the aftermath of war mean that these survivors are forced to live in close proximity with their abusers, many of whom, as in places such as Bangladesh, Afghanistan, and Lebanon, consolidate their political and economic bases at the end of conflict. For these survivors, the advancement of international law means very little, since they live ensnared by the memories of a nightmarish past and by the realities of the culture of impunity. What can be done to change these circumstances is a chapter in ethics, politics, and international law that remains to be written.

Notes

1.   Joanne Barkan, "As Old as War Itself: Rape in Foca," *Dissent*, Winter 2002, Available at: http://www.dissentmagazine.org/article/?article=633. Accessed October 3, 2011.

2. See 1241-42 and 1261-64 in the trial transcript, which is available at: http://www.icty.org/x/cases/kunarac/trans/en/000329ed.htm. Accessed October 3, 2011. For further information, see *Bridging the Gap between ICTY and Communities in Bosnia and Herzegovina*, Conference Proceedings, Foča, October 9, 2004, ICTY, UN. Available at: http://www.icty.org/x/file/Outreach/Bridging_the_Gap/foca_en.pdf. Accessed October 3, 2011.

3. Witness 50, UN: ICTY. Available at: http://www.icty.org/x/cases/kunarac/trans/en/000329ed.htm. See 1241-42, 1261-64. Accessed October 3, 2011. See also Barkan, "As Old as War Itself."

4. See note 2 above, *Bridging the Gap*.

5. Article 147 of the Fourth Geneva Convention defines war crimes as: "Willful killing, torture or inhuman treatment, including . . . willfully causing great suffering or serious injury to body or health, unlawful deportation or transfer or unlawful confinement of a protected person, compelling a protected person to serve in the forces of a hostile power, or willfully depriving a protected person of the rights of fair and regular trial, . . . taking of hostages and extensive destruction and appropriation of property, not justified by military necessity and carried out unlawfully and wantonly."

6. In Article 6 (c), the 1945 Agreement for the Prosecution and Punishment of the Major War Criminals of the European Axis and Charter of the International Military Tribunal (IMT) defined crimes against humanity as: "murder, extermination, enslavement, deportation, and other inhumane acts committed against civilian populations, before or during the war; or persecutions on political, racial or religious grounds in execution of or in connection with any crime within the jurisdiction of the Tribunal, whether or not in violation of the domestic law of the country where perpetrated." The list has been expanded since the ICTY and the ICTR to include rape and torture. The statute of the ICC expands the list to include enforced disappearance of persons and apartheid. Further, it contains clarifying language with respect to crimes of extermination, enslavement, deportation or forcible transfer of population, torture, and forced pregnancy.

7. Article 2 of the 1948 United Nations Convention on the Prevention and Punishment of the Crime of Genocide (CPPCG) defines genocide as "any of the following acts committed with intent to destroy, in whole or in part, a national, ethnical, racial or religious group, as such: killing members of the group; causing serious bodily or mental harm to members of the group; deliberately inflicting on the group conditions of life, calculated to bring about its physical destruction in whole or in part; imposing measures intended to prevent births within the

group; [and] forcibly transferring children of the group to another group." In the International Criminal Tribunal for Rwanda's (ICTR) 1998 case against Jean-Paul Akayesu, rape was found for the first time, at least in an international tribunal, to be an act of genocide. See "When Rape Becomes Genocide," *New York Times* (September 5, 1998). Available at: http://www.nytimes.com/1998/09/05/opinion/when-rape-becomes-genocide.html. Accessed October 3, 2011.

8. See Barkan, "As Old as War Itself."

9. International human rights law refers to the body of international law, much of it embedded in actions by the United Nations, designed to promote and protect human rights at the international, regional, and domestic levels. International human rights law is based on international treaties and customary international law. International humanitarian law, often referred to as the laws of war, is the legal corpus comprised of the Hague Conventions (1899, 1907), the Geneva Conventions (1949, plus the Additional Protocols to the Conventions, 1977), subsequent treaties, case law, and customary international law.

10. The dates refer to the year of adoption. Typically, the measures enter into force at a later time, when the necessary number of signatories has been obtained.

11. Article 2 (ii) Part 1, Convention against Torture and Other Cruel, Inhuman or Degrading Treatment or Punishment (CAT), December 9, 1975. Available at: http://www.hrweb.org/legal/cat.html. Accessed October 3, 2011.

12. EVAW defines violence against women as "any act of gender-based violence that results in, or is likely to result in, physical, sexual, or psychological harm or suffering to women, including threats of such acts, coercion, or arbitrary deprivation of liberty, whether occurring in public or private life." For the text of this United Nations declaration, see http://www.un.org/documents/ga/res/48/a48r104.htm. Accessed October 3, 2011.

13. CEDAW defines discrimination against women as "any distinction, exclusion or restriction made on the basis of sex which has the effect or purpose of impairing or nullifying the recognition, enjoyment or exercise by women, irrespective of their marital status, on a basis of equality of men and women, of human rights and fundamental freedoms in the political, economic, social, cultural, civil or any other field." For further information, see http://www.un.org/womenwatch/daw/cedaw/text/econvention.htm. Accessed October 3, 2011.

14. Text of the Optional Protocol to the Convention on the Elimination of All Forms of Discrimination against Women, Division for the Advancement of Women, Department of Economic and Social Affairs, United Nations (CEDAW).

Available at: http://www.un.org/womenwatch/daw/cedaw/protocol/text.htm. Accessed October 3, 2011.

15. The texts for the Geneva Conventions are available at http://www.icrc. org/eng/war-and-law/treaties-customary-law/geneva-conventions/index.jsp. Accessed October 3, 2011.

16. Fourth Geneva Convention (1949), Article 27. Available at: http://www.icrc. org/ihl.nsf/FULL/380?OpenDocument. Accessed October 3, 2011.

17. Article 27, however, leaves individuals vulnerable to activities of their own nation, because that article is silent on the actions of a state against its own people.

18. Judith G. Gardam and Michelle J. Jarvis, *Women, Armed Conflict and International Law* (The Hague: Kluwer Law International, 2001), 201. See also the First Geneva Convention (1949), Article 49 (http://www.icrc.org/ihl.nsf/ full/365?opendocument); Second Geneva Convention (1949), Article 50 (http:// www.icrc.org/ihl.nsf/full/370?opendocument);Third Geneva Convention (1949), Article 129 (http://www.icrc.org/ihl.nsf/full/375?OpenDocument); Fourth Geneva Convention (1949), Article 146 (see note 16 above). All accessed October 3, 2011.

19. The statute is available at: http://www.icty.org/x/file/Legal%20Library/ Statute/statute_sept09_en.pdf. See Articles, 2, 3, and 5. Accessed October 3, 2011.

20. For further detail on the events discussed in this paragraph, see the UN web site about the ICTY, which is available at: http://www.icty.org/sid/10058. Accessed December 12, 2011. See also David J. Scheffer, "Rape as a War Crime." This text, which consists of remarks made by Scheffer, the U.S. Ambassador-at-Large for War Crimes Issues, at Fordham University, New York, on October 29, 1999, is available at: http://www.converge.org.nz/pma/arape.htm. Accessed October 3, 2011.

21. Andrew Osborn, "Mass Rape Ruled a War Crime," *The Guardian*, February 23, 2001. Available at: http://www.commondreams.org/headlines01/0224-02. htm. Accessed October 3, 2011.

22. "Human Rights Watch Applauds Rwanda Rape Verdict," *Human Rights Watch News*, September 2, 1998. Available at: http://www.hrw.org/en/news/1998/09/02/ human-rights-watch-applauds-rwanda-rape-verdict. Accessed October 3, 2011.

23. See ibid.

24. See the Enough Project's report, "Wanted by the ICC: The LRA's Leaders,

Who They Are and What They've Done." Available at: http://www.enoughpro-ject.org/files/pdf/lra_leaders.pdf. Accessed October 3, 2011.

25. Nicola Henry, "Witness to Rape: The Limits and Potential of International War Crimes Trials for Victims of Sexual Violence," *The International Journal of Transitional Justice* 3 (2009): 115.

26. The indictment was broadened only after Navanethem Pillay's diligent questioning of witnesses, which elicited stories of rape, and through the intervention of NGO activists.

27. See the Institute for War & Peace Reporting (IWPR), "International Justice Failing Rape Victims," *TRI Issue* 483, February 15, 2010. Available at: http://www.iwpr.net/report-news/international-justice-failing-rape-victims. Accessed October 3, 2011.

28. Ibid.

29. See "Stankovic sentenced to 16 years imprisonment," Balkan Investigative Reporting Network (BIRN), November 14, 2006. Available at: http://www.bim.ba/en/36/10/1624/. Accessed October 3, 2011.

30. See the Institute for War & Peace Reporting (IWPR), "Foca Rape Sentence," *TRI Issue* 481, December 15, 2006. Available at: http://www.iwpr.net/report-news/foca-rape-sentence. Accessed October 3, 2011.

31. See Payam Akhavan, "Beyond Impunity: Can International Criminal Justice Prevent Future Atrocities?" *American Journal of International Law* 95 (2001): 7-31, and Laurel E. Fletcher and Harvey M. Weinstein, "Violence and Social Repair: Rethinking the Contribution of Justice to Reconciliation," *Human Rights Quarterly* 24 (2002): 573-639.

32. Eric Stover, *The Witnesses: War Crimes and the Promise of Justice in The Hague* (Philadelphia: University of Pennsylvania Press, 2005), 11.

33. Vanessa Pupavac, "International Therapeutic Peace and Justice in Bosnia," *Social and Legal Studies* 13 (2004): 377-401.

34. See, for example, ibid. and also the articles referenced in note 31 above.

35. Comments made by Judge Florence Mumba at the Avon Global Center Women and Justice Conference, National Museum for Women and the Arts, Washington, DC, March 12, 2010. The conference report, "Gender-Based Violence and Justice in Conflict and Post-Conflict Areas," is available at: http://www.lawschool.cornell.edu/womenandjustice/upload/Conference-report_Final-4.pdf. Accessed October 3, 2011.

Further Suggested Reading

Askin, Kelly D. "Gender Crimes Jurisprudence in the ICTR: Positive Developments," *Journal of International Criminal Justice* 3, no. 4 (2005): 1007-18.

Carpenter, R. Charli, ed., *Born of War: Protecting Children of Sexual Violence Survivors in Conflict Zones* (Bloomfield, CT: Kumarian Press, 2007).

Carpenter, R. Charli. *Forgetting Children Born of War: Setting the Human Rights Agenda in Bosnia and Beyond* (New York: Columbia University Press, 2010).

Chinkin, Christin. "Rape and Sexual Abuse of Women in International Law," *European Journal of International Law* 5, no. 1 (1994): 326-341.

Engle, Karen. "Feminism and its (Dis)Contents: Criminalizing Wartime Rape in Bosnia and Herzegovina. *American Journal of International Law* 99 (2006): 778-816.

Questions for Discussion

1. For the sake of peace in the aftermath of protracted conflict, countries have made the pragmatic choice for political reconciliation with war criminals, many of whom are responsible, directly or indirectly, for the commission of rape and sexual violence. Do you agree with such choices? To what extent do you think considerations of gender enter into them?

2. From what you have read, do you think international law offers protection to men and boys from sexual violence and rape? How? What are the challenges regarding recognition of male rape as a weapon of war and genocide?

3. Thousands of children have been born of wartime rape and sexual exploitation in conflict zones. What challenges do these children and their mothers face in the postconflict societies? Does international law take account of such challenges?

4. United Nations Security Council Resolution 1487, adopted on June 12, 2003, exempted American troops and personnel serving in any UN force in Iraq from prosecution for international war crimes under the Rome Statute of the ICC. What do such exemptions mean for accountability for war crimes in general and crimes against women and girls in particular?

6

Rape as a Tool of "Othering" in Genocide

James E. Waller

> The Interahamwe militia and FAR soldiers killed what I would
> have become.
>
> —*Pascasie Mukasakindi*

The selection I have chosen to orient this chapter is as disturbing and powerful as it is brief. In a few devastating words, a Tutsi woman named Pascasie Mukasakindi, who survived the 1994 Rwandan genocide, describes the unspeakable atrocities inflicted upon her by perpetrators who, with a vengeance, used rape in the service of genocide.[1]

> While the Interahamwe were placing dry tree branches around Marcel's house in order to burn it, Marcel told us to run out the back door. . . . While fleeing, I encountered a group of about fifty Interahamwe militia. They detained me near the bushes next to the Gasebeya River and stole everything I had: my bag, my shoes and my watch. I also had a bottle full of milk, and they threw that milk on me, saying that Tutsi were like cats because we all liked milk. . . . The men raped me, one by one. Even the youngest ones in the group raped me, and they looked like they were no older than thirteen. Almost fifty men raped me in one day. I was too numb to feel anything. . . . After they were done raping me, they shoved a nailed club into my vagina, threw me into a thorny bush and left me in that state . . . [Several days later] the Interahamwe spotted and captured me. . . . They tortured me in so many cruel ways, forcing me to take their penises in my mouth and shoving their penises

up my nose. Their sperm fell from my nose onto my body and into my mouth. I wanted to vomit. I felt so stupid, and I could do nothing. They insulted and humiliated me. They told me that I was ugly and dirty and that I stank. No one was there to help me . . . for two weeks many Interahamwe raped me every day, using me as their personal sex slave. . . . The Interahamwe militia and FAR soldiers who raped me did not think that I was a human being. . . . I feel the Interahamwe militia and FAR soldiers killed what I would have become.

Pascasie Mukasakindi was thirty-four years of age at the time when Hutu men assaulted her in 1994. Her voice provides excruciating testimony about the trauma she experienced when the cement of Rwandan society gave way during a 100-day spree of mass murder. Though sexual violence is a broader category (including rape, sexual mutilation, forced marriage, and sexual slavery), she reminds us that, in the context of genocide, sexual violence against women and girls generally takes the form of rape. Mukasakindi's testimony also reminds us that, while men and boys are subject to rape and sexual violence in genocidal conflict, the *modus operandi*, rooted in societies rife with gender inequality and discrimination, is men perpetrating sexual violence on women. Recent history has shown us that, in many cases of genocidal conflict, it is safer to be a soldier than a woman.

Mukasakindi's words give voice to the way in which rape creates submission and terror, humiliation, self-hate, ostracism or stigmatization, depression and suicide, poverty, and is devastating to physical health and ethnic and familial bonds.[2] The psychological impact of rape, manifest in her testimony, includes feelings of shame, intense shock, a paralyzing fear of injury or death, and a sense of loss of control over one's life. A study of Bosniak (Bosnian Muslims) and Croatian victims of rape during the 1992-1995 conflict in the former Yugoslavia, for instance, found that the rapes had deep immediate and long-term consequences on the mental-health of the assaulted women.[3] Jasmina, a survivor of sexual violence during the Bosnian war, told Amnesty International: "I can't sleep without pills. I still get upset easily when people mention the war. An image, a memory, a TV spot can be a spark. I can't stand it . . . I need help."[4]

Unfortunately, survivors of rape in genocidal societies are re-victimized as they find little support for their physical, psychological, economic, social, and spiritual recovery, even as many continue a life-and-death struggle against sexual diseases contracted during episodes of rape. In Rwanda, for instance, an estimated 70 percent of survivors of rape and sexual violence during the 1994 genocide are now HIV positive.[5] Mukasakindi was one of the victims who became HIV positive and whose victimization continues. In her words: "I am weak and constantly ill. I suffer from headaches, chest aches, backaches and pains in my vagina, and I have sinus problems as a result of the men who raped me in my nose. I live alone and have no one to help me, but I am surviving with the help of different organizations, which provide material and spiritual support."[6]

Mukasakindi's testimony, however, is also compelling for the questions it raises regarding the purposes of rape in genocidal conflict. Most often, when studied in the context of traditional warfare, rape is understood as a non-purposeful, incidental *by-product* of conflict—"bounty" or "spoils" in which males take advantage of the chaos of the conflict to claim their sexual just rewards. In genocidal conflict, however, rape often has what can be called a macro-level purpose; it is generally more "under control" of, and even central to, regime policy or directive. Here, as a political and social *tool* or *weapon*, rape can fulfill visions of genocide and ethnic cleansing by leading to physical death, community breakdown (including disruption of traditional gender roles), and the "dilution" of the next generation (including the intentional transmission of sexual diseases). As Catharine MacKinnon has written: "This is not rape out of control. It is rape under control. It is also rape unto death, rape as massacre, rape to kill and to make the victims wish they were dead. It is rape as an instrument of forced exile, rape to make you leave your home and never want to go back. It is rape to be seen and heard and watched and told to others: rape as spectacle. It is rape to drive a wedge through a community, to shatter a society, to destroy a people. It is rape as genocide."[7]

What has been relatively little discussed, however, and what I believe Mukasakindi's testimony clearly identifies, is the *micro-level purpose* of rape for the perpetrator. Rather than simply an extension of the regime's policy or directive, how does rape enable a perpetrator to do what he must do in the context of genocide? What is rape's instrumentality for the perpetrator? Rape and sexual violence are multi-functional for the perpetrator, but, this chapter will argue, one of their central purposes is defining the victim as "other" in such a way as to permit, and even justify, the atrocities. The goal of this chapter is to offer a psychological analysis of rape as a tool of "othering" in genocide.

Rape and Genocide

During genocide, rape occurs during attack, flight from attack, and, far too often, in camps for internally displaced persons and refugees. Perpetrators include police, security forces, paramilitary forces, military personnel, civilians, and, perhaps most disconcertingly, peacekeepers who egregiously abdicate their professional and moral responsibility for protection. For many reasons, precisely accurate counts about genocide-related victims of rape are impossible to obtain—governments and organizations may be resistant to collecting data; many victims are killed following rape; many more choose not to report their victimization due to stigmatization, shame, and the reality that rape investigations and trials can cause continuing psychological trauma; even more remain silent due to fear of reprisal and the expectation that justice will always be a dream deferred.

Despite these obstacles, however, we can at least offer some broad estimates of rape and sexual violence during genocide. During the Khmer Rouge's genocidal rule in Cambodia between 1975 and 1979, approximately 250,000 Cambodian women were forced into marriage.[8] As many as 64,000 internally displaced women experienced war-related sexual violence between 1991 and 2001 in Sierra Leone.[9] A mental health worker in that conflict said that "being raped is like being bitten by a mosquito, it's that frequent."[10] Between 250,000 to 500,000 women and girls in Rwanda were raped during the 1994 genocide (the lower figure underestimates as it is based on the number of subsequent pregnancies).[11] The atrocities in Rwanda led to a landmark judicial case in which rape was defined as a crime of genocide under international law.[12] Finally, in addition to Rwanda, the 1992-1995 Bosnian war clearly brought the world's attention to rape as a tool of genocide. During that time, an estimated 20,000 to 50,000 women, mostly Muslims, were raped by perpetrators, mostly

Serbs.[13] Most of the rapes occurred in places of detention and, to ensure that Muslim women would give birth to a Serbian child (since identity was paternally derived), many victims were held in custody until safe abortion was no longer possible or they actually gave birth.[14]

In recent years, rape and sexual violence during conflict have swept across Liberia (1999-2003), Kenya (December 2007-June 2008), Zimbabwe, Uganda, Burundi (November 2004 and November 2007), the Central African Republic (2002-2003) and the Democratic Republic of Congo (1998-ongoing). On March 4, 2009, the International Criminal Court (ICC) issued a warrant for the arrest of Sudan's president, Omar Hassan Ahmed Bashir (b. 1944), on two counts of war crimes and five counts of crimes against humanity against the Fur, Masalit and Zaghawa groups of Darfur. One of the five counts of crimes against humanity included "subjecting thousands of civilian women" from these ethnic groups to "acts of rape."[15] A common tactic has been for the *janjaweed* militia and Sudan's armed forces and security agents to lie in wait outside internally displaced persons camps to rape—and often to gang-rape—the women and girls who come out to collect firewood, grass, or water in order to survive. "Maybe around 20 men rape one woman," said one victim in a report cited by the prosecutor. "These things are normal for us here in Darfur. . . . They rape women in front of their mothers and fathers."[16] Children borne of these rapes are often subject to abandonment and infanticide. As another victim explained: "They kill our males and dilute our blood with rape. [They] . . . want to finish us as a people, end our history."[17] A second, supplemental arrest warrant for Bashir was issued on July 12, 2010, this time including three separate counts of genocide.

Rape as a Tool of "Othering"

Elsewhere, I have outlined a general explanatory model regarding the making of perpetrators of genocide and mass killing.[18] The model—drawing on existing literature; eyewitness accounts by killers, bystanders, and victims from a wide range of genocides and mass killings; and classic and contemporary research in social and evolutionary psychology—does not rely on a single broad-brush psychological state or *event* to explain the making of perpetrators. Rather, focusing less on the outcome, it is a detailed analysis of a *process* through which the perpetrators themselves—either in committing atrocities or in order to commit atrocities—are changed.

Most relevant to our understanding of rape and sexual violence as a tool of "othering" is an analysis of the obliteration of a common ground between perpetrators and victims. How do victims simply become objects of the perpetrators' actions? How do perpetrators define the target of their sexual violence in such a way as to "excommunicate" them from a common moral community? At least three mechanisms are central to understanding the psychological construction of the "other": us–them thinking, moral disengagement, and blaming the victims.

Us–Them Thinking. Human minds are compelled to define the limits of the tribe. Kinship, however defined, remains an important organizing principle for most societies in the world. Knowing who is one's kin, knowing who is in our social group, has a deep importance to species like ours. We construct this knowledge by categorizing others as "us" or "them." We have an evolved, universal capacity for us–them thinking in which we see our group as superior to all others and may even be reluctant to recognize members of other groups as deserving of equal respect.

Us–them thinking does not lead us to hate all out-groups. Social exclusion, let alone genocide and mass killing, is not an inevitable consequence of us–them thinking. We are reminded, however, that, once identified with a group, we find it easy to exaggerate differences between our group and others, enhancing in-group cooperation and effectiveness, and—frequently—intensifying antagonism toward other groups. This process helps us understand how the suggestive message of "us" against "them" can be ratcheted up to the categorically compelling "kill or be killed."

Moral Disengagement. The moral disengagement that often results from us–them thinking is not simply a matter of moral indifference or invisibility. Rather, it is an active, but gradual, process of detachment by which some individuals or groups are placed outside the boundary in which moral values, rules, and considerations of fairness apply. How do perpetrators regulate their thinking so as to disengage, or not feel, their moral scruples about harming others? How do they get to the point where, as Mukasakindi's testimony states, the perpetrators "did not think that I was a human being?"

Perpetrators use a variety of disengagement practices to make their reprehensible conduct acceptable and to distance them from the moral implications of their actions. For instance, mass murder can be made personally and socially acceptable and even morally justified if it is portrayed as serving socially worthy or ethical purposes. Perpetrators may believe this rationalization to such an extent that their evil is not only morally justifiable (right to do) but also morally imperative (wrong not to do it).[19] Perpetrators can then justify their evil as essential to their own self-defense—to protect the cherished values of their community, fight ruthless oppressors, preserve peace and stability, save humanity from subjugation, or honor their national commitments.

Moral disengagement also is facilitated by the dehumanization of the victims—identifying a group as inhuman either by categorizing them as subhuman creatures (that is, as animals of one kind or another) or by categorizing them as negatively evaluated superhuman creatures (demons, for example, or monsters). Mukasakindi's testimony regarding perpetrators' beliefs that "Tutsi were like cats" is illustrative of such dehumanization. Such dehumanization is most likely when the target group can be readily identified as a separate category of people belonging to a distinct racial, ethnic, religious, or political group that the perpetrators regard as inferior and/or threatening. These isolated subgroups are stigmatized as alien, and memories of their past misdeeds, real or imagined, are activated by the dominant group.

The dehumanization of victims helps perpetrators to justify their hurtful behavior. A common form of dehumanization is the use of language to redefine the victims so they will be seen as warranting aggression against them. Perpetrators so consistently dehumanize their victims that the words used to do so blur and trump perceptions that the victims are human beings. For example, the Hutu extremists called the Tutsi *inyenzi*, meaning cockroaches or insects, and treated the Tutsi accordingly. Haing S. Ngor, the late Cambodian doctor and actor who found fame for his role in *The Killing Fields*, the important 1984 film about the Cambodian genocide, notes the plight of those persecuted by the Khmer Rouge: "We weren't quite people. We were lower forms of life, because we were enemies. Killing us was like swatting flies, a way to get rid of undesirables."[20] Dehumanization also involves quantification in which victims merely become statistics—bodies to be counted, numbers to be entered into reports. Reduced to data, dehumanized victims lose their moral standing and become objects requiring disposal.

Such dehumanization often leads to an escalation of the brutality of the killing. Dehumanizing victims removes normal moral constraints against aggression. The body of a dehumanized victim possesses no meaning. It is waste, and its removal is a matter of sanitation. Dehumanization can remove every vestige of a moral or empathic context through which the perpetrator can relate to the victim as a fellow human being. As one witness to the Rwandan genocide recalled: "Assailants sometimes mutilated women in the course of a rape or before killing them. They cut off breasts, punctured the vagina with spears, arrows, or pointed sticks, or cut off or disfigured body parts that looked particularly 'Tutsi,' such as long fingers or thin noses. They also humiliated the women. One Tutsi witness from Musambira commune reported that after a massacre, she and about 200 other women were forced to bury their husbands and then to walk "'naked like a group of cattle' some ten miles to Kabgayi. . . . When the group stopped at nightfall, some of the women were raped repeatedly."[21] Another survivor of the Rwandan genocide recalls how a perpetrator argued that "it would be a great mistake if they killed me without humiliating me first."[22]

Dehumanization is particularly relevant for understanding rape and sexual violence because women, by far the most frequent targets, very often find themselves in patriarchal, male-dominated cultures where their "status" as humans is in question even in times of peace. In writing about the Universal Declaration of Human Rights, Catherine MacKinnon states: "Being a woman is 'not yet a name for a way of being human,' not even in this most visionary of human rights documents. If we measure the reality of women's situation in all its variety against the guarantees of the Universal Declaration, not only do women not have the rights it guarantees—most of the world's men don't either—but it is hard to see, in its vision of humanity, a woman's face."[23] As one Rwandan rape victim said following the genocide: "I wondered whether I was still a human being."[24]

Perpetrators further facilitate moral disengagement by using euphemistic language to make their atrocities respectable and, in part, to reduce their personal responsibility. By masking their evil in innocuous or sanitizing jargon, their actions lose much of their moral repugnancy. Mass murder becomes "ethnic cleansing," "bush clearing," or "liquidation." The camouflage vocabulary used by the Nazis to cover their extraordinary evil during the Holocaust was especially striking—"final solution," "special treatment," "evacuation," "spontaneous actions," "resettlement," and "special installations," among many others. Rwandan *genocidaires* repeatedly referred to their atrocities as simply their "work" and their rapes as getting a "taste" of Tutsi women.

Blaming the Victims. Finally, the psychological construction of the "other" feeds on itself and is driven by our brain's remarkable capacity to seek, and find, explanation in the events surrounding us, our actions, and the behaviors of people with whom we interact. We recognize that victims can be grouped in two broad categories—those who deserve their suffering and those who do not. We know that bad things do happen to good people. To a large degree, we recognize the reality that ours is not a just world. Nevertheless, we do not easily relinquish our hopeful illusion of a world that is fair and just. We hold on to that notion, however misguided, to give us the courage to go out into the world and to send our children out into the world. Our need to believe in a just world can and often does overwhelm our recognition that bad things can happen to good people. As a result, we often assume that victims deserve, and can be blamed for, their fates. Indeed, we show a hardy cognitive tendency to search for ways to blame individuals for their own victimization, a phenomenon often found in cases of rape when it is alleged that the victim's behavior was provocative or that "she was asking for it." On the whole, the general tendency to blame the victims for their own suffering is a central truth about human experience. For perpetrators, this tendency is instrumental in our striking propensity to devalue victims and their suffering. We will rearrange our perception of people and events so that it seems everyone is getting what they deserve. Victims must be suffering because they have done "something," must somehow be inferior or dangerous or evil, or because a higher cause is being served. The belief that the world is a just place leads us to accept the suffering of others more easily, even the suffering of people we ourselves have harmed.

It is not uncommon even to find victims blaming themselves for their own victimization, an internalization of rape by the victim. Frequently, victims will speak of "despising" or "hating" themselves and of their own "worthlessness." These patterns of self-blaming response often continue for years after a person's victimization in rape. As Clementine Nyinawumuntu (b. 1977), a rape victim and survivor of the Rwandan genocide, testified: "I do not love the person that I am. I have not grown up to be the person I wanted to be. I know that now, and I can never be that woman."[25]

Social Contexts of Cruelty

"Othering" is exacerbated by the real-time power of social influences on individual behavior. As we see in the myriad cases of genocide-related gang rape, a social context of cruelty makes each perpetrator believe that all people are capable of doing what they do. Such a context is morally inverted, shaped by a process of brutalization, in which right has become wrong, healing has become killing, and living requires killing. A social construction of cruelty envelops perpetrators in a social context that encourages and rewards evil. We must borrow the perspective of the perpetrators and view their actions not as the work of "madmen" but as the result of a clear and justified purpose—as defined by a social construction of cruelty. Three momentum-inducing features of a social construction of cruelty enable perpetrators to initiate, sustain, and cope with their cruelty: professional socialization, group identification, and binding factors of the group.

Professional Socialization. Perhaps most relevant to professional socialization is a merger of role and person through which evildoing organizations can change the people in them over time. When one performs the behaviors appropriate for a given role, one often acquires the attitudes, beliefs, values, and morals consistent with that role and its behaviors. Seen in this light, the egregious brutality of perpetrators does not automatically indicate an *inherent*, pre-existing brutality; not everyone playing a brutal role has to have sadistic traits of character. Rather, brutality can be a consequence, not only a cause, of being in a duly certified and legitimized social hierarchy committed to evil. In other words, the nature of the tasks of atrocity may have been sufficient to produce that brutality even if the perpetrators were not initially sadists. It may be a vicious social arrangement, and not the preexisting viciousness of the participants, that leads to the cruel behaviors exhibited by those who commit atrocities, including rape during war and genocide.

The merger of role and person has tremendous capacity for internalizing evil and shaping later evil behaviors. Most of us easily slip into the roles society provides us. A person who becomes invested in the logic and practices of an evildoing organization becomes owned by it. In a self-perpetuating cycle of evildoing, our behaviors and attitudes feed on each other as this altered psychological framework produces further changes in behavior that lead to more profound alterations in our psychological framework.

For the U.S. military, the real-life implications of the merger of role and person became disturbingly apparent in the spring of 2004 amid allegations of prisoner abuse in Iraq by American troops at the Abu Ghraib prison near Baghdad. The allegations were as graphic as they were sadistic—beatings with a broom handle and chair; threats with a pistol and military dogs; forcibly arranging detainees in sexually explicit poses; sodomizing detainees and attaching wires to their extremities. Subsequent investigation revealed photographic evidence of rape being carried out by American military personnel. While critics were quick to condemn the atrocities as "the miserable behavior of a few punks," social psychological research reminds us that, rather than an isolated "people" problem, the events at Abu Ghraib more clearly reflect a deeper, and more troubling, "systems" problem stemming from professional socialization into a context of cruelty that enabled these perpetrators to initiate, sustain, and cope with their evil.

Group Identification. Group identification—an emotional attachment to a group—is a potent influence on an individual's thoughts, emotions, and behaviors. Group identification, whether centered on race, ethnicity, tribe, kin, religion, or nationality, can become a central and defining characteristic of one's personal identity and may even overshadow the self. These group identities can even become such an important source of self-definition and esteem that other groups are perceived as threats—thus sowing the seeds for intergroup conflict by evoking suspicion of, hostility toward, and competition with an out-group. At the extreme, group identification may be mobilized into collective violence or a genocidal imperative as it is used to forge in-group solidarity and undermine the normal inhibitions against killing out-group strangers. We can identify with a group, and against other groups, to such a degree that group identification comes to dominate our individual thoughts, emotions, and behaviors, often against the interests and welfare of other groups.

Group identification carries with it a repression of conscience where "outside" values are excluded and locally generated values dominate. Such a repression of conscience serves a self-protective function, as well as having a progressively desensitizing effect on the perpetrators, and is facilitated in social contexts that promote diffusion of responsibility and deindividuation.

Diffusion of responsibility is accomplished by bureaucratic organization into cells and columns as well as by a routinization of bureaucratic subroutines—a segmentation and fragmentation of the killing tasks—in which responsibility for evil is divided among members of a group. Such division of labor, in addition to making the killing process more efficient and effective, allows perpetrators to reduce their identification with the consequences of their evil. Once activities are routinized into detached subfunctions, perpetrators shift their attention away from the morality of what they are doing to the operational details and efficiency of their specific job. They are then able to see themselves totally as performers of a role—as participants *in*, nor originators *of*, evil. It is easier for perpetrators to avoid the implications of their evil since they are focusing on the *details* of their job rather than on its *meaning*.

The segmented activities of bureaucratic organizations also provide a cloak of deindividuation that facilitates the committing of evil. Deindividuation refers to a state of relative anonymity in which a person cannot be identified as a particular individual but only as a group member. The concept usually includes a decreased focus on personal identity, loss of contact with general social norms, and the submergence of the individual in situation-specific group norms. Such conditions confer anonymity and increase the likelihood of evil as people partially lose awareness of themselves as individuals and cease to evaluate their own actions thoughtfully.

In addition, it is important to examine the ways in which group identification fulfills, and shapes, perpetrators' rational self-interests—both professionally and personally. Generally speaking, most perpetrators of genocide work within the context of a military or paramilitary organization. In that context, a logic of incentives enmeshed with professional self-interest—ambition, advancement, and careerism—plays a role in understanding their behavior. Moreover, there often is a mutually reinforcing, and deadly, compatibility of one's professional self-interests with a larger political, religious, or social interest in annihilation of a specific target group.

Genocide and mass killing are replete with examples of perpetrators who used the situations of extremity to advance their personal self-interest by claiming power, property, and goods. The following account of a Hutu perpetrator from the Rwandan genocide is illustrative of this reality: "A failed student turned killer, Shalom [Ntahobari] became a big man in Butare once the slaughter began. He swaggered around town with grenades hanging from his belt, often armed with a gun which he once aimed in insolent jest at a local burgomaster. One witness asserted that even military officers saluted Shalom. He controlled his own barrier in front of the family house near the university campus where he bullied his militia subordinates as well as passersby. One witness who had known Shalom as a fellow student witnessed him killing a man in order to rob him of his cattle."[26]

Binding Factors of the Group. Finally, a social construction of cruelty relies on binding factors of the group, or cementing mechanisms that endow a social context with at least minimal stability. Such binding factors are the pressures that work to keep people within an evildoing organization or hierarchy. They constitute the social authority of a group and hold the individual tightly to a rigid definition of the situation, closing off the freedom of movement to focus on features of the situation other than its authority structure.

One significant binding factor is the explicit, or implicit, dynamic of conformity to peer pressure. Military science is replete with assertions that the cohesive bonds soldiers form with one another in military and paramilitary organizations are often stronger than the bonds they will form with anyone else at any other point in their lifetimes. Among people who are bonded together so intensely, there is a powerful dynamic of conformity to peer pressure—or "mutual surveillance"—in which the individual cares so deeply about his comrades and what they think of him that he would rather die than let them down. Conformity to peer pressure helps sustain perpetrators' involvement in evil. It is difficult for anyone who is bonded by links of mutual affection and interdependence to break away and openly refuse to participate in what the group is doing, even if it is perpetrating atrocities.

Conclusion

In 2007, a report by the United Nations Secretary-General on the protection of civilians in armed conflict concluded: "In no other area is our collective failure to ensure effective protection for civilians more apparent—and by its very nature more shameful—than in terms of the masses of women and girls, but also boys and men, whose lives are destroyed each year by sexual violence perpetrated in conflict."[27] In the pursuit of ensuring more effective protection for civilians, this chapter has offered a psychological analysis of rape as a tool of "othering" in genocide. We are reminded how humanizing, de-categorizing, or personalizing others all create a powerful self-restraining effect on moral disengagement, while we also are cautioned against the power of contextual "systems" of initiation and socialization to encourage processes of brutalization. Only in paying heed to such reminders and cautions can we can begin to make strides on the long and hard road toward the effective protection of civilians in episodes of genocidal violence.

Notes

1.   Testimony of Pascasie Mukasakindi (b. 1959), a survivor of the 1994 Rwandan genocide, as recorded in *The Men Who Killed Me: Rwandan Survivors of Sexual Violence*, ed. Anne Marie de Brouwer and Sandra Ka Hon Chu (Vancouver: Douglas & McIntyre, 2009), 72-77. Quoted material is excerpted from 74-76. In her testimony, Mukasakindi refers to the Interahamwe and to FAR soldiers. The Interahamwe—the term means "those who attack together"—was a Hutu militia group, consisting mainly of young men, who were among the most brutal perpetrators of the Rwandan genocide. FAR stands for Forces Armées Rwandaises,

or Rwandan Armed Forces, the Hutu-dominated national army of Rwanda at the time of the genocide.

2. See the Center on Law and Globalization's "Overview: Rape and Genocide," which can be found at: http://clg.portalxm.com/library/evidence.cfm?format_tables=0&evidence_summary_id=250036. Accessed January 11, 2011.

3. M. Loncar, V. Medved, N. Jovanovic, and L. Hotujac, "Psychological consequences of rape on women in 1991-1995 war in Croatia and Bosnia and Herzegovina," *Croatian Medical Journal* 47 (2006): 67–75.

4. See "Bosnian Genocide Rape Victims Suffer in Silence" (October 1, 2009), which can be found at the Srebrenica Genocide Blog: http://srebrenica-genocide. blogspot.com/2009/10/bosnian-genocide-rape-victims-suffer-in.html. Accessed January 11, 2011.

5. de Brouwer and Hon Chu, eds., *The Men Who Killed Me*, 11.

6. Ibid., 76-77.

7. Catharine A. MacKinnon, "Rape, Genocide, and Women's Human Rights," *Harvard Women's Law Journal* 17 (1994): 11-12.

8. Amnesty International, *Making Violence Against Women Count: Facts and Figures—A Summary* (London, UK: Amnesty International, 2004).

9. Marie Vlachova and Lea Biason, eds., *Women in an Insecure World* (Geneva: Geneva Centre for the Democratic Control of Armed Forces, 2005).

10. Cited in Andrea Parrot and Nina Cummings, *Sexual Enslavement of Girls and Women Worldwide* (Westport, CT: Praeger, 2008), 40.

11. Organization of African Unity, *Rwanda: The Preventable Genocide* (Addis Ababa, Ethiopia: OAU, 2000).

12. See *The Prosecutor v. Jean Paul Akayesu (ICTR-96-4-T)* of the International Criminal Tribunal for Rwanda.

13. For an early report of the situation, see M. Valentich, "Rape Revisited: Sexual Violence against Women in the Former Yugoslavia," *Canadian Journal of Human Sexuality* 3 (1994): 53–64. Also significant is the contribution by the journalist-novelist Slavenka Drakulić, *S.: A Novel about the Balkans*, trans. Marko Ivić (New York: Penguin Books, 2001).

14. Patricia A. Weitsman, "The Politics of Identity and Sexual Violence: A Review of Bosnia and Rwanda," *Human Rights Quarterly,* 30 (2008): 561–78.

15. See http://www.icc-cpi.int/iccdocs/doc/doc639078.pdf for a complete copy of the arrest warrant. Accessed January 11, 2011.

16. David Scheffer, "Rape as Genocide in Darfur," *Los Angeles Times* (November 13, 2008), which is available at: http://www.latimes.com/news/opinion/commentary/la-oe-scheffer13-2008nov13,0,4968269.story. Accessed January 11, 2011.

17. Ibid.

18. See James Waller, *Becoming Evil: How Ordinary People Commit Genocide and Mass Killing*, 2nd ed. (New York: Oxford University Press, 2007).

19. In this chapter, I use the term *evil* and its variations (for example, *evildoing*) primarily to refer to the deliberate harming of humans by other humans. As I have said elsewhere, "Though evil may be difficult to define conceptually, we all are aware of its existence and pervasiveness at a concrete level. We know what it looks like, what it feels like, and how it can irrevocably alter our lives. . . . [My] behavioral definition . . . focuses on how people act toward one another. This definition judges as evil any human *actions* leading to the deliberate harming of other humans." Genocide and atrocities of the kind discussed in this book are instances of what deserves to be called *extraordinary* human evil. See ibid., 10-17.

20. Haing S. Ngor, *A Cambodian Odyssey* (New York: Warner, 1987), 230.

21. Weitsman, "The Politics of Identity and Sexual Violence," 575.

22. de Brouwer and Hon Chu, eds., *The Men Who Killed Me*, 101.

23. Catharine A. MacKinnon, *Are Women Human? And Other International Dialogues* (Cambridge, MA: Harvard University Press, 2006), 43.

24. de Brouwer and Hon Chu, eds., *The Men Who Killed Me*, 67.

25. Ibid., 111.

26. Quoted in Adam Jones, "Gender and Genocide in Rwanda," *Journal of Genocide Research* 4 (2002): 76.

27. United Nations Security Council, October 28, 2007, S/2007/643, paragraph 43, which is available at: http://www.securitycouncilreport.org/atf/cf/%7B65BFCF9B-6D27-4E9C-8CD3-CF6E4FF96FF9%7D/Civilians%20S2007643.pdf. Accessed January 11, 2011.

Further Suggested Reading

Allen, Beverly. *Rape Warfare: The Hidden Genocide in Bosnia-Herzegovina and Croatia*. Minneapolis, MN: University of Minnesota Press.

Butler, Christopher K., Tali Gluch, and Neil J. Mitchell. "Security Forces and Sexual Violence: A Cross-National Analysis of a Principal-Agent Argument." *Journal of Peace Research* 44 (2007): 669–87.

Denov, Myriam. "Wartime Sexual Violence: Assessing a Human Security Response to War-Affected Girls in Sierra Leone." *Security Dialogue* 37 (2006): 319–42.

Drakulic, Slavenka. *S.: A Novel About the Balkans*. Translated by Marko Ivić. New York: Viking Penguin, 1999.

Ducey, Kimberley A. "Dilemmas of Teaching the 'Greatest Silence': Rape-as-Genocide in Rwanda, Darfur, and Congo." *Genocide Studies and Prevention* 5 (2010): 310-22.

Green, Jennifer L. "Uncovering Collective Rape: A Comparative Study of Political Sexual Violence." *International Journal of Sociology* 34 (2004): 97–116.

Henry, Nicola. *War and Rape: Law, Memory and Justice*. New York Routledge, 2011.

Isikozlu, Elvan, and Ananda S. Millard. *Towards a Typology of Wartime Rape*. Germany: Bonn International Center for Conversion, 2010.

Kelly, Jocelyn. *Rape in War: Motives of Militia in DRC*. Washington, DC: United States Institute of Peace, 2010.

Questions for Discussion

1. This chapter states that, while the *modus operandi* is men perpetrating sexual violence on women, it is also possible for men and boys to be subject to rape and sexual violence in genocidal conflict. In what ways, if any, might male victims of rape and sexual violence be stigmatized differently than female victims?

2. In post-genocidal societies, how might the victims of rape and sexual violence be re-victimized? How might these challenges be best addressed?

3. This chapter reviews the micro-level purpose of rape for the perpetrator. Can you think of other purposes, not covered in this chapter, that rape might serve for the perpetrators?

4. What societal, cultural, or religious structures make it easier for perpetrators to define the targets of their sexual violence in such a way as to "excommunicate" them from a common moral community?

5. It has been said that the people most at risk in contemporary warfare are not soldiers but women and children. How has this chapter made you think differently about the protection of the populations most vulnerable in war?

7

Justice for Women? Rape as Genocide and the International Criminal Tribunal for Rwanda

Jessica A. Hubbard

> When asked about prosecuting those who raped her, Elizabeth
> said, "How can they be prosecuted? They are not even here."
> —*Binaifer Nowrojee, Shattered Lives*

Rwanda is located in the Great Rift Valley of central Africa. Bordering the Democratic Republic of Congo, Uganda, Burundi, Tanzania, and Zaire, this landlocked country, although smaller than the American state of Maryland, has a population of more than eight million, which makes it the most densely populated African nation. Rwanda also is one of Africa's poorest countries, and its economic problems include deforestation and severe erosion. Historically, while the Hutu ethnic group was the majority in Rwanda, German and Belgian colonizers gave the Tutsi authority and power. A hierarchy was established that favored Tutsi access to education, jobs, and government positions.[1]

The 1994 Rwandan genocide resulted in the deaths of more than 800,000 people. Overwhelmingly, the victims were Tutsi, but moderate Hutu, including some intermarried with Tutsi, were also among the slaughtered. In this genocide, rape was used in a systematic manner to destroy the culture of the Tutsi. This policy was devastating. Human rights groups estimate that every woman who survived the genocide was a victim of sexual assault.[2] Approximately seventy percent of the women raped were infected with HIV.[3] Here is an account regarding one Tutsi woman who survived genocidal rape in Rwanda.

Goretti, a twenty-six-year-old woman from Rusatira commune, Butare prefecture, was raped several times during the course of the genocide. When the violence began, the militia, who were all neighbors and even friends, told the women to go back to their land because they "did not have ethnicity" and that they were only killing the men. Nonetheless, after all her family was killed, she decided to hide in the bushes. She was soon discovered and held by a militiaman who raped her repeatedly over a period of two weeks. After the genocide, this man was arrested. Goretti explained how the militia behaved:

> The Interahamwe [Hutu militia group] shared women. Each one took a woman or a girl. The Interahamwe chased young girls and women—most were taken by two militia. I was taken by one who kept me for two weeks in mid-May. He told me that he would kill me after two weeks. Then he got tired of me and kicked me out.

Goretti was raped a second time after she managed to escape to nearby Songa. She was discovered by dogs that were sent to sniff out people hiding in the bush. She was caught and raped by two of the militia whom she did not recognize. She said:

> I was taken by force—they were like wild animals. You knew it was your last days, but I fought back anyway. They said that they had to take Tutsi women because before the war they were not able to take them. They said that Tutsi women stayed to themselves before.

Goretti concluded by saying that "most women were raped, if they are still alive. They [the Interahamwe] did whatever they wanted." She continued softly, "You can't ever forget. Now there's no one. Until I die, I'll always be sad."

Only the testimony of the women who were assaulted can begin to communicate what happens when rape becomes a weapon of genocide. Thus, the focal point of this chapter concentrates on excerpts from a Human Rights Watch report by Binaifer Nowrojee, a consultant to the Women's Rights Project. This report, which includes the testimony above, is called *Shattered Lives: Sexual Violence during the Rwandan Genocide and its Aftermath.* It is based on interviews and research conducted in

Rwanda in March and April 1996. (The report can be found in full at: http://www.hrw.org/en/reports/1996/09/24/shattered-lives.) I intersperse the excerpts within the chapter not only to let the victims speak for themselves but also to probe crucial issues about how, or even whether, justice can be obtained in the aftermath of genocidal rape.

Defining and Prosecuting Rape as Genocide

Crucial steps in the process of criminalizing sexual violence during war and genocide involved the establishment of the International Criminal Tribunal for Rwanda (ICTR).[4] Specifically, in the ICTR case (1996-1998) against Jean-Paul Akayesu (b. 1953), the Hutu mayor of the Taba commune in Gitarama prefecture, landmark actions included the following "firsts": (1) For the first time, an international tribunal found an individual guilty for committing the crime of genocide. (2) For the first time, an international tribunal defined the crime of rape, which previously had no commonly accepted definition in international law. The ICTR took rape to be "a form of aggression . . . a violation of personal dignity," which indicates that rape is one of the worst ways of inflicting harm because it produces intense psychological as well as physical suffering.[5] More specifically, the tribunal went on to define rape as "as a physical invasion of a sexual nature, committed on a person under circumstances which are coercive. Sexual violence which includes rape, is considered to be any act of a sexual nature which is committed on a person under circumstances which are coercive."[6] (3) For the first time, an international tribunal found an individual (Akayesu) guilty of rape not only as a crime against humanity but also an act of genocide. (4) For the first time, an individual's complicity in rape (Akayesu's) was interpreted as an instance of the crime of genocide.

Significantly, rape was not included in the original charge of genocide that was brought against Akayesu. It took the testimony of numerous women, relating their experiences of rape, the intervention of many women's human rights scholars and non-governmental organizations, and the strong insistence of South Africa's Navanethem Pillay, the tribunal's sole female judge, before the charges were amended to include rape as genocidal.[7] In these additional charges, the ICTR equated rape with torture, identifying how rape during the Rwandan genocide was used "for such purposes as intimidation, degradation, humiliation, discrimination, punishment, control, or destruction of a person."[8]

> *Marie-Claire* recounted how she was attacked by the military and the militia: "We were attacked by military together with Interahamwe. The Interahamwe were sent by the military. The Interahamwe were wild. To survive, you had to let yourself be raped. They told me to give them my money or my children." All but one of her children were killed by the militia. Marie-Claire was raped by a militia man whom she knew, a neighbor. "He is in Zaire now," she said. She continued:
>
> > He said many things during the rape and he hit and kicked me. He said "we have all the rights over you and we can do whatever we want." They had all the power—our men, our husbands, were all exterminated. We have no mother, no father, no brothers.

> *Clementine* and her husband and three children were separated as they fled from the militia in Kayenzi commune, Gitarama prefecture. After hiding for two days, thirty-eight-year-old Clementine was found by the militia one night as she hid in the bushes. They beat her badly before five of them raped both her and another woman hiding with her. "Two of the older militia refused to rape me," she said, "but they urged the younger ones to rape me and the other woman with me. They were saying 'we want to see how the Tutsikazi look inside. You can't shout—you must accept everything that we do to you now.'" After finishing the rapes, the older militia told the younger ones not to bother to kill Clementine because "you've already killed her." However, they killed the other rape victim before leaving the area. Clementine wandered around dazed looking for someone to help her. She knocked on the door of one house and when the owner opened the door, he said "you Tutsikazi are still alive. Why didn't they kill you?" Clementine later found refuge in the house of a woman who hid her until the RPF [Rwandan Patriotic Front, a Tutsi political and military movement] came in July 1994.

The ICTR identified how rape can be used systematically and intentionally to destroy a specific group of people. As illustrated by Clementine's narrative above, outright killing was not necessary to achieve that goal because rape's death-dealing consequences were so far-reaching. Following the 1948 United Nations Convention on the Prevention and Punishment of the Crime of Genocide, the ICTR defined genocide to mean:

> any of the following acts committed with intent to destroy, in whole or in part, a national, ethnical, racial or religious group, as such:
>
> (a) Killing members of the group;
> (b) Causing serious bodily or mental harm to members of the group;
> (c) Deliberately inflicting on the group conditions of life calculated to bring about its physical destruction in whole or in part;
> (d) Imposing measures intended to prevent births within the group;
> (e) Forcibly transferring children of the group to another group.[9]

The ICTR's definition of genocide, however, lacked an acknowledgment of the multiple ways in which women are affected when they experience genocidal rape. Although this chapter's testimonies from *Shattered Lives* show how devastating those effects can be, arguably even the more descriptive parts of the ICTR's judgment in the Akayesu case did not dwell sufficiently on this crucial aspect of the mass atrocities in Rwanda. While it is significant that the ICTR held that genocide can occur by forcibly impregnating women, or preventing birth in a group of women—thus destroying a group's identity and sustainability—genocidal sexual violence and rape should be understood as affecting women beyond their reproductive capacities.

When genocides are analyzed, the gender component as it extends beyond reproduction is often ignored. Arguably, genocide, as explicitly defined in international law, is gender neutral. Yet, as Lisa Sharlach cogently argues, "genocide has gender-specific effects. Girls and women are far more likely than are men to be the targets of sexual violence used as a component of genocide, but it is rare that analysts perceive rape to be a component of genocide."[10] As victims of genocide, men are beaten and killed. Sometimes they are raped as well. My analysis does not intend in any way to lessen the brutality or horror of such experiences, but its purpose is to highlight the fact that in genocide women are beaten and killed like men but also they are raped as only women can be.

Irreparable Harm

The ICTR held that rape and sexual violence "constitute genocide in the same way as any other act as long as they were committed with the specific intent to destroy, in whole or in part, a particular group, targeted as such." Hutu sexual violence in the 1994 Rwandan genocide served such a purpose—the intent was to destroy the Tutsi. As the ICTR put it, rape "resulted in the physical and psychological destruction of Tutsi women, their families, and their communities. Sexual violence was an integral part of the process of destruction, specifically targeting Tutsi women and specifically contributing to their destruction and to the destruction of the Tutsi group as a whole."[11]

Furthermore, the ICTR found that "the rape of Tutsi women was systematic and was perpetrated against all Tutsi women and solely against them."[12] Women were targeted because of their ethnicity and their gender, which includes their child-bearing potential. In genocidal rape these elements are likely to be inseparable, and thus genocidal rape is a weapon that does irreparable harm to a group in both the present and the future. As the ICTR said: "Tutsi women were subjected to sexual violence because they were Tutsi. Sexual violence was a step in the process of destruction of the Tutsi group—destruction of the spirit, of the will to live, and of life itself."[13]

> *Perpetue* was twenty years old and living in Runda commune, Gitarama prefecture, with her husband and child and her sister when the violence began. . . . She said:
>
> > On April 9, 1994, they found me. I was taken to the Nyabarongo River by a group of Interahamwe. When I got there, one Interahamwe said to me that he knew the best method to check that Tutsi women were like Hutu women. For two days, myself and eight other young

women were held and raped by Interahamwe, one after another. Perhaps as many as twenty of them. I knew three of them. Some Interahamwe watched over us while others went to eat and sleep. All the young women killed at that river were raped before being thrown in. I didn't know any of the other women. On the third day, one Interahamwe saw that I was not able to walk anymore. He told me that I had already died and could go. I tried to leave, but I could barely walk. There was blood everywhere and my stomach hurt. I walked towards Kamonyi and found refuge in an old church there. When I was going there, I saw that the Interahamwe had been burning people to death. I saw at least ten burnt bodies.

I was in the church building when the Interahamwe came there on May 15 and told us that it was our turn to be burnt. They took a lot of people outside to kill them. One Interahamwe chose me, but told me that he would protect me so that I would not be burnt to death. He took me to another building near the church and raped me there. Before he raped me, he said that he wanted to check if Tutsi women were like other women before he took me back to the church to be burnt. There were other women being raped there at the same time, maybe ten women and seven young girls. The next day, two Interahamwe watched over us while the others went to kill. The two were complaining they were feeling tired from all the killing. Then, one of them sharpened the end of the stick of a hoe. They held open my legs and pushed the stick into me. I was screaming. They did it three times until I was bleeding everywhere. Then they told me to leave. I tried to stand up, but I kept falling down. Finally I crawled outside. I was naked crawling on the ground covered in blood. I tried to ask someone on the road for help, but they thought I was a madwoman and just ignored me. I finally found a house where they gave me some medicine to apply to the area between my legs. They also gave me some clothes, but because I was bleeding so much the skirt became soaked with blood.

Perpetue stayed hiding in the bush for about one week until she found two men with a bicycle who were willing to take her to Gisenyi in the north-west part of the country. She thought that if she left the area where she was originally from, she would not be recognized as a Tutsi.

Unfortunately, when she arrived in Gisenyi at the end of May, she was recognized by an Interahamwe from her home area. He immediately notified the other militia that she was Tutsi and she was taken to a mass grave. Perpetue continued to recount her experience:

> I was told to give my clothes to them. The mass grave was for women and girls only and it was being organized by a woman they called Donatha. She had a long knife and cut me immediately behind the knee. One Interahamwe saw me and took me aside along with four other women. He explained to us that all the Gitarama people were going to be killed, but that he would protect us and that we could live with him. He took me to the lake. There, he raped me. I cried out because I was still wounded from before and he was opening all the wounds again. He beat me for crying and gagged my mouth. He told me that I was forbidden to cry because Tutsi had no rights at that moment. He also said that any Tutsi woman from Gitarama would be killed in an even worse way than what he was doing to me. After the rape, I was left alone and naked. I decided to try and escape. I couldn't walk properly and so I was on all fours. When people passed me, I sat down and stopped walking so they wouldn't know that I had been raped because I was ashamed. I crawled like that for two days in the bush. When I urinated, it came out like blood. Black, coagulated blood kept coming out of my vagina. . . .
>
> Since the war has ended, I have not had my monthly period. My stomach sometimes swells up and is painful. I think about what has happened to me all the time and at night I cannot sleep. I even see some of the Interahamwe who did these things to me and others around here. When I see them, I think about committing suicide.

Catharine MacKinnon believes that rape is committed against women—everyday, in all parts of the world—because they are women. But she contends that it is important to emphasize the ethnic component and the extent to which genocidal rape is a policy with the goal of destroying an ethnic group by assaulting the group's women. Unfortunately, the relationships between systematic assaults on women and genocidal attacks on ethnic groups are not always well understood. MacKinnon elaborates her view as follows:

The result is that these rapes are grasped in either their ethnic or religious particularity, as attacks on a culture, or in their sex specificity, meaning attacks on women—never both at once. Attacks on women, it seems, cannot define attacks on a people. If they are gendered attacks, they are not ethnic; if they are ethnic attacks, they are not gendered. One cancels the other. But when rape is a genocidal act, . . . it is an act to destroy a people. What is done to women defines that destruction.[14]

Further evidence about the irreparable harm that is done when rape is a genocidal act comes from a woman named Elizabeth, whose testimony is among those included in *Shattered Lives*.

> *Elizabeth* was twenty-nine years old and living in Kigali with her husband when the killing began. The militia came to their house while they were eating dinner with a group of people. She said:
>
>> About ten of them came. They picked two of the women in the group: a twenty-five year old and a thirty year old and then gang-raped them. When they finished, they cut them with knives all over while the other Interahamwe watched. Then they took the food from the table and stuffed it into their vaginas. The women died. They were left dead with their legs spread apart. My husband tried to put their legs together before we were told to get out of the house, and to leave the children behind. They killed two of our children. My husband begged them not to kill us, saying that he did not have any money on him, but that he had shoes and second-hand clothes that he sells at the market. He gave them all the clothes. Then, one Interahamwe said "you Tutsi women are very sweet, so we have to kill the man and take you."

Elizabeth's husband was killed and she was taken by the head of the militia to his house where she was raped. Ultimately, she managed to escape. She currently has no house and takes care of eight children—two of her own and six orphaned relatives. When asked about prosecuting those who raped her, Elizabeth said, "How can they be prosecuted? They are not even here."

The ICTR's recognition that rape can be a crime against humanity and an act of genocide has the potential to be an important step in increasing accountability for rape as a weapon of war and genocide.[15] But narratives like the ones above highlight important issues surrounding prosecution of those who have committed genocidal rape in Rwanda and elsewhere. In the case of Rwanda, many perpetrators of the genocide fled the country (see Marie-Claire's narrative above), but many Tutsi women had to continue living side by side with those who had raped them (see Perpetue's narratives above). Yet, it could also be said of these perpetrators, "How can they be prosecuted?" for even though they remain all-too-close, such perpetrators are akin to those who "are not even here" because constraining cultural norms do not favor the violated women and their testimonies. True, Jean-Paul Akayesu was convicted of genocide, and for the first time under international law, his complicity in rape was ruled to be genocidal. But as noted above, he was not originally indicted for rape. As the *New York Times* reported on September 5, 1998, "Despite extensive media reports of rapes, the tribunal investigators, at the time, virtually all men, could not find evidence to support an indictment. But during the trial a witness brought up rape in the cultural center. Questioned by Navanethem Pillay, a South African who is the tribunal's only female judge, the witness gave details. Other witnesses followed. Largely due to pressure from women's groups, the investigators went back to ask about rape, and those charges were added."[16] Akayesu's case, landmark and precedent-setting though it remains, is only one of the many that might have been tried but were not.

Testimony and Justice

For the Tutsi or any women who experience genocidal sexual violence, the issue of testimony is not a simple one. For example, despite the inclusion of rape in the Akayesu indictment, which created a space for testimony, justice for the victims of genocidal rape in Rwanda could scarcely be obtained because the multiple costs of breaking silence often outweighed the benefits. Jeanne, a young survivor interviewed by Human Rights Watch, believes that "Rape is a crime worse than others. There's no death worse than that. The problem is that women and girls don't say what happened to them."[17] Frequently, women will report the injury and death of family members but omit their own experience of sexual violence and rape. In telling authorities about the death of her daughter, one woman said: "I lost my daughter in a horrible way. . . . I did not mention the rape of my daughter. . . . I was only asked about the way my daughter was killed and if I saw it myself. I was crying. It was not worth it to say that she was raped."[18] This testimony, along with other narratives in this chapter, suggest that "the problem is not merely one of participation, but of how the 'conversation'—through its organization, forms, and traditions—excludes the particular things that cannot easily be said and heard."[19]

There seems to be an assumption or an expectation that verbalizing a trauma in the legal arena, in this case testifying about a rape, will allow individuals who have experienced extreme violence to obtain justice. But as an African proverb points out, "Truth is not always good to say."[20] Additionally, "if pain does not have a voice and trauma cannot be spoken, prioritizing speech over silence and assuming that peace-building and reconciliation rest primarily on verbalized accounts of the past events leaves the radical potential embedded in silence unexamined." [21]

The claim that truth leads to healing has to be placed within a specific cultural context. Societies construct meanings of justice, truth, forgiveness, reconciliation, and accountability, and those meanings need to be examined within the culture in which the process of justice is occurring. In this chapter, the focus has been on an international criminal tribunal, the ICTR. Such places tend to apply in a universal manner notions of justice that are Western and even Christian to a large degree.[22] Such approaches may overlook or underplay the necessity of recognizing the cultural differences of particular contexts, including the immensely important ways in which gender plays a part in constituting those differences. For example, adequate understanding of the meanings of sexual violence during war and genocide depends on grounding discussions of justice, truth, and reconciliation in specific contexts of culture and gender.

Years of research indicate that rape is not just an individual act of aggression perpetrated against another person but is also violence that occurs and is made more likely within specific cultural and social contexts. For instance, one factor that changes how women experience rape is the way that their society defines honor in relation to their community. In a cultural context that places great importance on the honor of a woman, rape is more successful in shattering a community. If cultural norms intensify the perception that the honor of a woman is violated through rape, if a culture's evaluation of gender deepens her sense of shame and increases the stigmatization of the rape victim's family, rape is more successful in achieving the intended goal of destroying a community.[23] As Dorothy Thomas and Regan Ralph aptly point out, "Soldiers can succeed in translating the attack upon an individual woman into an assault upon her community because of the emphasis placed . . . on women's sexual purity and the fact that societies define themselves, in overt or less clear-cut fashions, relative to their ability to protect and control that purity."[24]

Conclusion

In the Akayesu case, the ICTR took an important step for international law when it recognized that rape can be genocidal. Much remains to be done, however, before such tribunals or any other justice-oriented institutions can effectively combat the impunity with which such atrocities are committed and hold the perpetrators of genocidal sexual violence accountable. Steps in that direction depend on encouraging and supporting women who have the courage to testify about the sexual harm inflicted upon them and on vigorous efforts to hold perpetrators accountable for their actions. Even these steps, however, will be insufficient, for when genocidal rape takes place, the scales of justice scarcely can be balanced. Still, by paying attention to the first-hand accounts of women who have been the targets of genocidal rape, as this chapter has done by focusing on the Rwandan genocide, awareness may be created, including the understanding that rape is not merely a by-product of war and genocide but often central to the intentions that drive them both. That awareness and understanding, in turn, may lead to cultural and political changes that can help to curb if not eliminate, help to heal if not prevent, the widespread and long-lasting harm that is done to women, their families, and their communities when rape becomes a weapon of war and genocide.

Notes

1.   Catharine Newbury. "Background to Genocide: Rwanda," *Issue: A Journal of Opinion* 23 (1995):12-17.

2.   Binaifer Nowrojee, *Shattered Lives: Sexual Violence during the Rwandan Genocide and its Aftermath,* Human Rights Watch, September 1996. Available at: http://www.hrw.org/en/reports/1996/09/24/shattered-lives. Accessed October 10, 2011. The excerpts reprinted from *Shattered Lives* are used by permission from Human Rights Watch.

3.   Sherrie L. Russell-Brown, "Rape As An Act of Genocide," *Berkeley Journal of International Law* 21 (2003): 350-74.

4.   Based in Arusha, Tanzania, the ICTR was established by United Nations Security Council resolution 955 on November 8, 1994, for the purpose of prosecuting the primary perpetrators of the Rwandan genocide. At the time of this writing in 2011, the ICTR's work continues. Its web site is available at: http://www.unictr.org. Accessed October 10, 2011.

5.   Prosecutor v. Akayesu, Judgment (paragraph 597), International Criminal Tribunal for Rwanda, Case No. ICTR-96-4-T (1998). The entire Judgment is available at: http://www.unictr.org/Portals/0/Case%5CEnglish%5CAkayesu%5Cjudgement%5Cakay001.pdf. Accessed October 10, 2011. See also Richard J. Goldstone, "Prosecuting Rape as a War Crime," *Case Western Reserve Journal of International Law* 34 (2002): 277-86.

6.   Prosecutor v. Akayesu, Judgment (paragraph 598), International Criminal Tribunal for Rwanda, Case No. ICTR-96-4-T (1998), available at the site identified in note 5 above.

7.   Particularly significant in this regard was an important brief *amicus curiae* that pressed hard and effectively for the ICTR to "amend the indictment against Jean-Paul Akayesu to charge rape or other serious acts of sexual violence as crimes within the competence of the Tribunal." The key document is available at: http://www.iccwomen.org/publications/briefs/docs/Prosecutor_v_Akayesu_ICTR.pdf. Accessed October 27, 2011.

8.   Prosecutor v. Akayesu, Judgment (paragraph 597), International Criminal Tribunal for Rwanda, Case No. ICTR-96-4-T (1998), available at the site identified in note 5 above.

9.   "Statute of the International Criminal Tribunal for Rwanda," (1994), Article 2. See http://www2.ohchr.org/english/law/itr.htm. Accessed October 10, 2011.

10. Lisa Sharlach, "Rape as Genocide: Bangladesh, the Former Yugoslavia, and Rwanda," *New Political Science* 22 (2000): 89-102, especially 92. Available at: http://www.safhr.org/index.php?option=com_docman&task=cat_view&gid=1 37&Itemid=580&limitstart=10. Accessed October 12, 2011. See also Sharlach's article "Gender and Genocide in Rwanda: Women as Agents and Objects of Genocide," *Journal of Genocide Research* 1, 3 (1999): 387-99. Among other things, this article discusses how women, as well as men, can be—and have been—perpetrators of genocide.

11. Guglielmo Verdirame, "The Genocide Definition in the Jurisprudence of the ad hoc Tribunals," *The International and Comparative Law Quarterly* 49 (2000): 578-98. See also Prosecutor v. Akayesu, Judgment (paragraphs 731-74), International Criminal Tribunal for Rwanda, Case No. ICTR-96-4-T (1998), available at the site identified in note 5 above.

12. See "Historic Judgment Finds Akayesu Guilty of Genocide," ICTR Updates and Bulletins (September 2, 1998). Available at: http://ictr-archive09.library.cornell.edu/ENGLISH/PRESSREL/1998/138.html. Accessed October 10, 2011. See also paragraphs 731-34 of the ICTR judgment itself, available at the site identified in note 5 above.

13. See paragraph 732 of the ICTR judgment in the Akayesu case, which is available as indicated in note 5 above.

14. Catharine A. MacKinnon, *Are Women Human? and Other International Dialogues* (Cambridge, MA: Harvard University Press, 2006), 185.

15. Goldstone, "Prosecuting Rape as a War Crime," 277-86.

16. "When Rape Becomes Genocide," *New York Times*, September 5, 1998. Available at: http://www.nytimes.com/1998/09/05/opinion/when-rape-becomes-genocide.html?pagewanted=1. Accessed October 10, 2011.

17. See Nowrojee, *Shattered Lives*. Available at the site identified in note 2 above.

18. Ibid.

19. Marjorie L. DeVault and Chrys Ingraham, "Metaphors of Silence and Voice in Feminist Thought," in *Liberating Method: Feminism and Social Research*, ed. Marjorie L. DeVault (Philadelphia: Temple University Press, 1999), 183.

20. See Michael Ignatieff, "Articles of Faith," *Index On Censorship* 25 (1996): 110-22.

21. Tarja Väyrynen, "Narrativity and Silence in Conflict Resolution," in the proceedings of the 2007 convention of the International Studies Association (ISA),

p. 7. Available at: http://citation.allacademic.com/meta/p_mla_apa_research_citation/1/7/9/9/7/pages179979/p179979-1.php. Accessed October 10, 2011.

22. Kevin Avruch and Beatriz Vejarano, "Truth and Reconciliation Commissions: A Review Essay and Annotated Bibliography," *OJPCR: The Online Journal of Peace and Conflict Resolution* 4, 2 (2002): 43.

23. Dorothy Q. Thomas and Regan E. Ralph, "Rape in War: Challenging the Tradition of Impunity," *SAIS Review* (1994): 88-89.

24. Ibid., 89

Further Suggested Reading

Clark, Phil. *The Gacaca Courts, Post-Genocide Justice and Reconciliation in Rwanda: Justice without Lawyers*. Cambridge, UK: Cambridge University Press, 2010.

Cruvellier, Thierry. *Court of Remorse: Inside the Criminal Tribunal for Rwanda*. Translated by Chari Voss. Madison, WI: University of Wisconsin Press, 2010.

Human Rights Watch, September 2004. "Struggling to Survive: Barriers to Justice for Rape Victims in Rwanda." Available at: http://www.hrw.org/en/reports/2004/09/30/struggling-survive. Accessed October 10, 2011.

Leatherman, Janie L. *Sexual Violence and Armed Conflict*. Malden, MA: Polity Press, 2011.

Neuffer, Elizabeth. *The Key to My Neighbors House: Seeking Justice in Bosnia and Rwanda*. New York: Picador, 2002.

Salbi, Zainab. *The Other Side of War: Women's Stories of Survival and Hope*. Washington, DC.: National Geographic Society, 2006.

Questions for Discussion

1. Why are first-hand accounts important when examining an event such as the Rwandan genocide?

2. What factors make it difficult for some women to share what they experienced during the Rwandan genocide?

3. How did rape and sexual violence constitute genocide in Rwanda?

4. If justice cannot be obtained through a court, because events are too difficult to voice, what are some alternative approaches toward justice that might work better?

5. If you could meet the women whose testimonies appear in this chapter, what would you most want to hear from them and say to them? If you could meet Jean-Paul Akayesu, what would you most want to hear from him and say to him?

8

Guatemaltecas Have Not Forgotten: From Victims of Sexual Violence to Architects of Empowerment in Guatemala

Roselyn Costantino

Welcome to Guatemala, Heart of the Mayan World: Land where men, nature, and time have coincided and where they dwell together forever. More than 3000 years ago a people endowed with extraordinary skills formed one of the most well-known and most respected civilizations in history, the Maya. Guatemala is a country where the Mayan people live their traditions fully. They express their history and customs through their beautiful pottery, jade figures, and multicolor textiles, which is a true testimony of their ancient culture. It is an unbelievably beautiful, complex, and diverse country that has preserved their most precious heritage, its people.

—*INGUAT (Guatemalan Tourism Institute)*[1]

The words above may be true—unless you are a woman. For Maya women and girls in particular, daily life stands in stark contrast to the carefully crafted images that Guatemala's Tourism Institute distributes in travel posters and internet web sites. In these representations, one often sees a smiling but reserved, dark and exotic woman. In brilliantly colored, hand-woven native dress, she typically carries a healthy, wide-eyed and round-faced baby in a sling on her back. The profile of her real life experiences, however, is likely to reflect the worst indicators of human well-being in the Americas.

The State of Guatemala, which claims to promote women's rights, has not been an agent for change in correcting the many structural and cultural factors that are detrimental to the women of Guatemala. *Guatemaltecas* struggle daily against abject poverty, chronic malnutrition, illiteracy, alarmingly high rates of infant and maternal mortality, and lack of access to land, clean water, and medical care. Furthermore, and highlighting both the subject of this book and the focus of my chapter, extreme gender violence makes Guatemala one of the most dangerous places in the world to be a woman. To underscore that point, my brief chapter-focusing documents offer five glimpses of atrocities in Guatemala's genocidal history. As the subsequent analysis shows, these reports and testimonies about operations of the State do not depict rare and disconnected episodes. To the contrary, they illustrate the widespread and deep-seated violence that has made rape a weapon of war and genocide in Guatemala.

1. During a village massacre: "Fifteen years ago [1982], the women of Rio Negro [Guatemala Highlands], some of them pregnant, were dragged from their homes, forced to march to the top of a mountain, and there, along with their children, were raped, tortured and killed. 'The soldiers and the (paramilitary civil defense) patrollers started grabbing the girls and raping us,' recalls Ana, one of a handful of survivors of the massacre. 'Only two soldiers raped me because my grandmother was there to defend me. All the girls were raped.' In total, 177 women and children died that day. The village . . . disappeared. . . . Time and again women bore the brunt of men's crimes against humanity."[2]

2. At a clandestine torture center: "While he had sex with her, others masturbated, others licked her, they put their hands on her breasts, they punched her in the face, others put lit cigarettes on her chest; a few times she lost consciousness and each time she gained it, she would see another man on top of her, at least 20 judicials raped her; she lay in a pool of urine, semen, blood, it was really humiliating, a mix of hate, of frustration, and absolute impotence."[3]

3. At a school: "In June 1977, in the village of Tres Cruces, the municipality of Sipacapa, the department of San Marcos, members of the Guatemalan Army captured the teacher Eulabia de Díaz from inside

the Official Co-Ed Rural School. They tortured her and raped her to death. Then they took her dead body away."[4]

4. Seemingly random, but strategic acts of violence: "The women who were pregnant . . . one of them was in her eighth month and they cut her belly, and they took out the little one, and they tossed it around like a ball. Then they cut off one breast, and they left it hanging in a tree."[5]

5. At home: "I told no one, not even my husband, because he could have hit me and I was afraid. . . . That night they raped many women and their husbands didn't know about it because they were out doing their shifts."[6]

The Plight of *Guatemaltecas*

In Guatemala, women are targeted just for being women, and women of Maya descent are the least respected of all. Although the Guatemalan government ratified with no restrictions the 1979 United Nations Convention on the Elimination of All Forms of Discrimination against Women (CEDAW), studies confirm that instead of making progress, Guatemala has actually dropped twenty-two positions in the UN's Index of Institutional Quality: "There is no perception of any changes in the educational policies, nor in the media . . . [or] the cultural imagery of women's inferiority and subordination" that would indicate the State has generated the needed cultural revolution to allow women to enjoy their most basic rights, participate fully in political processes, work freely, and obtain adequate standards of living, including mental and physical health.[7] Nor has the State honored its commitments to alleviate child labor, slavery, prostitution, domestic abuse, and kidnapping with forced adoption. In periodic reports to the United Nations, the Guatemalan State touts major success in creating a safer, more equitable place for women, even as it continues to ignore or to claim ignorance about the ways in which the State's "self-interest" causes women to die horrible deaths through domestic abuse, disease and malnutrition, and in giving birth.[8] All are preventable except in Guatemala's masculine-dominated and ethnically racist society now deteriorating at a catastrophic rate.

What accounts for the disconnect between the daily lives of *Gautemaltecas* and the images created by the State of Guatemala and its Tourism Institute? Why is the site of one of the most advanced civilizations in world history also a brutally violent place that is extremely dysfunctional and dangerous for women and girls? The diverse cultures of Guatemala (Maya, European, and ladino, or mixed) all portray motherhood and mothers as "sacred." What explains the contradiction between the centrality of the role of women in the social imagination and the abuse, neglect, and violence to which real women are subjected? What does this divergence between imagined and lived reality mean in the day-to-day existence of Guatemalan women, and what have they done to remain resilient and to resist their plight?

My responses to these questions concentrate on rape as a weapon not only of war but also of *femicide,* two manifestations of violence against Guatemalan women that have marked the second half of the twentieth century and continue unabated in the twenty-first. Rape as a weapon of war refers specifically to the systematic and systemic deployment of rape as a military tactic to produce ethnic cleansing, intensify political terror, extract information, and reward soldiers. *Femicide* denotes the killing of a female because she is a female; concurrently, it connotes deep-seated misogyny and senses of power and impunity ingrained in a masculinist psyche.[9]

The term *femicide* entered legal, human rights, academic, and political parlance relatively recently, although the phenomenon it names—gendered violence against a woman that ultimately results in her death—is as old as patriarchal social institutions. In her foundational work, *Femicide in a Global Perspective,*[10] Diana Russell revived a nineteenth-century English legal term—*femicide,* the murder of a woman—and thus provided an initial step in articulating the gendered specificity of this criminal act by differentiating the intent, manner, and sanction of femicide from homicide.

Femicide and genocide are closely and usually—but not always—related. According to the United Nations definition, the term *genocide* refers to the intended destruction, in whole or in part, of "a national, ethnical, racial or religious group, as such." Debates continue about the UN's definition of genocide, because its enumeration of the groups that could be targeted for destruction in whole or in part seems too small and exclusive. Political groups, for instance, are not included in the UN's definition, although they definitely have been targeted for destruction that can rightly be called genocidal. Intentional destruction of groups, certainly as the UN defines genocide, cannot avoid targeting females, whose child-bearing role is essential for group survival. Genocide, however, is not restricted to killing the members of a targeted group. As the UN definition indicates, genocide can also result from inflicting other forms of harm—for example, "deliberately inflicting on the group conditions of life calculated to bring about its physical destruction in whole or in part." So genocide does not necessarily entail femicide, although usually the systematic killing of females for being female is inseparable from genocide. On the other hand, not all femicide is necessarily genocidal. Females could be killed as females, even to some extent systematically, without genocidal intent. A group's intention to secure its own strength and survival, for example, might result in policies—however problematic and unethical—to limit the number of females it contains. In sum, genocide is likely to entail femicide, but not necessarily, and femicide is likely to be genocidal, but, again, not necessarily. In the Guatemalan context, the femicide-genocide connection is very close, because murder of a female *for being female* can scarcely be separated from intended/genocidal destruction of groups.[11]

When one traces the antecedents of the recent Guatemalan incidences of strategic rape and femicide, it becomes evident that although the perpetrators and circumstances may morph along the time and space continuum of patriarchal social organization, neither the conditions that encourage femicide nor the perpetrators disappear.[12] Over the last decades, this realization has served as a catalyst for the courage and creativity that enable *Guatemaltecas* to execute the needed fundamental change to eliminate violence in its myriad forms despite regularly being threatened themselves for doing this work.

Historic Legacies of Violence against Women in Guatemala

In Guatemala, as in patriarchal societies worldwide, women are recognized as the givers of life, the transmitters of culture and tradition, and the pillars of family and community. To rape, torture, and kill a woman, especially in front of her family or community, dishonors not only the woman but also her family, community, and ethnic identity. Being raped in Hispanic Roman Catholic and traditional Maya cultures creates profound and traumatic shame and guilt. Such violence destroys a woman's emotional, physical, and mental health; it irrevocably damages familial and communal cohesiveness.

The unleashing of sexual violence against females and killing them because of their sex and constructed gender identity can be traced back in Guatemalan history at least to the sixteenth-century arrival of the Spanish. The cataclysmic encounter between the Spanish conquerors and the Maya still reverberates at all levels of Guatemalan social interaction. Conquest and colonization brought firearms, Spanish Roman Catholic ideologies, imperialist economics, rigid patriarchal hierarchy, racism, and genocide. Women have not fared well in such social or economic structures, which evolved over the centuries and depend on a female work force that is plentiful, pliable, and disposable.[13] For more than five hundred years, social, political, and economic institutions in Guatemala have created, maintained, and reinforced systemic obstacles to women's rights, blocked women's full participation in sociopolitical processes, and produced countless unspeakable atrocities.

After nineteenth-century independence from colonialism, and during early twentieth-century nation building and modernization processes, dominant Guatemalan economic and political elites reverted to the idealization of the family. But instead of advocating modernization that would eliminate archaic, traditional gender attitudes and obstacles to women's rights to own land, work without their husband's permission, and obtain education, the prevailing nationalist discourse of the period reinforced women's roles as selfless mothers and submissive wives who defer to male authority in exchange for protection. Rather than integrate women into economic or political spheres as productively equal members of society, these processes further restricted women's access to public spaces and resources, and, by means of controlling the female body, robbed women of autonomy as well. Twentieth-century economic growth—first, mega fruit and coffee plantations and, later, *maquiladoras*, multinationally-owned assembly plants advantaged by cheap labor, lucrative tax incentives, and weak enforcement of environmental and labor laws—required a submissive female workforce.

To secure this human capital, Guatemalan governmental institutions subjected women to sexualized violence by exerting ever-more intense masculine control over them—at home and in church, on the banana plantation and the *maquiladora* factory floor.[14] Ironically, exploiting Guatemalan "femininity" has had mixed results: it has transformed gender roles, family structures, and migration patterns that have simultaneously liberated women by providing income and generated a backlash by male family and community members who resent women's self-sufficiency and employment opportunities. Patriarchal institutions attempt to police women's institutional lives more than ever—for instance, by forcing *maquila* workers to show sanitary napkins or tampons monthly in order to prove they are menstruating and are not pregnant; by forcing sexual relations as a condition of getting a job or continued employment; by denying access to education, land, medical services, and other resources necessary for survival; and by limiting access to contraception and family planning, restrictions aimed at limiting a woman's power over her body, including the ability to determine when or if to become pregnant and how many children to have.

These myriad manifestations of violence against women are not only a *consequence* of discriminatory economic systems and socio-political structures inherited from the past, but they also constitute a *condition* of that structural design.[15] Since the sixteenth century, entrenched patriarchal institutions have subjected *Guatemaltecas* to an "insidious trauma" of female oppression characteristic of a male-dominated culture that normalizes and eroticizes sexual violence while continually attacking the physical and psychological integrity of women.[16] That subjugation both reflects and enhances the power of two central institutions: the military and the industrial capitalist system.

The Economics of Counting Bodies and Why Bodies Count

During the late nineteenth century, because of plentiful natural resources—mineral wealth, fertile tropical coastal and mountain areas, and plentiful human capital—Guatemala became a country of commercial and national security "interest" for the United States. American capitalism converted Guatemala into an exemplary "banana republic," a country controlled by exploitative foreign companies (often agriculturally based) that protect their interests by backing political coups and by supporting brutal dictatorships or puppet governments. U.S. officials with major investments in the United Fruit Company protected their interests despite the costs to poor and indigenous Guatemalans. The oppressive methods included secret operations, led by the Central Intelligence Agency (CIA), to support brutal puppet dictators and to crush resistance, and American military training of Guatemalan troops and police whose tactics to repress civil society often relied upon harsh interrogations, torture, rape, and extrajudicial executions. In 1954, a joint Guatemalan military-CIA coup overthrew a democratically-elected reformist president, ushering in a long line of military dictators and brutal repression of non-combatant Guatemalans.[17]

After this 1954 military coup, from 1960 to 1996 the Guatemalan military, paramilitary, and death squads terrorized Guatemalan citizens in a manner not seen in the Western Hemisphere since the sixteenth-century conquest: torture, mass rapes, genocide, and a scorched earth campaign ensued in what is sometimes called the Internal Armed Conflict. Labeling critical voices "communist," the terrorist State viewed anyone criticizing or revolting against extreme economic and social inequities as an obstacle to profit-making and to Guatemalan "modernization." Through a U.S.-style Cold-War counterinsurgency and with U.S. support and training, the Guatemalan State ruthlessly implemented an ideological cleansing of the body politic. In a total Guatemalan population of less than ten million at the time, the Guatemalan government and its agents murdered 150,000 mostly indigenous Maya and forcefully "disappeared" another 50,000, who came from diverse ethnic and social groups. The government's scorched earth and genocidal policies orphaned 250,000 children, widowed 80,000 women, produced 626 documented massacres, and wiped more than 400 indigenous communities from the face of the earth.[18] In response to the onslaught, 500,000 Guatemalans sought refuge in the jungle highlands of southern Mexico, and another 1.5 million persons became internally displaced, escaping extermination by abandoning their villages.[19] Those desperate steps had further devastating consequences because the people taking flight lost their land, which was confiscated by the government.

As part of the State's counterinsurgency, the Guatemalan military, paramilitary, civil defense patrols, death squads, and police forces targeted women and children for "special treatment" whether they were engaged in the conflict or not. They tortured, raped, mutilated, and murdered tens of thousands of mostly Maya women in front of their children—or their children in front of them—as State-sanctioned political acts.[20]

Females of every age suffered an indescribable level of cruelty designed to obliterate traditionally strong community ties essential to the survival of the Maya. For similar ends, boys and men, especially in rural villages, were forced to serve in Civil Defense Patrols, where, to "prove" they were not communists or guerrillas, they had to torture, rape, and kill their mothers, sisters, or neighbors. Refusal to do so condemned these boys and men to being tortured, raped, and killed themselves. Sometimes they also had to set fire to their homes, destroy village crops, and mutilate corpses. Wrecking the social fabric, most notably through the extreme violation and profound humiliation of the women, these genocidal acts systematically sought to eliminate the Maya and the insurgents alike.[21]

The State's militarized approach to resistance exacerbated misogyny and gender inequality in Guatemala, a nation with the most extreme gender inequities in the Western Hemisphere, and, as stated earlier, one of the most dangerous places in the world for women and girls.[22] The practices of State agents took femicide to epidemic levels. Since 2000, more than 4,800 women and girls, aged seven to eighty, have been kidnapped, tortured, raped, dismembered, and/or mutilated in Guatemala. Less than one percent of the perpetrators have been indicted, and only a small fraction of that number has been found guilty. Arguably, impunity for femicide, like that enjoyed by earlier genocidal war criminals, remains the most significant factor in the perpetuation of violence against women in Guatemala.

Women's Voices Breaking the Silence: Challenging Official History

The evidence presented above reveals the long-standing contradictions inherent between Guatemala's patriarchal and militarized image of women, on the one hand, and the women's life experiences, on the other. Equally important, however, is what contemporary *Guatemaltecas* are saying aloud about living within these contradictions, about the impact on their bodies of the terror and brutalization that attempts to obliterate their humanity. This chapter began with brief reports and testimonies about those genocidal policies. How can we further contextualize that testimony in order to understand the women's motivations for breaking silence long after the events took place? Why do the women bring up such devastating intimate violence in such public ways?

In part, making their voices heard and hearing themselves break the crippling silence surrounding their trauma provide both a healing therapy and a psychological-political discovery process that advances the women's struggle for justice, accountability, and reparations for the crimes committed against them.[23] "We must seek a way to heal the wounds in order to combat this culture of violence" argues Alba Maldonado, a lawyer and Congresswoman of the Unidad Revolucionaria Nacional Guatemalteca (URNG).[24] The wounds of the horrors she speaks of have been no secret in Guatemala; yet, terrorizing State forces kept most Guatemalans silent. International trading or investment partners refused to interfere in domestic affairs or perhaps underestimated the gravity of the crimes against humanity being committed. It has taken courageous, committed Guatemalans and their advocates to act upon their belief that healing is not possible without truth; no justice can be found without accountability from those who planned, enforced, or committed the crimes; and no reconciliation can occur without reparations to Guatemalan women, especially including indigenous Maya, who lost everything and yet still struggle for their children's survival and their own as well.

The healing process began with the ten-year negotiations (1986-1996) to end the Internal Armed Conflict. The persistence of Guatemalan women forced the State and United Nations negotiators to open a space at the table for representatives of a broad array of women's organizations. This presence at the negotiating table significantly recognized the victimization of women during the war and also acknowledged the broad scope of gender violence in Guatemalan society. Other important developments included three documents that took steps toward empowering women, restoring their human dignity and their rights, by inscribing women's experiences in Guatemala's historical narrative: (1) The Human

Rights Office of the Archdiocese of Guatemala's comprehensive study, *Guatemala, Never Again!* (Nunca Más)/ *REHMI, Recovery of Historical Memory Project*; (2) *Guatemala: Memory of Silence*, a 1999 report based on findings by the Guatemalan Truth Commission (CEH); (3) the UN-brokered 1996 Peace Accords. First-hand testimonies gathered for these documents—they include content highlighted at the start of this chapter—demonstrate that sexual violations constituted much more than physical attacks against women. They evidence the profound emotional, psychological, and social consequences of that violence: serious and chronic medical problems, psychological damage, infectious and stress-related diseases, forced pregnancy, infertility, and stigmatization, including rejection by family members and communities.[25]

It has been essential for *Guatemaltecas* to speak their truth to power and for us to listen, as both constitute acts in defiance of the silencing of this history not only in Guatemala but also in the United States, which bears considerable responsibility for the atrocities inflicted on Guatemalan women in recent decades. With that responsibility in mind, you may want and need to read again the excerpts at the beginning of this chapter. They show that the surviving women are giving testimony, speaking out, and demanding justice for what they and their sisters and mothers experienced as well as for the 50,000 plus *Guatemaltecas,* the vast majority Maya, who did not survive the violence to tell their stories.

As difficult as it is to relive their experiences of violence, *Guatemaltecas* continue to insist that moving forward requires not only sharing their memory of atrocity but also ensuring that awareness of atrocity enters into Guatemala's collective consciousness. One significant step toward that goal was taken in 2010 by the broad coalition of women's organizations that initiated the Guatemalan Tribunal of Conscience, a public hearing in Guatemala City with media coverage that reached a national and international audience. Although their testimonies were not heard in an official courtroom, but before symbolic judges, women came from far and wide, especially from rural villages, to testify about the atrocities they suffered almost thirty years earlier. Nevertheless, despite the passage of time, the mostly Maya women still were shielded behind screens so that their identities would not be revealed as they spoke publicly about crimes the perpetrators still want forgotten.[26]

One sad reality about this national trauma is that the impact of the violence has not ceased. The loss of a generation of intellectuals and artists, human rights advocates, labor organizers, university students, and Maya women continues to haunt and impoverish Guatemala. Memorializing their traces in ceremonies or on plaques can do little to rectify the gruesome history inscribed in the Guatemalan national psyche and on the bodies of all, but especially women who survived the war and who continue to pay the highest price.

From Victims to Architects of Change

This world's not going to change unless we're willing to change ourselves.[27]

In the early twenty-first century, Guatemala faces a meltdown of those social and political institutions that should guarantee the security and well-being of its citizens. An epidemic of hostility still rages: homicide, gang warfare, organized crime and narco-trafficking, the repression of human rights workers, labor organizers, journalists, judges, and artists, and high levels of gender violence. At the same time, *Guatemaltecas* are developing ways to translate trauma and almost hopeless economic situations into the transformation, albeit slow, of their communities and nation. Innovative approaches by women's organizations model a robust transformative response to gender violence. These approaches include capacity building for women's initiatives, non-hierarchal organizational practices, and legal, legislative, and political actions that advance solutions to issues of particular concern to women. *Guatemaltecas* are constructing a civil society from the grassroots to provide the services to women and children that the State either cannot or will not supply. They have painstakingly documented the adverse conditions to which women are subjected because of their gender. For example, the Grupo Guatemalteco de Mujeres (1988) has produced an important report, "Situational Diagnosis of the Violent Deaths of Women in Guatemala," which formalized the concept and documented the phenomenon of femicide in Guatemala and has served as a model for such documentation in other countries. [28]

Other groups, such as the National Union of Guatemalan Women (1980), National Coordinating Committee of Widows of Guatemala

(1988), New Horizons (1989), Survivors' Foundation (2001), and Coordinating Group of Traditional Midwives of the State of Quetzaltenango (CODECOT, 2001) have moved beyond earlier obstacles to women's collaboration—for instance, differences of socio-economic status, ethnic group, language, religion, geographic location—and consolidated efforts to enhance security and social justice for women. They design development projects and promote political participation; they create coalitions of lawyers, psychologists, and forensic scientists to force access to mass grave sites and military records as they resist abusive militarization of the country. Women are supporting and promoting women in the social sciences and other professions to undertake the profound transformation required to address Guatemala's gross economic inequality.[29] Until 2005, the NGO New Horizons provided what was often the *only* safe house in the country for abused women and girls.[30] More recently, networks throughout Guatemala have been formed to extend shelter and legal, psychological, and social assistance for young and adult women victims of domestic and non-domestic violence. The umbrella group CODECOT's multi-faceted approach exemplifies the methodology being employed by numerous organizations. It promotes theoretical and practical knowledge of traditional Maya medicine and true collaboration between medical practitioners and midwives; improves maternal/infant health in rural communities; strengthens the coordinating group through ongoing technical health training and training in community organizing and leadership; and promotes participation in local, state, and national political spheres to improve public health policies.[31]

Another notable accomplishment resulted when the efforts of a broad coalition of women's organizations and individual feminist activists and professionals successfully impacted legislative and judicial institutions to secure the passage of the 2008 Law Against Femicide and Other Forms of Violence Against Women. This internationally unprecedented law writes into the legal code an expansive definition of gender violence against women. It defines femicide as the "violent death of a woman by virtue of her gender, as it occurs in the context of the unequal gender relations between men and women," and then identifies four types of violence against women punishable by law: femicide; physical/sexual violence; psychological violence; and economic violence. The law establishes a specialized judicial court charged with investigating cases of gendered violence as well as Centers of Integral Support for Female Survivors of Violence, which provide much-needed shelter, medical care, and therapy to female victims of domestic violence and their children.[32]

Resistance against these initiatives remains entrenched and strong. As women's advocates advance legal and judicial reform and as members of women's organizations investigate gender crimes, excavate mass graves, decipher military files, and defend women victims of wartime rape and femicide, they continue to receive death threats against themselves and their families, and numerous organizations' headquarters have been raided and evidence destroyed.[33] The message conveyed by this terror: keep silent. *Guatemaltecas'* response: Watch us, not as objects of your terror but as the agents of change we are.

What Can We Do?

One of this chapter's goals is to create a critical framework from which to explore both the root causes and recent manifestations of violence against women in Guatemala and the responses of *Guatemaltecas* to their plight. The critical lens incorporates the role of social memory in the perpetration, perpetuation, and transformation of that violence. Developing the skills to "see" history and to "read" current events permits us to be aware of hidden realities, including what is done in our name. For citizens of the United States, those skills permit and even require interrogating how the "American way of life" is connected to the horror and tragedy women and girls endure elsewhere. Insight about those connections can create responsibility to do something about them. What might such actions look like? Here are ways to make a difference suggested by *Guatemaltecas* and their allies:[34]

1. Be informed. Consult online sources, beginning with the Guatemala Human Rights Commission/USA.[35]

2. Read about the impact of the U.S.-Central American Free Trade Agreement on small farmers, co-ops, and women artisans. Commit to buying only "fair trade" coffee, chocolate,

woven clothing, and other popular items that Maya and women's cooperatives produce.[36]

3. Call, send emails, and/or join lobbying efforts to tell congressional representatives that you know how military aid to Guatemala results in sexual violence that women continue to suffer.

4. Actively support the International Violence Against Women Act (IVAWA) and demand protection of children, women, and other vulnerable populations worldwide.[37]

5. Start a campus organization grounded in the belief that through collective actions we *do* make a difference. Invite speakers to address structural causes of violence against women. Write letters to school and local newspapers. Start a blog. Teach others to sharpen how they "see" history and "read" public discourse.

6. The next time you say or hear someone say "never again," ask what she, he, or you have done to be sure that *never again* means something.

I have worked in Guatemala and Mexico for more than twenty years. During that time, I have interacted with women organizers and political operatives, lawyers and abused wives, professors and elementary school children, women who are educated and wealthy, and those who are so poor that they cannot provide adequate nutrition for their children. Perhaps the most salient truth made clear to me by these experiences is that violence against women is not a Guatemalan, Mexican, Congolese, or Chinese problem but rather that violence against women has occurred whenever hierarchical structures give advantage to males over females and as long as self-authorized men have written foundational histories to validate the repression and violent death of women.

The gender-violence issues facing the Guatemalan and global community are of such far-reaching importance that we must draw from the skill and knowledge of all persons of good will to improve the odds in favor of social justice and peace. *Guatemaltecas* understand the urgency of this need. Despite their daily challenges, these women keep working to achieve those goals. *Nunca Más*, they insist, requires calling on social memory to look back and never forget, while looking forward and creatively transforming.

Notes

1.   This INGUAT statement appeared particularly in the early years of the twenty-first century, when Roberto Robles directed the Guatemalan Tourism Institute, a government agency. Robles resigned his position in November 2010.

2.   Jennifer Harbury, "War Crimes: Women Begin to Speak. The rape of indigenous women in the 1970-1980 Guatemalan Civil War." *CERIGUA Weekly Briefs* 48 (December 11, 1997). Available at http://www.libertadlatina.org/LatAM_ Guatemala_Indigenous_Rape_In_Civil_War.htm. Accessed October 17, 2011.

3.   "Violations of Human Rights: Sexual Violence Against Women." in *Guatemala: Memoria del Silencio*, (see especially sections 28 and 50). English translation adapted by the author. The findings in this document are based on evidence and testimony from the Guatemalan Truth Commission (CEH). Available at http://shr.aaas.org/guatemala/ceh/mds/spanish/cap2/vol3/vol3. html. Accessed October 17, 2011.

4.   *Guatemala, Never Again!* (Nunca Más)/*REHMI: Recovery of Historical Memory Project*. The official report of the Human Rights Office, Archdiocese of Guatemala, headed by Bishop Juan Gerardi (Maryknoll, NY: Orbis Books, 1999), Case 8068. The findings in this report are based on evidence and testimony obtained by the CEH (Guatemalan Truth Commission).

5.   Ibid., Case 6335.

6.   See, as cited in note 3 above, *Guatemala: Memoria del Silencio*, sections 48 and 110. English translation adapted by the author.

7.   CLADEM-Guatemala, "Alternative Report on the Observance by the State of Guatemala of the Compromises of the Convention on the Elimination of All Forms of Discrimination against Women, CEDAW," 2008. See chapter 1. Available at: http://www2.ohchr.org/english/bodies/cedaw/docs/ngos/ CLADEM_Guatemala43_en.pdf. Accessed October 17, 2011. CLADEM is the abbreviation for the Latin American and Caribbean Committee for the Defense of Women's Rights.

8.   See ibid.

9.   Apparently ignoring the myriad differences among and between women in multicultural, multilingual, multiethnic Guatemala, the government and the military have regarded women as a class, especially when targeting the rural and urban poor and Maya women in particular.

10.   Diana E. H. Russell, "Introduction: The Politics of Femicide" in *Femicide in Global Perspective*, ed. Diana E. H. Russell and Roberta A. Harmes (New York: Teachers College Press, 2001), 3-11. See also Jill Radford and Diana E. H. Russell, eds., *Femicide: The Politics of Woman Killing* (New York: Twayne Publishers, 1992).

11. See further, Article II in the 1948 United Nations Convention on the Prevention and Punishment of Genocide. Available at: http://un.org/millennium/law/iv-1.htm. Accessed October 17, 2011.

12.   Russell, "Introduction," in *Femicide in Global Perspective*, 3-11.

13.   Melissa Wright, *Disposable Women and Other Myths of Global Capitalism* (New York: Routledge, 2006).

14.   Sexual violence includes any coerced sex in marriage and intimate relationships, rape by strangers, sexual harassment, forced prostitution and sexual trafficking, early marriages, virginity testing and proof, and other forms of practices that control a woman's use of her body. For further information on gender and the *maquiladora* factories, see Leslie Salzinger, "Making Fantasies Real: Producing Women and Men on the Maquila Shop Floor," in *The Body Politic: Gender in the New World Order*, Vol. 34 (March/April 2001) of the North American Congress on Latin America's (NACLA) Report on the Americas, 13-19.

15.   Patricia de Fuentes, ed. and trans., *The Conquistadors: First-Person Accounts of the Conquest of Mexico* (Norman, OK: University of Oklahoma Press, 1993), 138.

16.   Laura S. Brown, "Not Outside the Range: One Feminist Perspective on Psychic Trauma." *American Imago* 48 (1991): 119-33.

17.   The School of the Americas trained more than 1,500 Guatemalans between 1946-1995. Many of the trainees perpetrated egregious human rights abuses but continue to hold positions of power in Guatemala's government and military. Further information about some of these men is available at http://www.derechos.org/soa/guat-not.html. Accessed October 17, 2011.

18.   For statistics and background on the violence in Guatemala, see further, Roselyn Costantino, "Femicide, Impunity, and Citizenship: The Old and The New in the Struggle for Justice in Guatemala" in *Chicana/Latina Studies* 6 (Fall

2006); the many documents on the Human Rights Watch (www.hrw.org) website about violence over the years in Guatemala; "Guatemala: Violence and Inequality Still Blocking Solutions for IDPs" found at http://www.internal-displacement. org/8025708F004CE90B/%28httpCountries%29/ADC95A48885DA5B38025 70A7004CF4E3?OpenDocument; and "The Genocide of Guatemala's Mayans" in Adam Jones, *Genocide: A Comprehensive Introduction,* 2nd ed. (New York: Routledge, 2011), 139-48. Web sites accessed October 17, 2011.

19. According to the UN High Commission for Refugees (UNHCR), "Internally displaced people, or IDPs, are often wrongly called refugees. Unlike refugees, IDPs have not crossed an international border to find sanctuary but have remained inside their home countries. Even if they have fled for similar reasons as refugees (armed conflict, generalized violence, human rights violations), IDPs legally remain under the protection of their own government—even though that government might be the cause of their flight. As citizens, they retain all of their rights and protection under both human rights and international humanitarian law." An externally displaced person, or refugee, on the other hand, is a person who has crossed international borders "owing to a well-founded fear of being persecuted for reasons of race, religion, nationality, membership of a particular social group or political opinion, is outside the country of his nationality, and is unable to, or owing to such fear, is unwilling to avail himself of the protection of that country." See further, www.unhcr.org for definitions and more information. Accessed October 17, 2011.

20. See Judith N. Zur, "The Psychological Impact of Impunity," *Anthropology Today* 10, 3 (June 1994): 12-17, and *Violent Memories: Mayan War Widows in Guatemala* (Boulder, CO: Westview Press, 1998), 1-25.

21. See Daniel Wilkinson, *Silence on the Mountain: Stories of Terror, Betrayal, and Forgetting in Guatemala* (Boston: Houghton Mifflin Company, 2002).

22. María Eugenia Villarreal, "Women in Peace Building in Guatemala." Paper presented at *HiPeC International Peace Building Conference*, Hiroshima, Japan. March 8-9, 2007. Available at http://home.hiroshima-u.ac.jp/hipec/confer-ence/009.pdf. Accessed October 17, 2011.

23. See Consoricio Actoras de Cambio, *Breaking the Silence: Justice for the Women Victims of Sexual Violence during The Guatemala Armed Conflict*, trans. of Spanish title (Guatemala City: ECAP, UNAMG and F&E, 2006).

24. Quoted in Adrián Reyes, "Guatemala: Brutal Killings of Women Recall Counterinsurgency Techniques." *IPS News*, June 22, 2005. Available at: http://ipsnews.net/print.asp?idnews=29187. Accessed October 17, 2011. The URNG

was an umbrella insurgency network during the Internal Armed Conflict. After the Peace Accords, it became a political party.

25. Elisabeth Rehn and Ellen Johnson Sirleaf, *Women, War and Peace: The Independent Experts' Assessment on the Impact of Armed Conflict on Women and Women's Role in Peace-building* (New York: United Nations Development Fund for Women, 2002).

26. *Impunity Watch*, "Guatemalan Women Hold Tribunal of Conscience" (8/4/2010). Available at: http://www.impunitywatch.org/en/publication/67. Accessed October 17, 2011.

27. The quotation is from Rigoberta Menchú Tum, the indigenous Guatemalan who won the 1992 Nobel Peace Prize. See http://www.betterworldheroes.com/menchu.htm. Accessed October 17, 2011.

28. This report is not available in English, but its content is reflected in the work of CLADEM-Guatemala. See note 7 above.

29. Further information related to these points can be found at the following web sites: http://www.conamgua.org and http://www.unamg.org and http://conavigua.org.gt. Accessed October 17, 2011.

30. The web site for New Horizons is available at http://www.ahnh.org. Accessed October 17, 2011.

31. For more information, see the CODECOT web site as http://www.codecot.org. Accessed October 17, 2011.

32. For an important analysis, see "Guatemala's Femicide Law: Progress Against Impunity?" This article comes from the Guatemala Human Rights Commission/USA (GHRC/USA) and is available at: http://www.ghrc-usa.org/Publications/Femicide_Law_ProgressAgainstImpunity.pdf. Accessed October 17, 2011.

33. For further information on these points, consult the following web sites: http://www.sectordemujeres.org/ and http://www.sobrevivientes.org/ Accessed October 17, 2011.

34. The suggestions that follow emerged from discussions in Guatemala supported by the GHRC and, in particular, by its "Women's Right to Live" initiative. For related information see the GHRC web site at http://www.ghrc-usa.org. Its links to Programs and How You Can Help are especially relevant. Accessed October 17, 2011.

35. See note 30 above.

36. For further information on these aims, see http://www.ghrc-usa.org/

HowYouCanHelp/Shop.htm and "DR-CAFTA in Year Two: Trends & Impacts," which is available at: http://www.ghrc-usa.org/Publications/CAFTA_impacts_ year_two.pdf. Accessed October 17, 2011.

37. For further information on these points, see http://www.womenthrive.org/. Its link to Violence against Women explores the IVAWA. Accessed October 17, 2011.

Further Suggested Reading

Amnesty International. *Guatemala's Lethal Legacy: Past Impunity and Renewed Human Rights Violations*, 2002. Available at: http://www.amnesty.org/en/ library/info/AMR34/001/2002/en. Accessed October 17, 2011.

Bastick, Megan, and Karin Grimm Rahel Kunz. *Sexual Violence in Armed Conflict: Global Overview and Implications for the Security Sector.* Geneva, Switzerland: Geneva Centre for the Democratic Control of Armed Forces, 2007.

Jonas, Susanne. *Of Centaurs and Doves: Guatemala's Peace Process.* Boulder, CO: Westview Press, 2000.

Menchú, Rigoberta. *I, Rigoberta Menchu: An Indian Woman in Guatemala.* Translated by Ann Wright. London: Verso, 1984.

Paz y Paz Bailey, Claudia. "Guatemala: Gender and Reparations for Human Rights Violations." In *What Happened to the Women? Gender and Reparations for Human Rights Violations*, edited by Ruth Rubio-Marín. New York: Social Science Research Council, 2006.

Questions for Discussion

1. What is the relationship between genocide and femicide?

2. Why did the Guatemalan State use sexual violence as a weapon of war in its bloody counterinsurgency during the Internal Armed Conflict? Was there anything distinctive about the Guatemalan use of this tactic of war, or do events there largely replicate what has happened in other conflict zones?

3. Considering the level of violence against women throughout much of the world, can such violence be stopped? For that to happen, what changes would need to occur? What are the greatest obstacles to those changes? If those changes could take place, what would the benefits be?

9

My Name Is Mwamaroyi: Stories of Suffering, Survival, and Hope in the Democratic Republic of Congo

Lee Ann De Reus

If I were given the floor, I would speak up and tell people that rape and violence have had terrible consequences. Please, it is time for the violence to stop.

—Mwamaroyi, a woman in the Democratic Republic of Congo

On May 21, 2009, the research I was doing in eastern areas of the Democratic Republic of Congo (DRC, formerly Zaire) took me to a rural clinic, where I had the opportunity to interview a remarkable 46-year-old mother of six. Using a pseudonym to safeguard her identity and to respect her privacy, I shall refer to her as Mwamaroyi (Mwah-mah-ROY-ee).

Mwamaroyi has a broad smile, laughs easily, and shyly tilts her head when making new acquaintances. Her spirit is strong, her eyes convey compassion, her walk and posture reveal determination. When we met, Mwamaroyi was wrapped in traditional brightly colored fabrics. Pinned to her T-shirt was a V-Day "Stop Violence against Women" button—an unexpected western emblem in an African village but a badge she wore proudly. To orient this chapter on the catastrophic sexual violence that has been rampant in the DRC, here is a part of what Mwamaroyi told me on that spring day.

> If I were given the floor to tell other people in the world about myself and the women in Congo, I would first say that the women live in peace. The second is that I would tell the people that all this violence, which is done to women, is a consequence of two countries' misunderstanding. If they cooperated, then the wars would end, and women would be safe from rape and violence. The third thing I would tell them is that Congolese women are neglected because no one talks about the rape and violence we have suffered through.
>
> In 2004, my youngest child was 4 years old when my country was invaded. I was raped by rebels from the National Congress for the Defense of the People. There were three men. I was raped until my womb fell out. I suffered so much. I went to a hospital in Katana, and they tried to repair and heal me. But I still suffer some pain.
>
> In 2006, I went to visit my friend in a nearby village. While I was traveling there, we were attacked by another rebel group, the Democratic Forces for the Liberation of Rwanda. I was raped again. There were five men, and this time, it was worse. I had surgery again to try to repair the damage. The surgery helped, but sometimes my feet still swell, and I get terrible headaches.
>
> After the first rape, my husband left me. He said I must be contaminated. So he doesn't want to be contaminated by me. He just fled.
>
> The wars have very negatively affected my life. I was living peacefully in my home with my husband and my children and now, because of war, he is gone. I live alone with the children, trying to carry the burden myself, and provide for my children's education, food, and health. So all this I do alone, and I am weaker because of the rapes.
>
> I leave this to God and people of good will. I rely on an organization that sometimes gives me some money to support

my children. My children are succeeding. One of them is about to take the national examination. Another has acquired skills in woodwork and completed his studies. Another has studied mechanics, and he is looking for work. We also harvest beans, potatoes, and cassava, and sell them at the market. So we get by. This is how we survive.

I also work to sensitize other survivors of rape. I educate them and tell them they should not feel guilty, that the guilty ones are the men who rape. I tell the survivors it is not their fault.

I would like to ask, would it be possible to offer workshops that will empower women, and give them the tools to speak up?

My greatest hope is one day to see women in Congo stand up and cry out about what has happened to us, and to be advocates for our cause. If the women in Congo can stand up and say that we are at peace, it will bring me joy.

If I were given the floor, I would speak up and tell people that rape and violence have had terrible consequences. Please, it is time for the violence to stop.

Mwamaroyi's story is important for several reasons. First, her words put a human face on the war against women in eastern DRC. Like women everywhere, Mwamaroyi is a mother, a sister, a daughter, and a provider for her family; she wants the best for her children and a life without fear or want. As human beings, we are the same. But Mwamaroyi lives in a place now labeled as the "worst place in the world to be a woman."[1] Only by chance does that fate set her apart from most of the readers of this book. Second, her story reflects the horrific nature and frequency of attacks against Congolese women as evidenced by the number of attacks and assailants she reports and her lasting injuries—physical, psychological, and economic. Third, the complexity of the conflict in eastern DRC is represented by the two different armed groups responsible for the assaults against her. Fourth, the abandonment by her husband is indicative of the severe stigma associated with rape and speaks to the shame and humiliation so many abused women endure. Fifth, Mwamaroyi's struggle to support, feed, educate, and care for her family reflects the immense insecurities that women face in the wake of sexual violence unleashed during war and genocide. Finally, despite the harsh realities, Mwamaroyi's story embodies the resilience, courage, and hope of survivors who still perform essential daily tasks, hold their families together, and believe that peace is achievable.

How does a woman like Mwamaroyi find the strength to carry on despite her trauma, physical injuries, and daily struggles with poverty? Why was she attacked—not once but twice? Why did her husband abandon her? What will it take for the violence to stop? These were some of the questions I posed to thirty rape survivors in eastern Democratic Republic of Congo in the summers of 2009 and 2010. As an activist scholar, I was there to collect stories for a research project about how women cope with the stigmatization of rape. But more importantly, I wanted to raise awareness in the United States about the crisis for women in the DRC.

"The Worst Place in the World to be a Woman"

The DRC, Mwamaroyi's homeland, is located in central Africa. The second largest African country in area, it is approximately the same size as the United States east of the Mississippi River. The DRC's population numbers about 71 million, making it the fourth most populous nation on the continent. The major languages are French (for the educated) and Swahili for those, such as Mwamaroyi, who have not attended school. Christianity, predominantly Roman Catholicism, is the dominant religious faith. Approximately 70 percent of the people identify with that tradition. The average per capita income is about $189, which makes the DRC one of the poorest countries in the world. Life expectancy is 54 years for men and 57 years for women.[2]

Life for Congolese women and girls is particularly difficult. According to a recent study by Women for Women International, for every hundred women in the DRC:

40	are displaced
75	do not own a mattress
40	never attended school

50	eat only one meal a day
75	earn $1 or less per day
80	think a lot about upsetting events
65	think about hurting themselves
80	are from villages that have been attacked
75	think their current village will be attacked
50	of their spouses left because of war
50	are afraid to work outside of their home
80	are unhappy with their life today[3]

Rampant gender-based violence worsens these dire straits. Accounts of sexual violence such as Mwamaroyi's are all too common in the DRC. The United Nations estimates that at least 200,000 women and girls have been raped "since open hostilities began in 1996," but the true extent, though not precisely known, is considerably higher.[4] In the DRC's South Kivu province alone, the International Rescue Committee provided assistance to more than 40,000 Congolese survivors of sexual violence between 2002 and 2009.[5] Indeed, Margot Wallström, the UN's special representative on sexual violence in conflict, has described eastern DRC as the "rape capital of the world."[6] Missing from the figures above are the number of men who have been victimized by sexual violence and the number of women and girls held as sex slaves and forced wives. The world has never known levels of sexual violence more extreme than those in the DRC in the early twenty-first century. Yet, this humanitarian crisis is largely ignored by the global community.

The causes of rampant sexual violence in the eastern DRC are complex. A thorough explication of them is more than any book chapter can provide. Simply put, however, the DRC is a failed state and unable to protect its citizens. The result is a myriad of armed groups that terrorize local populations with complete impunity for their crimes. Long-standing land disputes among the nation's many ethnic groups, struggles to control the DRC's vast mineral resources, contested citizenship rights, displaced populations—these are only some of the factors that drive the conflict. Complicating matters further, none of these circumstances can be adequately understood without attention to historical context and, in particular, the brutal reign of King Leopold II of Belgium (1877-1908), colonial Belgian rule (1908-1960), and the autocracy of Mobutu Sese Seko (1930-1997).

The Mobuto regime (1971-1997)—the country was called Zaire at the time—was characterized by severe corruption, political repression, and human rights violations. Put in place by an American-backed coup, Mobuto received support from the United States government as a Cold War ally until the collapse of the Soviet Union. In the aftermath of the 1994 genocide in neighboring Rwanda, violence erupted in eastern DRC in 1996 when Rwandan Hutu militia forces (perpetrators of the Rwandan genocide) combined forces with the state military against Congolese ethnic Tutsis. Armies from Uganda and Tutsi-led Rwanda consequently attacked with the intent of overthrowing Mobutu. Known as "Africa's World War," this escalating and protracted conflict, which eventually involved eight African nations and about twenty-five armed groups, officially ended with peace agreements in 2003, but subsequent starvation, disease, and continuing violence brought the death toll to an estimated 5.4 million by April 2007.[7]

This African warfare has been the deadliest since World War II. Despite various peace agreements, at the time of this writing in late 2011, the fighting continues in eastern DRC with extreme sexual violence inflicted on women and girls. As a weapon of war, rape is used to demoralize and shame populations into submission.[8] The systematic mutilation and destruction of women shreds the social fabric of families, communities, and regions, enabling armed militias to gain power and maintain control.[9]

The Wounds and Children of Rape

The physical injury and psychological damage to Congolese women are represented by Mwamaroyi, who spoke of her need for surgery and the ailments from her attacks, which linger even after medical treatment. In 2008, Panzi Hospital in Bukavu, South Kivu province, received more than 2,000 women in need of gynecological services due to rape. These numbers were comparable in 2009 and even larger in 2010. Many of the symptoms reported by the abused women were the consequence of infections (sexually transmitted and urinary) or internal injury. More than one-third of the women were seeking help for incontinence (leaking of urine or feces)[10] or what is referred to as a "fistula"—a rupture usually between the vagina, rectum, and bladder.[11] Such damage is most often associated with complications of pregnancy and childbirth, but in the DRC these injuries are largely due to violent rape with objects—gun barrels, for example, or sticks and bottles—that perforate the vagina and other organs. Dr. Denis Mukwege of Panzi Hospital is the chief surgeon who has perfected the repair of fistulas, attempting to restore women's physical bodies and dignity.[12] The surgery is difficult because the tissue is so delicate, and often women must have repeat procedures to end their incontinence.

For many women, the psychological wounds from sexual violence are worse than the physical injuries. The trauma results in depression, nightmares, sadness, anger, fear, anxiety, and shame.[13] At its worst, the stigma associated with rape and fistula leads to the abandonment of women by husbands, families, and villages. A violated woman is considered "damaged." If she smells of bodily waste, she is not only unclean but also regarded as ruined and worthless. The cultural conceptualization of women as property is at the root of this harsh stigma. In my research, a majority of the women who suffered war-related sexual violence were rejected by husbands and to varying degrees by family, friends, and villages. It is common for raped women to be victimized again, publicly by individuals who hurl taunts and insulting remarks at them or privately by husbands who shame them with verbal and sometimes physical abuse. When I asked the women how they responded to such public or private humiliation, they spoke of walking silently in disgrace, hanging their heads, and saying nothing in their defense. Most reported crying later in their homes when alone.

The psychological consequences of sexual violence and its stigma underscore the paramount need for psychological counseling for the abused women as well as education about the value of women, which especially needs to be directed toward men and boys. In the case of Panzi Hospital, only two psychologists were available to more than three hundred abused women. Trained therapists—Congolese or culturally competent non-Congolese—and the money to hire such staff are both in short supply. Although some significant educational programs can be found (for example, Women for Women International's Men's Leadership Program in the DRC), there are far too few of them.

Trauma was evident among many of the women I interviewed. For example, not one of the women cried as she shared her story—possibly because they simply had no more tears or perhaps because, as a means of survival, they had repressed their feelings. One woman, Fatima, was tortured and raped in 2006 and again in 2007. She has a three-year-old daughter, born from an attack. Mother and child are HIV positive. Although Fatima did not exhibit overt symptoms of trauma during our brief time together, I later learned from hospital staff that she had attempted suicide after arriving at Panzi and that she had been caught beating her daughter on two occasions. Although Fatima had recovered from her physical injuries and was soon to be discharged, all of her family members had been killed, and she had no place to go. The hospital was not equipped to house her or the thousands of women like her who were largely destitute, abandoned or without relatives and the means to support themselves. In Fatima's case, the hospital staff was concerned not only about what would happen to her once she was on her own but also about her daughter's health and safety in circumstances where the mother's behavior toward her child could not be monitored. The suffering created by rape during war and genocide escalates because it extends to the children produced by such violence.[14]

The rape of women has produced thousands of children in the DRC. But the birth rates and levels of acceptance or rejection are not known. Only anecdotal evidence indicates infanticide, abortion, and stigma as responses to "children of the enemy."[15] My 2010 interview with a social assistant at Panzi Hospital indicates that the rejection of children and the desire to end unwanted pregnancies caused by rape were identified as major challenges facing the women and staff.

Pregnant women often arrive at Panzi wanting an abortion—this procedure is illegal in the DRC—and sometimes women neglect their children. Occasionally, a child is left behind by a woman when she leaves Panzi. Through counseling, however, the hospital's staff has worked successfully with many abused women to prevent and overcome such rejection. One social assistant observed that while most of the rape victims treated at Panzi are mothers, the majority do not reject their children. In fact, I met women who named their children "Hope," or "Luck," demonstrating the mothers' resilience and capacity for positive coping.

By no means was stress removed, however, if mothers accepted the children born of rape. Seeking medical care for the long-term aftereffects of rape, a mothers' trip to Panzi Hospital usually entailed leaving some or all of her children behind. During interviews, the women expressed great anxiety as they worried about how their children were faring with other family members, neighbors, or on their own.

Perpetrators, Mass Destruction, Resilience, Religion, and Hope

During the interviews I conducted with abused women in the DRC, I asked them *why* they thought the sexual violence was occurring. All of them indicated it was because of "the conflict." With little access to reliable news sources, the women had meager information about the ever-changing particulars of the crisis, but for them, the only way to stop the raping was to stop the fighting.

Soldiers from the Democratic Forces for the Liberation of Rwanda (FDLR) or Interahamwe (former members of the Hutu militias and Rwandan armed forces responsible for the 1994 genocide) had sexually assaulted a majority of the women I interviewed in the DRC. Other frequently reported perpetrators came from the Forces Armées de la République Démocratique du Congo (FARDC, the DRC's army)—the very forces who were supposed to protect the nation's citizens. In Mwamaroyi's case, she was attacked in 2004 by men from yet another group of perpetrators, the Congrès National pour la Défense du Peuple (CNDP, the National Congress for the Defense of the People), Laurent Nkunda's Congolese militia, which fought against the DRC's military. In 2006, she was raped by soldiers from the FDLR. Congolese women have endured sexual brutality inflicted by diverse and conflicting perpetrators.

In the thirty interviews I conducted, the women all spoke of the difficulties created by the fighting in the DRC. The destruction of homes caused displacement and loss of livelihood. The murder of family members had devastating consequences for those who survived. The fear of rape kept women from working in the fields, which contributed to a lack of food. Again and again, the fear of rape was entirely justified, and the women I interviewed recounted details of horrific attacks they had experienced directly or witnessed. Attacks typically occurred in a woman's home or while she was working in the fields. Sometimes the women were ambushed on the way to market. The number of assailants ranged from a single perpetrator to eighteen of them. According to the reports I received, the women were held captive and brutalized for lengths of time that ranged from hours to two years.

Most astonishing about Mwamaroyi and many of the others who entrusted stories to me was the resilience these women displayed. Despite the horrors inflicted upon them, the women still function and perform daily tasks. They care for themselves and their children, interact socially, and try their best to move forward. Some, including Mwamaroyi, have become advocates who transcend their pain by comforting, educating, and striving to empower other sexually abused women.

I asked the women, "How do you get through the difficult times?" "What gives you strength?" "What gives you hope?" Their answers invariably revolved around the women's religious beliefs. They emphasized faith, belief in God, and prayer as sources of inspiration. The women's views about forgiveness were particularly remarkable. When I asked the women what should happen to the men who raped them ("Should they be imprisoned, executed or forgiven?"), their answers overwhelmingly stressed the importance of forgiveness. The judgment of these men "was up to God." This cultural preference toward forgiveness may have direct implications for legal assistance programs. While the women's emphasis on forgiveness does not rule out desires for justice that include prosecuting those who assaulted them, the majority of the women I interviewed were not much interested in legal assistance.

Clearly, the women wanted to move on with their lives. Several significant factors may have contributed to this sentiment. For example, the women may perceive legal assistance as too expensive or as re-traumatizing if they must face their attackers and relive what happened as they testify against them. Furthermore, a lack of understanding about human rights may inhibit them from taking legal action. That said, perhaps the act of forgiveness incorporates or transcends justice for these women. Or forgiveness may be a means for restoring dignity because it is a hallmark of a "good" Christian. In the context of sexual violence in the DRC, many questions about the meaning, place, and value of forgiveness remain. The feasibility and success of legal assistance programs for rape survivors and ending impunity for perpetrators of sexual violence in the DRC will depend on careful and sensitive analysis of these complexities.

Trying to end our time together as positively as possible, I concluded my interviews with the Congolese women by asking them about their hopes. Significantly, the women's responses focused primarily not on themselves but on their children. The women hoped that their daughters and sons, including those born of rape, would be "provided for" and that they would be "able to attend school." While it may have been a function of mistranslation, it was interesting that the women seemed to frame their response about provision with the possibility that they would be unable to provide for their children. In other words, if the mother was absent, for whatever reason, the hope was that her children would still have care. When I pressed the women about their hopes for themselves, they wished for good health so they could once again provide for their families. It was clear from the interviews that these women prided themselves on their ability to "dig in the fields" and harvest a crop that fed their families and livestock, and perhaps generated income when sold at the market. Often weak from injury and without the physical strength to farm, the women were further compromised by the loss of the provider role. But when asked if they considered themselves "victims or survivors," virtually all of the women chose "survivor," and while the women considered themselves to be "weak in body," they often described themselves as "strong in mind and spirit."

In a single word—*peace*—the women interviewed expressed their most fervent hope for the women of the DRC. That outlook was strongly reflected in their responses to my final interview question: "If you could send a message to people all over the world, what would you tell them? What would you want people to know?" The following statement, from the last woman I interviewed, captures best what was said by all.

I would ask them to pray for us. But also to do what they can so that peace can be restored. Peace is beyond all kind of aid they can send. Because whatever aid they send, if there is no peace, what will you be eating then? It is better that you eat vegetables having it salt or not, oil or not, when you know that you are quiet, you eat, you go in your bed, you sleep. These little children can be sent to school, old women can be taken care of, and men can go to job. This is the good thing I could ask people.

Then she turned, looked me right in the eye, and said, "I could ask you to go and tell other people."

Problematic Approaches to Advocacy and Policy

Despite the obviously complex reasons for the DRC's widespread sexual violence, the Congolese crisis is often grossly oversimplified by advocacy/policy organizations and by media sound bytes, such as those claiming that "cell phones cause rape." The latter assessment refers to minerals such as tin, tantalum, tungsten ("the 3 Ts") and gold, which are necessary elements in the manufacture and operation of many electronic devices—not only cell phones but also computers, digital cameras, and various game devices. Mines in eastern DRC hold large deposits of these valuable and profitable minerals. Many armed groups benefit from their exaction and trade—often with slave labor under unsafe and deplorable conditions.

The prevailing discourse, particularly in the activist community, is that these "conflict minerals" support the militias that perpetrate sexual violence. Hence, the insatiable global consumption of electronics, particularly in the West, drives the extraction and sale of the minerals and, at least indirectly, implicates each of us consumers in the DRC's gender-based violence. As with the African traffic in "blood diamonds," the remedy sought through U.S. legislation has emphasized control and transparency of the supply chain, the tracking of minerals, and ultimately the "certification" and labeling of electronics as "conflict-mineral free."

While it is true that armed groups profit from the mineral trade, buy weapons, and commit rape, regulation of the mineral supply chain is no silver bullet. The militarization of mines in the DRC is one consequence of a failed state. Thus, the current crisis in eastern DRC is best understood with analysis of the existing government headed by Joseph Kabila (b. 1971), who took office in January 2001, the contributing historical factors, and the present role of countries such as Rwanda, Uganda, and the United States. Conspicuously missing from the advocacy campaigns and policy debates in the United States is consideration of questions such as: What is the supply chain not just for conflict minerals but for the weapons used in the DRC? Why are women's bodies the battleground of this conflict? Which groups and individuals outside the DRC are providing financing, resources, leadership, and strategy for the warring militias? Did American legislation put an end to the traffic in "blood diamonds?" Are the problematic strategies employed in that case worth replicating? Who benefits financially from the crisis in eastern DRC? How do land rights, corporate interests, control over the DRC's vast mineral resources, citizenship rights, and displaced populations factor into the current conflict?

Making a Difference for Mwamaroyi and Her Congolese Sisters

As an activist scholar, my research and advocacy are reciprocally motivated by a quest for social justice. This orientation has implications for research methodology. When I interviewed abused women in the DRC, I took great care to minimize re-traumatization for Mwamaroyi and the other women. While the sharing of painful experiences can be therapeutic and healing, the potential for renewed distress remains real. Thus, the staff at Panzi Hospital was careful at the outset to identify the women most likely to cope with and benefit from participation in the study. Each participant was guided through the informed consent process; the interviews were held in private spaces with the woman seated closest to the exit. Participants could refuse to answer any question or stop the interview at any time, and a therapist was available if anyone experienced difficulty during or after an interview.

Protecting the identity of the women was, and continues to be, a necessary and important priority. Armed groups such as the FDLR operate on a sophisticated level that includes attention to websites. Given the computer savvy and access to information that these forces possess, we must prevent the possible nefarious use of photographs—video or still images—of the women. Once a woman's story of rape, her name, and other identifying information are documented in a book or newspaper article or on a website, the likelihood of retaliation against her escalates. Thus, any photos or artist's renditions that I have used always obscure and protect the identities of the abused women.

Unfortunately, the guiding principle of anonymity is not shared by all advocacy and policy organizations. It is common to see the photographs and testimonies of rape survivors used in ways that ignore the importance of anonymity and violate privacy. While the reporters or authors may claim they received informed consent, it is highly unlikely, for example, that a woman with no experience of the internet, which would be the case with regard to most abused women in the DRC, can adequately understand what appearing in cyberspace could mean. Even if the chances of retaliation are low, putting the women at further risk is irresponsible.

None of the thirty brave women I interviewed had to share their story with me. No material incentives were offered. But they entrusted painful memories with the hope that doing so *might* make a difference. This is an awesome responsibility and it is now my duty to serve as witness, messenger, and advocate on their behalf. To do otherwise would violate their trust and result in re-victimization.

As an activist scholar, I do not distinguish between the "personal" and the "professional"; my activism, passions, and research not only inform each other but also my life as a whole. This way of "being in the world" is not unique to me. It is open to everyone. I am fortunate to combine what I find most meaningful in such a way that "work" on behalf of women in the DRC is not my occupation but rather a vocation and way of life. When people ask what they can do to make a difference, I offer several suggestions.

First option: Be informed. Even if that is the totality of your involvement, you will likely operate differently in the world as a consumer, voter, and as a caring human being. The simple act of sharing what you have learned—informally with friends and family or more formally, perhaps through a blog—is often how grassroots change begins, one or just a few persons at a time. There are many helpful websites, books, and reports to utilize. Several are included at the end of this chapter.

Second option: Lobby your elected officials. Ask them questions like those posed in this chapter. American legislation will not single-handedly end any conflict on another continent, but laws that influence U.S. foreign policy, such as the International Violence against Women Act, call attention to issues and can move us in a forward direction. Only constituent pressure and persistence will put crises such as the DRC's on a representative's radar screen.

Third option: Host a fund raiser. Many non-profits are doing invaluable work in the DRC, but they tend to be sorely underfunded. For individuals with no time but with some money to spare, even small donations can add up and go far to improve the lives of individuals. Successful events can recruit hundreds of people or a small group of friends who gather for dinner and an opportunity to learn more about the DRC.

Fourth option: Make a private donation. For those who want to get involved on an individual level, Women for Women International is a well-respected and effective non-profit that enables sponsors to directly assist a woman in need. Panzi Hospital and Heal Africa are two other worthy recipients of contributions. As the largest hospitals in eastern DRC, they provide extraordinary life-saving services to rape survivors.

Fifth option: Use your voice! Writing letters to the editor, blogging, speaking to groups are all effective ways to get involved, raise awareness, and bring change. Only with our collective voices can we begin to create the political will needed to end the suffering for all people in the DRC.

This chapter began with words from Mwamaroyi: "If I were given the floor, I would speak up and tell people that rape and violence have had terrible consequences. Please, it is time for the violence to stop." Her words remind me of Ubuntu, a South African concept. Simply stated, it means "I am, because we are." In other words, what has dehumanized Mwamaroyi and the tens of thousands of women and girls like her in the DRC also dehumanizes me and you. Each time a Congolese woman is sexually violated, all of us are diminished, and we lose some of our humanity. My hope is that the experiences of Mwamaroyi and her Congolese sisters recounted here will bind us together with them, inspire action, and make us all more fully human.

Notes

1.   Human Rights Watch, "Soldiers Who Rape, Commanders Who Condone: Sexual Violence and Military Reform in the Democratic Republic of Congo," July 16, 2009. Available at: http://www.hrw.org/reports/2009/07/16/soldiers-who-rape-commanders-who-condone. Accessed October 18, 2011.

2.   The data in this paragraph can be confirmed and amplified at the following web sites: https://www.cia.gov/library/publications/the-world-factbook/geos/cg.html and http://www.state.gov/r/pa/ei/bgn/2823.htm. Accessed October 18, 2011.

3.   See the Women for Women International briefing on the status of women in the DRC, "Stronger Women, Stronger Nations," July 2010. Available at: http://www.womenforwomen.org/news-women-for-women/assets/files/Congo-Briefing.pdf. Accessed October 18, 2011.

4.   United Nations Security Council, Report of the Secretary-General pursuant to Security Council resolution 1820, U.N. Doc. S/2009/362, July 15, 2009. Available at: http://www.securitycouncilreport.org/atf/cf/%7B65BFCF9B-6D27-4E9C-8CD3-CF6E4FF96FF9%7D/WPS%20S%202009%20362.pdf. Accessed October 18, 2011.

5.   International Rescue Committee, "Level of Brutality Against Women and Girls in Congo Increasing; UN Must Do More to Protect Them," December 10, 2009. Available at: http://www.theirc.org/news/level-brutality-against-women-and-girls-congo-increasing-un-must-do-more-protect-them-irc-press. Accessed October 18, 2011.

6.   United Nations News Centre, April 27, 2010. See http://www.un.org/apps/news/story.asp?NewsID=34502. Accessed October 18, 2011.

7.   Berkeley-Tulane Initiative on Vulnerable Populations, "Living with Fear: A Population-Based Survey on Attitudes about Peace, Justice, and Social Reconstruction in Eastern Democratic Republic of Congo," August 2008. Available at: http://www.law.berkeley.edu/HRCweb/pdfs/LivingWithFear-DRC.pdf. Accessed October 18, 2011.

8.   For further discussion about the victimization of men and boys, see Maria Eriksson Baaz and Maria Stern, "The Complexity of Violence: A Critical Analysis of Sexual Violence in the Democratic Republic of Congo (DRC)," 2010. Available at: http://nai.diva-portal.org/smash/record.jsf?searchId=1&pid=diva2:319527.

After reaching this site, go to File Information and click on FULLTEXT02. Accessed October 18, 2011.

9. For more on these points, see H. Patricia Hynes, "On the Battlefield of Women's Bodies: An Overview of the Harm of War to Women," *Women's Studies International Forum* 27 (2004): 431-45, and Kevin Gerard Neill, "Duty, Honor, Rape: Sexual Assault against Women during War," *Journal of International Women's Studies* 31 (2000): 1-10.

10. Statistics provided by Panzi Hospital staff in email dated August 11, 2010.

11. For discussion of fistulas, see Mathias Onsrud, Solbjorg Sjøveian, Roger Luhiriri, and Denis Mukwege, "Sexual Violence-Related Fistulas in the Democratic Republic of Congo," *International Journal of Gynecology and Obstetrics* 103 (2008): 265-69.

12. To learn more about Dr. Denis Mukwege and his work visit http://www.panzihospital.org. Accessed October 18, 2011.

13. Harvard Humanitarian Initiative, "Now, the World Is without Me: An Investigation of Sexual Violence in Eastern Democratic Republic of Congo," April 2010. Available at: http://hhi.harvard.edu/images/resources/reports/final%20panzi%20hhi%20-%20oxfam%20report%20compressed_1.pdf. Accessed October 18, 2011.

14. For further information about this widespread problem, which is by no means confined to the DRC, see R. Charli Carpenter, ed., *Born of War: Protecting Children of Sexual Violence Survivors in Conflict Zones* (Bloomfield, CT: Kumarian Press, 2007); R. Charli Carpenter, *Forgetting Children Born of War: Setting the Human Rights Agenda in Bosnia and Beyond* (New York: Columbia University Press, 2010), and Jonathan Torgovnik, *Intended Consequences: Rwandan Children Born of Rape* (New York: Aperture, 2009).

15. Kathryn Jefferis Birch, "If We Could Read & Hear Their Stories: A Comparative Analysis of Perpetrator Patterns & Community Responses to Sexual Violence in Liberia & Eastern Democratic Republic of the Congo," April 2008. To access this document, put If We Could Read & Hear Their Stories into the Google search engine, and a link to the document will appear. Accessed October 18, 2011.

Further Suggested Reading

Hochschild, Adam. *King Leopold's Ghost*. Boston: Mariner Books, 1999.

Lemarchand, Rene. *The Dynamics of Violence in Central Africa*. Philadelphia: University of Pennsylvania Press, 2009.

Prunier, Gerard. *Africa's World War: Congo, the Rwandan Genocide, and the Making of a Continental Catastrophe*. Oxford: Oxford University Press, 2009.

Shannon, Lisa. *A Thousand Sisters: My Journey into the Worst Place on Earth to be a Woman*. Berkeley, CA: Seal Press, 2010.

Wrong, Michela. *In the Footsteps of Mr. Kurtz: Living on the Brink of Disaster in Mobutu's Congo*. New York: Perennial, 2000.

Helpful Websites for DRC Updates

http://www.drccoalition.blogspot.com/

www.enoughproject.org

www.friendsofthecongo.org

www.genocideintervention.net

www.hrw.org

www.panzifoundation.org

www.womenforwomen.org

Questions for Discussion

1. What is your reaction to the story of Mwamaroyi?

2. Most Americans are unaware of the crisis in eastern Democratic Republic of Congo (DRC). Why?

3. Why should the average citizen and the global community care about what is happening to women and girls in the DRC?

4. In your opinion, what are some possible solutions to the sexual violence crisis in eastern DRC?

5. If you could write a letter to Mwamaroyi, what would you say?

10

Weapon of Sadness: Economic and Ethical Dimensions of Rape as an Instrument of War

Julie Kuhlken

The little daughter's on the mattress,
Dead. How many have been on it
A platoon, a company perhaps?
A girl's been turned into a woman,
A woman turned into a corpse.
—Aleksandr Solzhenitsyn, Prussian Nights

The document that I have chosen to orient this chapter consists of key paragraphs from the 2007 "Report of the United Nations' Secretary-General on the protection of civilians in armed conflict" (United Nations S/2007/643).[1] They are reprinted here with the appropriate subheadings and paragraph numbering.

Conduct of hostilities: further erosion of the principles of distinction and proportionality

21. The first issue is the further erosion of the principles of distinction and proportionality. The principle of distinction requires belligerents to distinguish at all times between combatants and civilians and to direct attacks only against combatants and other military objectives. In

accordance with the principle of proportionality, deaths of, or injuries to, civilians and damage to civilian objects must not be excessive in relation to the direct and concrete military advantage expected from the attack. On a number of occasions in recent and ongoing conflicts, we have witnessed intentional targeting of civilians and also a tendency to interpret the principle of proportionality in a way that leads to an unjustified and troubling expansion of what constitutes permissible civilian casualties. . . .

B. A more robust response to sexual violence

43. In no other area is our collective failure to ensure effective protection for civilians more apparent—and by its very nature more shameful—than in terms of the masses of women and girls, but also boys and men, whose lives are destroyed each year by sexual violence perpetrated in conflict.

44. Sexual violence, including rape, is a war crime and may, in some situations, be of such dimensions as to constitute a crime against humanity. Sexual violence has been used as a calculated method of warfare in places such as Bosnia and Herzegovina, Liberia, Rwanda, Sierra Leone and Somalia, and is currently practiced in the Central African Republic, the Democratic Republic of the Congo and the Sudan, where its use by Janjaweed and Government soldiers was described by the International Commission of Inquiry on Darfur as widespread and systematic. As a method of warfare, sexual violence is aimed at brutalizing and instilling fear in the civilian population through acts of deliberate cruelty, weakening their resistance and resilience, through humiliation and shame, and destroying the social fabric of entire communities. Victims are often left with horrific physical and psychological scars and, worse still, may have contracted a sexually transmitted disease, including HIV and AIDS. In some cases, they are shunned and abandoned by their families and communities.

45. While such violence is not confined to the Democratic Republic of the Congo, the grueling situation in the eastern provinces of Ituri

and the Kivus epitomizes the devastating effect of sexual violence in conflict. The United Nations Special Rapporteur on violence against women notes that in South Kivu province alone, where 4,500 cases of sexual violence were recorded in the first six months of 2007, acts of rape and sexual slavery perpetrated by armed groups were aimed at the complete physical and psychological destruction of women, with implications for the entire society. Women were brutally gang-raped, often in front of their families and communities. In numerous cases, male relatives were forced at gunpoint to rape their own daughters, mothers or sisters. Frequently women were shot or stabbed in their genital organs, after being raped. Women who survived months of sexual enslavement were forced to eat excrement or the flesh of murdered relatives. In the same province, units of the Congolese army were reported to have targeted communities suspected of supporting militia groups and committed acts of gang rape and murder. Individual soldiers or police officers also committed such acts, considering themselves to be above the law. These are not random acts of violence in the theatre of war but a deliberate attempt to dehumanize and destroy entire communities.

46. In Equateur province, the police and army are reported to have responded to civil unrest with armed reprisals against civilians that involve torture and mass rape. The Panzi hospital in Bukavu, which specializes in treating victims of sexual violence, receives annually 3,500 women who suffer fistula and other severe genital injuries resulting from sexual violence. That is just one institution, in one province, in a conflict-affected country the size of Western Europe.

47. The perpetrators of sexual violence regularly go unpunished. Their crimes may go unreported because of shame or fear on the part of the victims; because of the absence of assistance or mechanisms for reporting such crimes; because of a lack of faith in reporting systems; or because the victims did not survive. It is believed that for every rape that is reported, as many as 10 to 20 may go unreported. In most conflict settings, though, impunity frequently prevails because of the lack of action by those with a duty to respond—a failure that denies justice to those affected and reinforces a climate in which violence of this nature is inexplicably considered normal.

48. The international community's revulsion towards sexual violence is clear, as demonstrated in General Assembly resolution 61/134 and Council resolutions 1325 (2000), 1674 (2006) and others. Evidently, though, more decisive and rigorous action is needed to bridge the gap between the rhetoric of those resolutions and the reality on the ground and to treat acts of sexual violence for what they are—despicable war crimes and crimes against humanity that must be punished. To do otherwise, to continue standing by, year after year, violates the obligation to punish such acts and belies the solemn commitment made at the 2005 World Summit to protect civilians.

49. First, at the national level, and in accordance with the obligation to search for and prosecute persons suspected of genocide, war crimes and crimes against humanity:

(a) States within whose jurisdiction acts of sexual violence amounting to these offences occur, or where perpetrators or victims are present, must investigate, prosecute and punish perpetrators. In the case of the armed forces and the police, this should include the commanders under whom they serve if the commanders failed to take measures to prevent the violations;

(b) Where necessary, States should:

(i) Enact new laws that criminalize sexual violence;

(ii) Review overly narrow rape laws;

(iii) Resolve conflicts between the application of statutory and customary laws;

(iv) Significantly improve access to justice for victims, including the possible establishment of ad hoc judicial arrangements for dealing with these crimes;

(v) Strengthen national and local investigatory and prosecutorial capacity.

50. Second, prevention and response activities by humanitarian actors must be strengthened and better coordinated. In addition to work

undertaken within their respective mandates, 12 United Nations entities have formed United Nations Action against Sexual Violence in
Conflict, which aims to amplify programming and advocacy, improve
coordination and accountability and support national efforts to prevent sexual violence and respond effectively to the needs of survivors.
However, given the magnitude and complexity of the issue, there is still
a need to establish a clear and dedicated "institutional home" within the
United Nations that would:

> (a) Coordinate the activities of agencies involved in this area,
> including systematic information collection and coordinated
> needs assessments;

> (b) Ensure the provision of expertise and support to the field;

> (c) Develop system-wide advocacy on the issue;

> (d) Act as repository of best practices for prevention of and
> response to sexual violence.

51. In a related context, combating sexual violence committed by
peacekeeping personnel and humanitarian workers remains an important challenge within the United Nations and for troop- and police-
contributing countries. In July 2007, the General Assembly adopted
amendments to a model memorandum of understanding for troop and
police contributors participating in peacekeeping missions (see resolution 61/291). It assigns contributing countries the responsibility to
investigate sexual exploitation and abuse by members of their national
contingents and grants them exclusive jurisdiction over any offences
committed. Having recognized this responsibility, Member States must
fully discharge their duties and ensure that the United Nations policy of
zero-tolerance is uniformly applied.

As a weapon of war and genocide, rape serves a variety of ends. It
can be used to gratify sexual urges as in the case of "comfort women"
forced into prostitution by the Japanese Army during World War II; it
can be practiced to exact revenge as in the case of the advancing Red
Army described by Alexsandr Solzhenitsyn in the passage from *Prussian
Nights* that serves as this chapter's epigraph; it can turn women and their

reproductive capacity into spoils of war, as in "The Rape of the Sabine Women"; or used systematically, it can sow the seeds of genocidal terror such as in Rwanda and the Democratic Republic of Congo (DRC).[2]

Especially the last possibility concerns me here, because it is particularly prone to instrumentalization, meaning the intentional cultivation as a means: Once rape is recognized as a useful weapon of war, women are not victimized because they happen to be in the wrong place at the wrong time; they are intentionally sought out as legitimate targets. No spontaneous sexual impulse or even retrospective desire for revenge explains why it becomes a *routine* practice to cut off labia or shove sticks and knives into the vaginas of women and girls.[3]

Because what is happening is both the rape and mutilation of individuals, as well as an attack on women as such (as one sixteen year old victim from Bukavu explained, "I know they didn't target me—any [woman] would have had the same thing happen."[4])—any account of the misogynistic nature of the violence must take into account both its strategic usefulness, on the one hand, and how this usefulness feeds an escalation of violence, on the other. To this end, two factors in particular come to the fore: first, the economic value of controlling women's unique place at the intersection of productive and reproductive labor; second, the ethical impact of terroristic violence and its special relation to women. Neither of these factors is adequately acknowledged by the current international framework for the protection of civilians in conflict, which, in turn, may explain that framework's impotence when faced with instrumentalized rape.

The Erosion of Principles

As the 2007 UN "Report of the Secretary-General on the protection of civilians in armed conflict" explains, "sexual violence perpetrated in conflict" demonstrates most clearly "our collective failure to ensure effective protection for civilians."[5] As a "calculated method of warfare," sexual violence poses a particular threat to the international legal framework governing war because it erodes both the principle of distinction as well as that of proportionality. The principle of distinction was firmly established by the Hague Conventions of 1899 as a way of limiting "the rights of belligerency to a particular class of participant,"[6] and consequently "requires belligerents to distinguish at all times between combatants and civilians."[7]

If maintained, this distinction ideally sets up a space of neutrality for humanitarian organizations on the model of the International Committee of the Red Cross to act between a "reasonable," professional army of occupation, on the one hand, and a passive (even "innocent") population of non-combatants, on the other.[8] This neutral space insulates the population from sexual violence by insisting that the private lives and needs of the population should be addressed separately from the theater of war. However, this shielded space disappears if it is not the aim of combatants to establish political authority on the model of the territorial state, but rather, as in the case of the DRC, to control primary commodity resources.

The pursuit of an economic agenda by military means puts belligerents into direct competition (and cooperation) with civilians. The resulting "relations of protection, service [and] delivery, [but also] extraction, and abuse"[9] intimately involve belligerents in the private lives of civilians without simultaneously upholding mechanisms for the safeguard of legal rights and protections. These circumstances very easily lead to an environment of impunity where the "perpetrators of sexual violence regularly go unpunished."[10]

The environment of impunity is further aggravated by a decline in the protections afforded civilians by the principle of proportionality. First enshrined in the 1949 Fourth Geneva Convention after the devastation of World War II, the principle of proportionality extends protections directly to civilians, who are "seen as a distinct category under international law"—rather than just to state-based actors as in the case of the Hague Conventions.[11] Combined with the outright ban of certain practices such as rape and torture, the principle of proportionality's demand that "deaths of, or injuries to, civilians and damage to civilian objects must not be excessive in relation to direct and concrete military advantage"[12] means that civilians should be insulated from all forms of sexual violence. However, because the underlying assumption of humanitarian law—namely, that "noncombatants have no strategic value"[13]—is questionable in civil conflicts driven by greed,[14] the value of attacking and exploiting civilians, including sexually, enters the utilitarian calculations of militias in such a way as to encourage "a climate in which [sexual] violence of this nature is inexplicably considered normal."[15]

Focused on the DRC, the 2009 Human Rights Watch (HRW) report *You Will Be Punished* notes that more than one thousand members of the murderous Hutu FDLR (Democratic Liberation Forces of Rwanda) were repatriated to Rwanda in 2009. That action, however, still left civilians at risk to such an extent that for every FDLR combatant who left the DRC, "one civilian has been killed, *seven women and girls have been raped*, eight homes have been destroyed, and nearly 900 people have been forced to flee for their lives."[16] To understand this devastating escalation, it is necessary to consider the particular economic significance of women, and how their labor becomes a target of extreme sexual violence.

The Significance of Women

Women occupy an unusual role within the political economy of labor because their efforts contribute significantly to both the production of goods and services as well as to the reproduction of human life. In contrast, men are largely occupied only with the first of these endeavors, and are biologically excluded from a significant part of the latter by the natural inequality of reproductive labor.[17] As has been noticed by thinkers stretching back to Plato (429-347 BCE), these two types of activity— production and reproduction—operate according to very different rhythms, a difference that led Hannah Arendt (1906-1975), a political philosopher concerned with the preservation of rights under extreme political situations, to suggest that we distinguish them terminologically as *work* on the one hand, and *labor* on the other. Productive *work* creates durable items, which when taken together give us a sense of having a stable world where our actions have meaning. By contrast, *labor* is undertaken as a "monotonous performance of daily repeated chores"[18] that serve to sustain life, but as such, are consumed by it. As particularly tied to the cycle of life, women's involvement in laboring connects them to natural processes, whose productivity is the surplus of fertility—that is, even as an endless cycle, labor creates more than what is needed for survival and allows for the generative act of reproduction.[19]

If one projects the distinction between work and labor into the context of war, one recognizes that war traditionally has targeted the products of work.[20] The demolition of buildings and bombing of factories deprives one's enemy of the infrastructure he needs in order to pursue his worldly interests. In the process, individuals lose their lives, but the reproductive basis of life in laboring is spared. The rape that occurs in such traditional war settings retains its link to the gratification of life impulses—sexual and reproductive. Things are very different, however, if the aim is to disable the laboring capacity of one's enemy. In this case, one attempts to deprive one's enemy of fertility itself, and force her back into a painful state of sheer physical need. The pain inflicted by brutal rape is almost a perfect weapon in such a war, fought against laboring capacity. Hannah Arendt describes the paralyzing effect of such pain when she says, "Nothing . . . ejects one more radically from the world than the exclusive concentration upon the body's life, a concentration forced upon man in slavery or in the extremity of unbearable pain."[21] In an attack upon the reproducible basis of labor, the mutilation of sex organs and the maximization of humiliation—such as has occurred in the DRC where fathers have been forced to rape daughters[22]—heightens the effectiveness of the assault.

Furthermore, because it targets life processes, instrumentalized rape often has an environmental dimension that makes aggression against women a particularly effective way of attacking whole communities and their economies. The area that has seen the worst of the sexual violence in the DRC, for instance, is the eastern Kivu region, into which fled both refugees and *genocidaires* from Rwanda in 1994. The large camps that were set up to house these fleeing Hutus were both politically destabilizing and ecologically destructive, and to the extent that the region is agriculturally divided between roving livestock-raising pastoralists and sedentary farmers,[23] as well as being rich in mineral wealth, the conflict is one where land use is being contested. As in Darfur, where rape has also been widespread in a conflict that pits pastoralists against sedentary farmers, women's connection to the land makes them especially likely to become targets.

Such jeopardy is particularly the case in the DRC, where women do as much as 80 percent of the agriculture.[24] As agricultural laborers, they are essential to what Vandana Shiva calls the "sustenance economy," which "provides for the biological survival of the marginalized poor and the reproduction of society."[25] Thus, these women are in the frontline defense of the economic interests of local communities against those of the export market for primary commodities, which, according to Paul Collier, is the chief motor of civil conflict.[26] From the perspective of militias fighting for control of "lootable resources," women's laboring capacity within the "sustenance economy" is much like a natural resource to be conquered and exploited. By targeting women, militias disrupt community-based sustenance economies dependent upon women's laboring capacity. In the escalation of extreme sexual violence, such that women are "brutally gang-raped, often in front of their families and communities," or "forced to eat excrement or the flesh of murdered relatives," the perpetrators sow terror that disables the targeted communities.

As the 2007 UN report succinctly expresses it, "these are not random acts of violence in the theatre of war but a deliberate attempt to dehumanize and destroy entire communities."[27] In other cases, women are abducted and enslaved by militia groups, who exploit their labor—sexual and productive—sometimes for many months at a time. Both the abductions and the terror generated by the gratuitous sexual violence bar women from undertaking the environmental practices that maintain the sustenance economies of their communities.[28] In order for these communities and the environments that sustain them to recover and thrive, it is not just the legal tools of justice outlined in the 2007 UN document that must come into play.[29] The environmental and economic value of women's labor within the sustenance economy must also be politically acknowledged. This acknowledgement was made, at least at the international level, in the awarding of a Nobel Peace Prize in 2004 to the Kenyan environmental political activist Wangari Maathai (1940-2011), whose Green Belt Movement builds on the links between the preservation of the environment, the empowerment of women, and the advance of democracy. At the 2004 awards ceremony, it was optimistically projected that "in a few decades time, the relationship between the environment, resources and conflict may seem almost as obvious as the connection we see today between human rights, democracy and peace."[30]

The Ethical Effects of Instrumentalized Rape

The optimism expressed at the 2004 Nobel Peace Prize Ceremony will only be justified, however, if progress on the economic front is matched by sensitivity to the profound ethical effects of instrumentalized rape. That rape victims in Rwanda were told that they were being kept alive in order to "die of sadness"[31] captures the extreme demoralization wrought by rape. In all parts of the world, the shame of rape shrouds the crime with silence, but the humiliation is particularly acute in Africa where, as one victim put it, "after rape, you don't have value in the community."[32] It is not uncommon for rape victims to be socially shunned, unable to marry or even return to their families. This social exclusion is a reflection of the moral paradox rape poses for a community: the raped woman embodies the inversion of a community's normal relations to outsiders. Whereas men are traditionally the outward face of a community, rape forces women into intimate contact with outsiders, assaulting their customary insulation within the domestic sphere. This inversion morally guts the community, and the exclusion of the raped woman is the social reaction. As Hugo Slim remarks in his thorough account of what he calls the "seven spheres of suffering" experienced by civilians in war: "In many societies at war . . . it is hard for a raped woman to keep a central place in her family and community. Whereas many of us expect compassion and care to greet someone who has been raped, women often experience the opposite in war."[33]

One of the earliest accounts of the long-term ethical effects of social exclusion as a consequence of instrumentalized rape is presented by Frantz Fanon (1925-1961) in *The Wretched of the Earth*. Fanon worked as a psychiatrist during Algeria's War of Independence and relates as his first case study the situation of B— whose wife is raped by French soldiers when detained for questioning about his whereabouts. Ashamed by her dishonor, B—'s wife "asked him to forget her," saying that he "ought not to think of taking up their life together again."[34] However when B— tries to socially exclude her, he develops a set of disorders, including impotence, serious enough to make him a patient of Fanon. What B— realizes in talking through his case is that his wife's reduction to moral nullity through dishonor was paradoxically due to her morally courageous refusal to give the French any information about himself or his comrades. As B—describes the situation, "it was the rape of an obstinate woman, who was ready to put up with everything rather than sell her husband. And the husband in question, *it was me.*"[35] B—'s moral dilemma—acknowledge his wife's brave loyalty at the price of dishonor, or exclude her to preserve honor but at the cost of bearing an unpaid debt to her for having probably saved his life—indicates the degree to which instrumentalized rape morally paralyzes a community, exposing it to manipulation and control.

Given the humiliating nature of the crime, documented accounts of the conscious use of rape as a method of control are not easy to obtain. Nevertheless, one well-studied institution that relied on systematic, instrumentalized rape is that of slavery in the U.S. South.[36] There, as in the current situation in the DRC, the destruction of a community and its social ethic was undertaken for economic reasons, and was done by means of a social inversion, such that black women were placed between black men and the white community, with which they worked in much closer contact than black men. The African-American feminist, bell hooks (b. 1952), has written at length on the "mass brutalization and terrorization" experienced by black female slaves, saying that the "female slave lived in constant awareness of her sexual vulnerability and in perpetual fear that any male, white and black, might single her out to assault and victimize."[37] Caught between racist white women and sexist black men, black women were completely exposed to systematic rape by white men, who saw it as a tool for gaining the obedience of the black community: "The political aim of this categorical rape of black women by white males was to obtain absolute allegiance and obedience to the white imperialistic order . . . it was in fact an institutionalized method of terrorism."[38]

Thus at the extreme, ethical manipulation by means of rape establishes the conditions of terror under which "guilt and innocence [such as that of B—'s wife or the black female slave who accepts gifts from her white master in exchange for sex] become senseless notions."[39] For Hannah Arendt, whose philosophical analysis of the Holocaust provides a unique insight into the conditions of terror, the disappearance of the distinction between guilt and innocence reflects the "rightlessness" of terror's victims. Instrumentalized rape generates "rightlessness" by means of three weapons of dehumanization, all of which one finds in survivor accounts.

The first weapon attacks the judicial existence of the victim by placing her outside the protection of the law. The instrument of this attack is very often the active or passive participation of the regular police or military forces, which in Rwanda, for instance, organized and supported the Interahamwe militias,[40] and in the DRC are supported even by UN peacekeepers. As the 2007 UN report admits: "combating sexual violence committed by peacekeeping personnel and humanitarian workers remains an important challenge."[41] Both Susan Brownmiller (b. 1935) and Catherine MacKinnon (b. 1946), who have written extensively about rape, describe military culture as fostering a permissive "ideology of rape,"[42] which at least partially accounts for the otherwise incomprehensible participation of "peacekeepers" in attacks.

The second weapon undertakes "the murder of the moral person" of the victim.[43] This assault occurs both in the shame that silences her, thereby shutting her off from the "grief and remembrance" of "human solidarity,"[44] and in the denial of the victim's right to moral choice. The latter denial is starkly illustrated by the story of Marie G., who when kidnapped with two other girls, initially attempted to resist being raped only to have her crying companions tell her, "Accept it; there is nothing you can do."[45]

The third weapon transforms human beings into "specimens of the human animal."[46] By the "killing of [a woman's] individuality, of the uniqueness shaped in equal parts by nature, will, and destiny,"[47] and treating her as something of the specimen "woman," instrumentalized rape deprives the victim of her special claim to her own victimization. It is something that happens to *a* woman in general, not to her in particular. The sixteen year old in Bukavu, who said that "'I know they didn't target me—and any [woman] would have had the same thing happen,'"[48] is a victim of this third use of instrumentalized rape. She has been disabled at the level of her sense of self, left without even the consolation of the personal will that things could be otherwise. When the will to spontaneous action disappears, so does the human freedom that is necessary for a full sense of selfhood and the conviction that one has rights as a human being. Women are particularly exposed to this kind of moral disablement: On the one hand, because of the devaluation of their activities even in times of peace, such as is illustrated by the economic analysis of instrumentalized rape, and on the other, because of the double exposure to violence made possible by sexism as it is combined with racism (or its opposite, the denial of difference in legal "universalism"[49]) and/or the natural inequality of reproductive labor.

Conclusion

Rape is a sadly effective weapon of war. It attacks simultaneously the economic and moral basis of a community. It attacks the economic basis by undermining the "sustenance economy" that reproduces the day to day existence of individuals as well as the on-going maintenance of human life. It attacks the moral basis of community by gutting its solidarity, undermining the conviction that basic human rights exist, creating a culture of "rightlessness," and threatening impulses to intervene in favor of those in distress. In response, the international community needs both to affirm the moral responsibility to intervene, such as through the "Responsibility to Protect" doctrine alluded to in the 2007 UN report,[50] and to hold individuals accountable for their crimes, such as one sees in the ground-breaking trial (1996-1998) of Jean-Paul Akayesu (b. 1953) in the International Criminal Tribunal for Rwanda. In addition to these legal actions, ongoing social action to increase recognition of the value of women and their economic activities is also needed. Without such economic and ethical recognition, women will continue to suffer from the use of rape as a brutal weapon of ongoing sadness in war and genocide.

Notes

1.   In 2007, the UN Secretary-General was Ban Ki-moon (b. 1944). The full text of the report is available at: http://www.securitycouncilreport.org/atf/cf/%7B65BFCF9B-6D27-4E9C-8CD3-CF6E4FF96FF9%7D/Civilians%20 S2007643.pdf. Accessed October 19, 2011.

2.   For further information on rape as a weapon of genocide, see Carol Rittner, "Using Rape as a Weapon of Genocide," in *Will Genocide Ever End?* eds. Carol Rittner, John K. Roth, and James Smith (St. Paul, MN: Paragon House, 2002), 91-97. "The Rape of the Sabine Women" is a tale from the founding legends of Rome, according to which the mostly male followers of Romulus abducted women from the Sabines after the latter refused to let the Romans marry them peaceably. It is recounted by both Plutarch and Livy.

3.   Relating the story of a young Congolese woman named Monique who bravely refused to submit to her attackers, Hugo Slim makes the observation that her slow death by sexual mutilation is an "example of the calm intent and precision butchering" that has "become routine in a continent where machetes and knives are always to hand." See Slim's *Killing Civilians: Method, Madness and Morality in War* (New York: Columbia University Press, 2008), 65-66.

4.   Quoted in *The War within the War: Sexual Violence in Eastern Congo* (New York: Human Rights Watch, 2002). Interview was undertaken October 19, 2001.

5.   "Report of the Secretary-General on the protection of civilians in armed conflict" (New York: United Nations Security Council, 2007), S/2007/643.43. See note 1 for access information.

6.   Karma Nabulsi, "Evolving Conceptions of Civilians and Belligerents: One Hundred Years after the Hague Peace Conferences," in *Civilians and War*, ed. Simon Chesterman (Boulder, CO: Lynne Rienner Publishers, 2001), 15.

7.   S/2007/643.21.

8.   Nabulsi, 16-17.

9.   Bruce D. Jones and Charles K. Cater, "From Chaos to Coherence? Toward a Regime for Protecting Civilians in War," in *Civilians in War*, 254.

10.   S/2007/643.47.

11.   Nabulsi, 19.

12.   S/2007/643.21.

13.   Jones and Cater, "From Chaos to Coherence," 246.

14.   This is a reference to Paul Collier's thesis that the "true cause of much civil war is not the loud discourse of grievance but the silent force of greed." See Collier's "Doing Well Out of War: An Economic Perspective," in *Greed and Grievance: Economic Agendas in Civil Wars,* ed. Mats Berdal and David M. Malone (Boulder, CO: Lynne Rienner Publishers, 2000), 101.

15. S/2007/643.47.

16. *You Will Be Punished: Attacks on Civilians in Eastern Congo* (New York: Human Rights Watch, 2009), 45-46 (my emphasis).

17. The "natural inequality of reproductive labor" is the fact that women undertake nearly all of the labor of reproduction but can claim only 50 percent of the result (i.e., the child).

18. Hannah Arendt, *The Human Condition* (Chicago: University of Chicago Press, 1998), 100.

19. As Hannah Arendt puts it in *The Human Condition*, "The fertility of the human metabolism with nature, growing out of the natural redundancy of labor power, still partakes of the superabundance we see everywhere in nature's household" (106).

20. Adrienne Christiansen analyzes how this traditional conception of war in terms of work and its destruction makes it difficult for women to raise the topic of rape in deliberations about war. See Christiansen's "Rhetoric, Rape, and Ecowarfare in the Persian Gulf," in *Ecofeminism: Women, Culture, Nature*, ed. Karen Warren (Bloomington, IN: Indiana University Press, 1997), 239-59).

21. Arendt, *The Human Condition*, 112.

22. S/2007/643.45.

23. Herbert Weiss. "War and Peace in the Democratic Republic of Congo" *American Diplomacy* 5, 3 (Summer 2000). Available at: http://www.unc.edu/depts/diplomat/AD_Issues/amdipl_16/weiss/weiss_congo1.html. Accessed October 19, 2011.

24. "Women, Agriculture and Rural Development: A Synthesis Report of the Africa Region," Food and Agriculture Organization (FAO) of the United Nations document (1995). Available at: http://www.fao.org/docrep/x0250e/x0250e03.htm. Accessed October 19, 2011.

25. Vandana Shiva, *Earth Democracy: Justice, Sustainability, and Peace* (Cambridge, MA: South End Press, 2005), 5.

26. Collier, "Doing Well Out of War," 93. Collier provides a useful explanation for why primary commodity exports are so instrumental in accounting for the incidence of civil war. First, compared with manufacturing, the barriers to entry are lower and the infrastructure needed to maintain extraction operations is less complex. Second, such exports are highly profitable, both because they are "based on the exploitation of idiosyncratic natural endowments rather than the

more competitive level playing fields of manufacturing," and because long trade routes allow for the imposition of "predatory taxation" by militias. Further, this taxation can be high and easy to collect since it can be "levied in kind." Finally, these illegitimate sources of wealth are easier to hide since primary commodities are "generic rather than branded products, and so their origin is much more difficult to determine" (93-94).

27. S/2007/643.45.

28. "Local people attributed a food shortage in Uvira in late 2001 in part to the refusal of women to go tend their fields outside Uvira, a refusal motivated by fear of rape and other kinds of attacks by soldiers and other combatants" (Human Rights Watch, 2002).

29. S/2007/643.49-50.

30. Ole Danbolt Mjøs, Chairman of the Norwegian Nobel Committee, Oslo City Hall, Norway, December 10, 2004. The programs currently run by the UN Food and Agriculture Organization, which attempt to restore agriculture in areas of the DRC specifically by working with women, acknowledge the same links as the Green Belt Movement.

31. *Shattered Lives: Sexual Violence during the Rwandan Genocide and its Aftermath* (New York: Human Rights Watch, 1996), 1. Available at: http://www.hrw.org/reports/1996/Rwanda.htm. Accessed October 19, 2011.

32. Ibid., 25.

33. Slim, *Killing Civilians*, 66.

34. Frantz Fanon. *The Wretched of the Earth*, trans. Constance Farrington (New York: Grove Press, 1963), 255.

35. Ibid., 257-58.

36. According to Susan Brownmiller in her groundbreaking book on rape, *Against Our Will* (New York: Simon Schuster, 1975), the first substantial account of rape as a weapon of war was made during the English occupation of Scotland in the mid-eighteenth century (38-40). She also recognizes that slavery in the U.S. South is "a perfect study of rape in all its complexities, for the black woman's sexual integrity was deliberately crushed in order that slavery might profitably endure" (153). For a firsthand account of the female slave experience, see Harriet A. Jacobs (1813-1897), *Incidents in the Life of a Slave Girl* (New York: Signet Classics, 2010). The book was originally published in 1861.

37. bell hooks, *Ain't I a Woman: Black Women and Feminism* (Boston: South End Press, 1981), 19 and 24, respectively.

38. Ibid., 27.

39. Hannah Arendt, *The Origins of Totalitarianism* (New York: Harcourt, 1951), 465.

40. *Shattered Lives*, 40.

41. S/2007/643.51.

42. For Susan Brownmiller, see *Against our Will* (New York: Simon and Schuster, 1975). For Catherine MacKinnon, see in particular "Rape, Genocide, and Women's Human Rights," *Harvard Women's Law Journal,* 17 (1994): 5-16. A helpful summary of these arguments and an analysis of the international legal framework that addresses wartime rape is offered by Sally Scholz in "Human Rights, Radical Feminism, and Rape in War," *Social Philosophy Today,* 21(2005): 207-24. The phrase, "ideology of rape," is Wilhelm Reich's (quoted by Brownmiller, 12).

43. Arendt, *The Origins of Totalitarianism*, 451.

44. Ibid., 452.

45. Human Rights Watch, 2002. Interview from October 19, 2001 in Murhesa. The exclusion from the realm of human solidarity is illustrated by Antionette E., interviewed in Sake on October 21, 2001: "Twenty-year-old Antoinette E. was raped after school one day in early 2000 when she went to get water. An RCD soldier from the nearby military camp came down the hill from the camp toward her, offering to help carry the water, but then turned on her and raped her. When she resisted, he cut her shoulder with a knife, leaving a thick scar. She cried and went home but did not seek medical attention. She became pregnant as a result of the rape. At that time she lived with her family and went to school. As a result of the rape, the family rejected her and she had to leave school. She now has the sole care of the baby, who is handicapped, and survives by washing clothes or working as a laborer on other people's land. 'The RCD soldiers do whatever they want,' she said."

46. Arendt, *The Origins of Totalitarianism*, 455.

47. Ibid., 454.

48. *The War within the War*. Interview was undertaken October 19, 2001.

49. The fact that the genderless nature of human rights has made it hard to acknowledge wartime rape as a crime against humanity is a striking case of how legal "universalism" can combine with sexism to leave women especially

vulnerable. See the articles by MacKinnon and Scholz cited in note 42.

50. S/2007/643.48.

Further Suggested Reading

Maathai, Wangari. *The Challenge for Africa.* New York: Random House, 2009.

Pillay, Navanethem. "Sexual Violence in Times of Conflict: The Jurisprudence of the International Criminal Tribunal for Rwanda." In *Civilians and War*, edited by Simon Chesterman. Boulder, CO: Lynne Rienner Publishers, 2001.

Plumwood, Val. *Feminism and the Master of Nature.* New York: Routledge, 1993.

Prunier, Gérard. *Africa's World War: Congo, the Rwandan Genocide, and the Making of a Continental Catastrophe.* New York: Oxford University Press, 2009.

Warren, Karen J. *Ecofeminist Philosophy: A Western Perspective on What It Is and Why It Matters.* Lanham, MD: Rowman & Littlefield, 2000.

Questions for Discussion

1. How can the pursuit of economic gain create a climate in which women and girls are vulnerable to sexual atrocities?

2. Instrumentalized rape exploits women's labor as if it is a replaceable natural resource. How and why? What can be done to combat these abuses?

3. How does instrumentalized rape undermine justice? What actions do you recommend to restore justice and the credibility of human rights for women who have endured rape as a weapon of war and genocide?

4. You have been hired by the United Nations to chair a new committee charged with addressing rape as a weapon of war and genocide. What would be your top priorities for this committee's platform for action?

11

Genocide, Rape, and the Movies

Paul R. Bartrop

> *"Wie oft?"*—"How often?"
>
> —*A Woman in Berlin*

Mass rape has long been associated with violent conflict, explained away as "collateral damage" or "spoils of war." Not until the late twentieth century did the concept of rape as a genocidal objective become apparent. The essays in this volume form part of a growing literature considering that phenomenon from a variety of perspectives.

Despite the obvious temptation of movie makers to exploit sexuality through nudity, violence, and sex, rape scenes in films about war and genocide are relatively rare. Why this should be the case is obvious: for a rape scene to be effective, a director must have an acute sense of understanding and imagination, and have access to skilled actors and actresses who can convincingly depict the most violent and intimate forms of assault that human beings can inflict and experience. Overwhelmingly, women and girls are the targets of rape that is driven by war and genocide. Some brave and highly talented actresses, the very finest in their craft, are able to represent such harrowing scenes; many others cannot. And movie makers—writers, actors, directors, production and set designers, camera operators, and so on—are often wary of touching on this topic, which is fraught with moral and psychological, as well as technical, dangers.

This chapter primarily concentrates on six key movies that illustrate the significance of cinematic responses to rape as a weapon of war and genocide. The films discussed are by no means an exhaustive listing of

movies relating to rape during genocide and war. In fact, the idiosyncratic nature of the selection could suggest all manner of limitations on
the author's part, in areas such as genre, origin, box-office appeal, historical situation, and the like. However, one thing remains constant for
all historians, including historians who employ film for their insights,
namely, chronology. Thus, in this short listing of six films, I take a number of movies that consider rape in war and genocide, and simply place
them according to the historical time frame with which they deal. Hence,
I start with the Nanking massacre of 1937, and move to the aftermath
of World War II in Germany, the wars of Yugoslav disintegration in the
1990s (starting with Croatia, and then moving to Bosnia), and finish with
the Rwandan genocide of 1994. After a consideration of these five motion
pictures, I then examine briefly what some regard as the archetype of all
documentaries that deal with rape in warfare and genocide situations,
again as it applied to Bosnia. At the chapter's end, some additional relevant films are identified and annotated.[1]

Black Sun: The Nanking Massacre

Directed by Mou Tun Fei, this 1994 Hong Kong film—also known as *Men
behind the Sun 4*—is set in the year 1937, when Japanese soldiers occupied the Chinese city of Nanking. Over the course of a few months, up to
300,000 innocent civilians and refugees perished in a brutal occupation
at the hands of the Japanese.

In its portrayal of the cruelty and viciousness of the occupation,
Black Sun is generally recognized as one of the most disturbing films ever
released. Its incessant depiction of the atrocities inflicted by the Japanese
has led to both criticism and commendation. One of the major issues to
be confronted is whether the filmmaker should have attempted to be as
unrelenting as he was in his depiction of violence and gore, or whether he
should have left some things to the imagination—or, better yet, just left
some things alone altogether.

This film is unyielding in showing the sadistic cruelty of the Japanese.
Mou has Japanese soldiers machine gunning and driving bayonets into
helpless civilians, and engaging in a contest to see who can decapitate the
greatest number with their samurai swords. Chinese women are rounded

up to serve as "comfort women" for the sexual gratification of Japanese troops. We also see other forms of sexual violence, as a monk is forced to have sex with a woman the Japanese have captured. Upon his refusal—in yet another scene of horror—he is castrated.

This movie, filmed in Cantonese in Steven Spielberg-style black and white, is difficult to watch. While the scenes of mass murder and rape are tough enough, one scene—of a pregnant woman slit open by a Japanese bayonet, and her fetus borne aloft by the offending soldier—is so shocking that it makes one wonder as to the psychological health of the screenwriter and director. In another dreadful scene, towards the end of the movie, a toddler is picked up by the leg and dropped head-first into a cauldron of boiling water.

In addition to violent murder, rape is an ever-present theme. Insofar as there is a character development in the film—and this is a sketch rather than a full-blown plot—a family in hiding is viciously attacked in their home by Japanese troops. As the eldest son flees along with two smaller children we know as John and Jean, the parents and an elderly grandmother hold off the soldiers. Later, the son returns home to find that the parents are dead, the mother having been stripped naked and raped. The grandmother, alive but also a victim of rape, lies half-naked on the floor. When John and Jean return, they see their grandmother about to burn the bodies of their parents and immolate herself in the process. A squad of Japanese troops, seeing the children, begins to advance on Jean, who must be no more than ten years of age, with the intention of raping her. We hear her screams as the grandmother pushes John outside, locks the door, and sets the house on fire. We are left to assume that all inside, rapists and raped, murderers and murdered, are caught in the ensuing blaze.

Finally, after a long period, the Japanese generals decide that the mountains of corpses throughout the devastated city must be disposed of in order to prevent disease. After soldiers spend days dousing the tens of thousands of bodies with gasoline, the grisly spectacle is ignited. The smoke from the conflagration blots out the very light of the sun, giving the movie its title.

Black Sun is a truly disturbing portrayal of rape and murder in wartime. Director Mou's realism is interspersed with authentic footage and survivor accounts, adding to the discomfort that viewing this movie intensifies. The film is an uncompromising portrayal, and its consistent representation of the barbaric cruelty with which the occupying army raped, pillaged, and terrorized its victims marks it as a truly horrifying movie, and a model within its genre.

A Woman in Berlin

Known in Germany as *Anonyma—Eine Frau in Berlin*, this 2008 movie is a film version of a book first published in the United States in 1954.[2] It is an account of the fate of the civilian population of Berlin at the hands of the occupying Soviets at the end of World War II in Europe, between April and June 1945. When the book was published, its author's identity was suppressed to guarantee her safety. (In 2003, it was revealed that she was Marta Hillers, a journalist, German patriot, and one-time Nazi propagandist.) The book described the nature of the Soviet occupation of the city, detailing the many struggles the local population was forced to endure at the hands of a Red Army keen to ensure that the Germans suffered as Russians had suffered at the hands of the Nazis. In particular, the book described graphically the author's experiences as a victim of repeated rape during the Soviet occupation of the city.

The historical details of the Soviet occupation make for grim reading. It is believed that an estimated two million German women were raped as the Soviets moved in from the East, 100,000 of them in Berlin alone. So far as anyone could tell, in 1946 almost 4 percent of Berlin-born children were estimated to have been the offspring of Russian fathers.

The book's appearance unleashed a storm. German men were simultaneously outraged and ashamed, mainly by the sense that they had been unable to protect their women from the violations they suffered. In East Germany, and indeed, throughout the Soviet bloc, there was further outrage at the suggestion that Soviet troops would have behaved in such an undisciplined and brutal manner. Yet although the sexual violence of the Red Army in Germany at the end of World War II was widely known, the widespread and systematic rape of German women was nonetheless swept under the carpet in the decades that followed.

Given this background, when the film was made in 2008, its director, Max Färberböck, was prepared for a critical reception. Nina Hoss, the actress playing Marta Hillers, was equally aware that this was a role that would be at the same time demanding and controversial. The challenges facing Hoss were multiple because of Marta Hiller's complex character, for this victim of vicious and repeated rapes had also been a convinced Nazi working for Hitler's regime. No doubt the rape scenes were physically and emotionally challenging, but Hoss's feeling that she had a responsibility to the past and to the future was a motivating force that resulted in her stunning performance.

The film's narrative turns on a decision by Marta Hillers, after being raped by a number of Soviet soldiers, to live no matter what compromises she has to make with her sense of morality. For the sake of her physical survival, she vows to take some measure of control over her circumstances. She resolves to seek out a protector from among the Soviet troops, entering into a sexual relationship with him that will at least bring otherwise random assaults from all and sundry under control. Several of the other women living in the ruined apartment building where much of the action of the film takes place adopt the same strategy.

The movie is thus a lens through which modern filmgoers, who know nothing of the time in question, can view the horror of war and the compromises needed to survive it. Färberböck even provides an opportunity for an exchange between two women that was common in Berlin at the time, as they greet each other with the phrase "*Wie oft*?"—"How often?" That is, "How often have you been raped by Russian soldiers?" Such down-to-earth conversation exemplified how much German women, imprisoned in Berlin, suffered at the hands of the Soviet soldiers.

A Woman in Berlin is a film that considers the nature of violent sexual crime, and the moral compromises that can enter into the struggle for survival when a woman is trapped by such violence. Färberböck's approach is to emphasize the women's fear, the nature of the sudden violence that confronts them on a daily basis, and their struggle to survive and to hold on to their dignity in spite of the degradation that confronts them.

Vukovar

Known in the former Yugoslavia as *Vukovar Poste Restante*, this 1996 film, set during the 1991 siege of Vukovar, a small Croatian city of about 50,000 people adjacent to the Serbian territory of Vojvodina, is a Romeo-and-Juliet love story about a Serb, Toma (played by Boris Isaković), and his childhood sweetheart Ana (Mirjana Joković), a Croat. Vukovar was the scene of a destructive siege of World War II-style proportions between September and November 1991. From early August, the city center had been subjected to sporadic bombing from Croatian Serb paramilitaries and elements of the Yugoslav People's Army (*Jugoslovenska Narodna Armija*, or JNA), but this assault escalated into a full-scale siege during that September. In the carnage that followed, Vukovar was reduced to rubble as Serb big guns and aircraft bombed the town incessantly. The city's defense was brave and stubborn before being overwhelmed by the Serb onslaught. Generally speaking, Vukovar was probably the most thoroughly devastated town in any of the wars in the former Yugoslavia between 1991 and 1995.

Directed and co-written by Boro Drasković, *Vukovar* begins on Toma and Ana's wedding day in 1989, when they are married with the blessings of both their families. This is the same day the Berlin Wall falls, and with a portent of things to come, we see the procession of their wedding party blocked by Croatian and Serbian demonstrations. Very soon, as the country of Yugoslavia begins to split into warring ethnicities bent on the creation of their own independent states, the happiness accompanying this mixed marriage is shattered. Toma is drafted into the Serbian-dominated JNA, and Ana, by this time pregnant, desperately tries to find ways to stay alive as Vukovar comes under constant bombardment. Moving in with her parents after her neighborhood turns into a war zone, she soon finds there is no escape from the war. One day, while she is out trading gold for bread, her parents are killed when a stray shell hits their house.

After her parents are killed, Ana finds herself alone in an environment that is now strange and terrifying. Rape, robbery, and murder are everyday realities. Although she pines for Toma—as he does for her—the possibility of a reunion appears remote. Houses and businesses have been razed, a pall of death and smoke lies over the ruins, and Ana tries to find some sort of connection with other human beings if only to survive in the vestiges of her now-shattered city.

Knowing what Ana's happy past had been like makes her violation at the hands of Serb soldiers all the harder to bear. In a scene nearly as difficult to watch as it must have been to make, Ana and her friend Ratka (Monica Romić) are alone in the house, with Ratka's small daughter asleep in another room. As Serbian soldiers burst into the house intent on looting the place, Ratka asks "Who are you?" A soldier, in response, claims "We're the dogs of war." (This phrase is taken from Shakespeare's *Julius Caesar*: "Cry 'Havoc,' and let slip the dogs of war." The term *havoc* is of even older derivation, and is based on a military order from the Middle Ages that directed soldiers to engage in pillage and to create pandemonium.) Ana and Ratka are then brutally raped by several soldiers, while Ratka's young daughter watches, held tenderly in the arms of one of the soldiers. The whole scene is emotionally draining, and is hard to take for even seasoned movie-goers.

It could be said that the women's experience is a metaphor for the city of Vukovar itself, which was ravaged by the conflict and then left to fend for itself after the men were done. Meanwhile, in the remaining part of the movie, Ana finds herself foraging for survival in bombed-out rubble, clearly striving to ensure that her unborn child will not become a victim even before entering the world. Toma's unit, closing in on the city as it slowly capitulates, eventually engages in combat with Croatian militiamen very close to where Ana is staying. Ultimately, in an irony worthy of Shakespeare or the Bible, Toma is shocked to see Anna in his gun sights, and he shoots at the house in which she is hiding. Whether or not the two will see each other again, and be reunited in a "happy-ever-after" scenario, is one of the features of the movie that keeps viewers' attention riveted right through to the end.

Vukovar was filmed during 1994 in strife-torn Bosnia, with many scenes shot in the shell of what had been the city itself. While this is the story of two fictional children of Vukovar, its authenticity sometimes makes it difficult to distinguish between fiction and documentary. In the movie's compelling final sequence, the camera surveys mile after mile of charred wasteland as it pans what is left of Vukovar and its suburbs. As it does so, the absence of any living creatures, human or otherwise, is left for our attempts to comprehend what has taken place.

Savior

This 1998 movie is related to rape during genocidal war, but *Savior* differs from many others in that it focuses on the aftermath of rape rather than on the crime itself. Produced by Oliver Stone and directed by the Serbian Peter Antonijević, the movie is based on the true story of an American mercenary in Bosnia. Robert Orr, who wrote the screenplay, had been a photographer's assistant during the Bosnian war, and he knew first-hand the situation he was describing.

Mass rape, as practiced during the conflicts in the former Yugoslavia, became institutionalized. There is little doubt that it was applied as a matter of policy by many Serbs, and it is known that a succession of Serb-run "rape camps" appeared, particularly in 1992 and 1993, intended to add to the climate of fear and to encourage the process of forced evacuation of Bosnian Muslims (Bosniaks) from towns and villages throughout Bosnia and Herzegovina. The policy put all women on notice that if they did not leave they could be subject to rape, and by virtue of that experience they would frequently be ostracized upon returning to their communities. Were they to fall pregnant—an objective of the rapes, in many cases— they would be doubly "tainted" upon returning home. Children born of rape would be perceived as of mixed ethnicity, and not as members of the community into which they were born. Thus, the central idea behind the mass rapes was to weaken the fabric of the ethnic group. While it has been demonstrated that the policy of genocidal rape took place at the hands of the Serbs against the Bosniaks, it is certainty also true that Serb women were targeted at times by some Bosniaks.

Savior considers this phenomenon, but with a twist: here, Vera, the female lead (Nataša Ninković), is a young Serb woman who has been raped by Bosniaks and fallen pregnant as a result of her ordeal. Guy (Dennis Quaid), an American anti-Muslim mercenary fighting for the Serbs, is sent to a United Nations-supervised checkpoint to help oversee a prisoner exchange of Serb and Bosniak civilians during a brief cease-fire. The heavily pregnant Vera is one of these civilians. Guy and his partner, a Serb soldier named Goran (Sergej Trifunović), put her into Goran's car in order to return her to her village.

Goran has little interest in Vera's situation, and blames her for engaging in sex with a Muslim instead of killing herself—and, once realizing she is pregnant, for not committing suicide out of shame. In a particularly brutal scene, Goran stops the vehicle in a tunnel, throws Vera out of the car and begins beating her. Once she is on the ground, he then repeatedly kicks her distended stomach, determined to kill her and her "Muslim bastard child." His actions bring on premature labor. Guy, watching all this from the car, tries to stop Goran, but when Goran persists, Guy finds he has no option but to shoot (and kill) him. Guy then helps Vera deliver her baby.

While this scene of salvation should give some measure of hope for Vera and the child, Antonijević does not give us this relief. Instead, we see that Vera's immediate response is to reject the baby and attempt suicide. Stopped from doing so, she then refuses to feed or take care of her newborn child. Upon arriving at her village, she is in turn rejected as her father recoils from the daughter who has betrayed the family honor and would have been better off killing herself. In his view, by "allowing" herself to be raped, she has brought shame upon him. Guy then has no alternative but to try to find refuge for her at a United Nations refugee camp.

In the climax of the movie, in order to emphasize his detestation of war, Antonijević introduces vicious fighters from the Croat forces into his schema, completing the trinity of belligerents who combined to make the Balkan conflict such a complex and violent one. By the end, one tends not so much to hate Serbs, Bosniaks, or Croats, but rather to loathe the war for the actions it led some people from all three groups to inflict on others. The consequences, as shown unflinchingly in scenes of atrocities that are among the most graphic ever shown in a serious motion picture, are always tragic, confronting, and disturbing. *Savior*'s scenes of dehumanization and butchery show how this war turned seemingly ordinary people into murderers, torturers, and rapists.

Un dimanche à Kigali

Known in English as *A Sunday in Kigali*, this film, a Canadian movie made in French in 2006, is set during the Rwandan genocide of 1994. If for no other scene—and there are many memorable ones—it is notable for an especially violent, even sadistic episode of rape late in the film.

Based on the novel *A Sunday at the Pool in Kigali* by Canadian writer Gil Courtemanche, and directed by Robert Favreau, *Un dimanche à Kigali* concerns the story of Bernard Valcourt, a white filmmaker and journalist. He falls in love with a young Rwandan woman, Gentille Sibomana, who works at the *Hôtel Des Mille Collines* (made famous for the rescue efforts of its manager, Paul Rusesabagina, whose own story was dramatized in the 2004 film *Hotel Rwanda*, directed by Terry George). Gentille (played by Senegalese-born actress Fatou N'Diaye), an ethnic Hutu often mistaken for a Tutsi, is a waitress at the *Mille Collines*, where Valcourt (Canadian actor Luc Picard) is staying while making a documentary about AIDS.

The movie is told partly in flashback, partly in real time. As Valcourt and Gentille realize the depth of their love for each other, larger events overcome their relationship. As the extremist Hutu Power government increasingly encourages violence against Tutsis, Gentille, by virtue of her appearance and demeanor, is taken increasingly to be a Tutsi, and her life is endangered. Valcourt tries to get her out of Rwanda and into Canada, but bureaucratic red tape blocks the way. Despite the deteriorating situation, Valcourt refuses to leave Rwanda, and the two are married—only to be separated at a Hutu checkpoint, with machete-wielding thugs demanding to see the couple's wedding certificate. Valcourt's last vision is of Gentille being dragged away to what, he can only conclude, must be a horrible death by machete.

After the genocide, when he can return to Kigali, Valcourt, filled with despair, decides to find out what happened to Gentille, and with his camera sets out to reconstruct her final days. In doing so, he learns more and more about the reality of the genocide, and of what had happened to others he had known just a few months before. Some became killers. Some were murdered. And others were viciously gang raped, prior to being killed.

In search of Gentille, Valcourt has precious little to go on. There are few leads and not many witnesses who are prepared to talk in the post-genocide climate of fear. The viewer, however, does know what has happened to her. In the horrific scene mentioned at the start of this section, Gentille is thrown into a cell, beaten, degraded, and repeatedly raped by members of the *Interahamwe* militia. The ferociousness of their assaults is aggravated by their contempt for a woman who had the audacity to consort with a white Westerner, and their attitude is that they will teach her appropriate humility and her "proper place" in the new society. As the main torturer comes to assault her one last time, he tells her, with deliberate control: "You're covered in blood, but still you scorn me. . . . Think you're better, but you're nothing." He then smashes a bottle, and drives it into her vagina. With a piercing scream, she collapses into unconsciousness, as he finishes his work by using the bottle to mutilate her face.

When Valcourt finally does locate Gentille in the post-genocide Rwanda, she is barely recognizable, and at first she refuses to show her face to him. When finally she does, she says, very deliberately and slowly, "I'm not the woman you loved. I'm no longer a woman." While the film then moves quickly to an ending that is anything but happy, director Favreau has by this stage made his point. The beauty of the love story, contrasted with the horror of the genocide, provides us the glimpses of both the best and the worst that humanity has to offer, within the framework of a movie that is at the same time agonizing and immensely powerful.

Calling the Ghosts: A Story about Rape, War and Women

This Emmy Award-winning documentary depicts the experiences of two women who became victims of mass rape during the Bosnian War of 1992-1995. Jadranka Cigelj and Nusreta Sivac, friends since childhood and both lawyers from the Bosnian town of Priejdor, were two Muslim women living "normal" lives as late-twentieth century professionals, until, in the spring of 1992, they were forced from their homes by Serbian troops and imprisoned at the notorious Omarska concentration camp. Along with hundreds of other Bosniak and Croat women, they were systematically and repeatedly raped, brutalized, and forced to witness countless atrocities and murders. The documentary is supplemented by original footage of the conditions at Omarska taken by British journalists in 1992 and 1993.

Directed by Mandy Jacobson and Karmen Jelincic in 1996, *Calling the Ghosts* does more than recount the women's experiences. It also chronicles their battle to get rape classified as a major war crime by the International Criminal Tribunal for the former Yugoslavia (ICTY) in The Hague. We see Jadranka and Nusreta, as they travel to the Netherlands to attend the ICTY, showing how they have converted their personal struggles for survival into a larger project in which they fight to assist other women similarly brutalized.

Their recollections go beyond personal confession, as the women testify about many of the crimes that occurred. When the camps were first uncovered by journalists such as Ed Vulliamy and Roy Gutman, whose accounts were then broadcast around the world, the Serbs controlling places like Omarska decided that their captives should be released, but the trauma the women suffered obviously remained with them afterwards.

This movie is essential viewing when attention concentrates on genocidal rape in warfare. The main focus of Jadranka and Nusreta's post-camp experiences is one of bearing witness to what had happened, and letting the world know about it, but accompanying this commitment is a concern: rape is not a pleasant topic of discussion or of public revelation, and the bravery shown by these two women in coming forward is far from common to all. Should they keep silent, or should they speak out? This dilemma is faced by many victims of rape, and in the case of genocidal rape the problems are compounded by the willingness to listen and believe—or not—of those to whom the story is to be told. But these women are determined to let the world know of the atrocities that occurred—not only for their own sakes but also in memory of those who suffered and died in the camps.

The importance of having their voices heard and of being believed thus becomes a major part of Jadranka and Nusreta's post-camp lives. Both women engage in outreach to others who have suffered: Jadranka interviewing rape victims for the Croatian Information Center, and Nusreta helping refugees with legal issues as she works for the Association of Women of Bosnia and Herzegovina.

Related Films and Dilemmas

Especially in film, there are dangers in dealing with rape in war and genocide, including abuses that can be called "genocide pornography."[3] But for responsible filmmakers and sensitive viewers, movies can be useful in providing a window to advance awareness of sexual violence and what is necessary to prevent it from happening again and again. This is not to say that all the answers can be found in movies; indeed, rape is a phenomenon that is likely to be more inexplicable than understandable. At the very least, however, these cinematic depictions of rape as a weapon of war and genocide raise questions that may lead to deeper insight.

Calling the Ghosts, for example, proclaims overall not only that human beings can be tortured and mutilated but also that the human spirit can transcend even the most horrendous of assaults. Is such a claim overly optimistic and too triumphal? All six of the films discussed above raise profound questions of that kind. They include: What needs to be done so that additional films about rape as an instrument of war and genocide are not needed? Rather than leaving us stunned and paralysed, how can cinematic studies of rape in wartime and genocide transform us from being passive viewers to becoming agents for healing change? Primarily dealing with wartime and genocidal circumstances different from those referenced above, here are other related films that can help to advance such inquiry.

Ararat (2002, Canada): Director: Atom Egoyan; Producers: Atom Egoyan and Robert Lantos; Writer: Atom Egoyan. Starring: Charles Aznavour, Christopher Plummer, Arsinée Khanjian, Simon Abkarian, David Alpay, Marie-Josée Croze, Elias Koteas, Brent Carver, Eric Bogosian.

Ararat is one of only a very few major motion pictures taking the Armenian genocide as its theme. The somewhat convoluted plot involves a series of intertwining subplots, the unifying theme revolving around a Canadian Armenian film director making a movie about the genocide, and the people who surround him in his efforts: Ani, the art historian hired as consultant; her son Raffi; Ali, an actor hired to play a Turkish officer; and David, a customs officer. At the premiere of the movie-within-the-movie, a vicious rape of an Armenian woman is shown, her small daughter hidden but holding her mother's hand as she undergoes her ordeal.

Attack on Darfur (2009, USA; also released as *Darfur*): Director: Uwe Boll; Producers: Uwe Boll and Dan Clarke; Writers: Uwe Boll and Chris Roland. Starring: Edward Furlong, Billy Zane, Kristanna Loken.

Six Western journalists and their escort of African Union peacekeepers visit a small village in Darfur, western Sudan. Upon hearing that a

Janjaweed militia unit is on its way to the village, they are faced with an impossible decision: leave Sudan and report the atrocities to the world, or risk their own lives and stay in the hope of averting what would be certain slaughter. When the *Janjaweed* enters the village, they begin to rape, torture, and kill all the villagers. This movie is acknowledged as the first non-documentary motion picture to be made about the Darfur tragedy.

City of Life and Death (2009, China): Director: Lu Chuan; Producers: Lu Chuan, Han Sanping, and John Chong; Writer: Lu Chuan. Starring: Liu Ye, Gao Yuanyuan.

The most recent recounting of the story of the Rape of Nanking, this film is set in 1937 during the Imperial Japanese Army's capture and subjugation of what was then the Chinese capital. The film tells the story of several real and fictional figures. The battle sequences are considered among the finest filmed in a motion picture, and the scenes of violence show an intense level of cruelty.

My Mother's Courage (1995, Germany, as *Mutters Courage*): Director: Michael Verhoeven; Producer: Veit Heiduschka; Writers: George Tabori (story), Michael Verhoeven. Starring: Pauline Collins, George Tabori, Ulrich Tukur.

One of the very few films to include a scene of rape of a Jewish woman during the Holocaust, this film is an adaptation of Hungarian author George Tabori's autobiographical novel, in which he describes how his mother Elsa escaped a deportation train of 4,000 Jews from Budapest to Auschwitz in July 1944. The rape scene relates to a Jewish deportee who rapes Elsa while actually on the train.

Ravished Armenia (1919, USA; also released as *Auction of Souls*): Director: Oscar Apfel; Producer: William Nicholas Selig; Writers: Harvey Gates, Aurora Mardiganian, Nora Waln. Starring: Aurora Mardiganian, Irvin Cummings, Anna Q. Nilsson, Henry Morgenthau, Lillian West.

Arguably the first motion picture to feature scenes of genocide, the theme of genocidal rape is embedded in the film's very title. There are no known complete copies of the film in existence today, but a restored and edited 24-minute segment of the historic motion picture exists, and was released in California in 2009. The movie, as it is recalled in contemporary print sources and in the restored fragment, shows young Armenian women flogged and crucified for their refusal to enter Turkish harems as sexual slaves.

Soldier Blue (1970, USA): Director: Ralph Nelson; Producers: Gabriel Katzka and Harold Loeb; Writers: Theodore V. Olsen (novel, *Arrow in the Sun*), John Gay. Starring: Candice Bergen, Peter Strauss, Donald Pleasence.

This stereotype-breaking revisionist Western centers on a young white woman, Cresta Lee, and young United States cavalry private, Honus Gant. The only survivors of an attack on a cavalry unit by the Cheyenne Indians in 1864, Honus and Cresta try to find their way to safety at Fort Reunion. The climax of the film is one of the most brutal sequences ever filmed by a Hollywood studio, as the rape, massacre, and mutilation of Cheyenne and Arapaho at the hands of a unit of Colorado volunteer cavalry at Sand Creek is re-enacted with an eye to absolute authenticity.

Two Women (1960, Italy, as *La ciociara*): Director: Vittorio De Sica; Producer: Carlo Ponti; Writers: Vittorio De Sica and Cesare Zavattini, from the novel by Alberto Moravia. Starring: Sophia Loren, Jean-Paul Belmondo, Eleonora Brown, Carlo Ninch, Raf Vallone.

A mother and her 12-year-old daughter struggle to survive in wartime Italy, towards the end of Mussolini's regime. After the liberation, as they try to return to Rome, they are gang raped by Moroccan soldiers serving in the allied Free French forces. This film earned Sophia Loren, who portrays the mother, an Academy Award for Best Actress.

Town without Pity (1961, USA/West Germany): Director: Gottfried Reinhardt; Producers: Eberhard Meichsner and Gottfried Reinhardt; Writers: George Hurdalek, Jan Lustig, Silvia Reinhardt, Dalton Trumbo (uncredited), from the novel by Manfred Gregor. Starring: Kirk Douglas, Christine Kaufmann, E. G. Marshall, Barbara Rütting, Robert Blake, Richard Jaeckel, Frank Sutton.

In a case of post-World War II rape by occupying soldiers, four American GIs are accused of raping a teenage girl from a German village.

Major Steve Garrett is assigned to defend them. During the investigation for the trial, Garrett uncovers some unsavory truths concerning the girl's family and its relationship with the other residents of the village. To defend the men, he must destroy the girl's reputation in court. If he fails, the four soldiers will be executed.

Conclusion

Sadly, the occasions for films about rape as an instrument of war and genocide are scarcely diminishing, and undoubtedly there will be more films made about such catastrophes. In multiple languages, filmmakers will need to keep raising the question found in *A Woman in Berlin*: "*Wie oft?*"—"How often?" If film about rape as an instrument of war and genocide can make its viewers not only ask that question but *feel* its poignancy and its plea for our accountability, then the work of daring filmmakers, actors, and actresses may make an invaluable ethical and political contribution, one that perhaps can be made in no other way.

Notes

1.   The films discussed in this chapter are more-or-less available in VHS or DVD format or by downloading from online sources. Some are available through Netflix or through Amazon.com. By entering the film titles into an internet search engine, additional information will be available.

2.   See Anonymous, *A Woman in Berlin: Eight Weeks in the Conquered City*, trans. Philip Boehm (New York: Henry Holt, 2005).

3.   See Catherine A. MacKinnon, "Turning Rape into Pornography: Postmodern Genocide" in *Mass Rape: The War Against Women in Bosnia-Herzegovina*, ed. Alexandra Stiglmayer (Lincoln, NE: University of Nebraska Press, 1994), 73-81.

Further Suggested Reading

Although there is a substantial literature relating to movies about the Holocaust—and a developing literature on film and genocide—relatively little has been written about films focused on wartime and genocidal rape. The following suggestions reference a small sampling of sources that essentially relate to film and the Holocaust. While movies that portray rape during the Holocaust are extremely rare, nonetheless many of the themes embedded in these works can be applied to other cases of genocide; the key is to encourage further research in the area, and to launch new initiatives that are at present unconsidered and under-represented within the literature.

Baron, Lawrence, *Projecting the Holocaust into the Present.* Lanham, MD: Rowman and Littlefield, 2006.

Doneson, Judith, *The Holocaust in American Film.* Syracuse, NY: Syracuse University Press, 2002.

"Films of the Holocaust, Genocide, and Futuristic Destruction." In *Encyclopedia of Genocide,* edited by Israel W. Charny, vol. 1, 228-40. Santa Barbara, CA: ABC-Clio, 1999.

Haggith, Toby and Joanna Newman, eds., *Holocaust and the Moving Image: Representations in Flim and Television since 1933.* London: Wallflower Press, 2005.

Insdorf, Annette, *Indelible Shadows: Film and the Holocaust*, 3rd ed. Cambridge, UK: Cambridge University Press, 2003.

Shofar: An Interdisciplinary Journal of Jewish Studies 28 (Summer 2010): Special issue on Holocaust and Genocide Cinema, edited by Lawrence Baron.

Wilson, Kristi M. and Tomas F. Crowder-Taraborrelli, eds., *Film and Genocide.* Madison, WI: University of Wisconsin Press, 2012.

Questions for Discussion

1. As you consider, perhaps by viewing, one or more of the films discussed in this chapter, how useful may the film/films be in developing an understanding of the causes and nature of rape in warfare and genocide?

2. Do you think that films about rape as an instrument of war and genocide tell you more about that subject than you can find out from other sources? Why do you think so?

3. Do films about rape in wartime and genocide tend to have "biases?" What points of view do the filmmakers display? Could you tell if the director of a film that deals with rape in war and genocide is a man or a woman? How? Do you think the film would be different if the alternative was the case?

4. As you consider films about rape in wartime and genocide, are you likely to be able to relate personally or identify with any of the characters in these films?

5. If you were to make a film on the subject of rape in war and genocide, how would you approach that task? Or do you think that the subject of rape as a weapon of war and genocide is not one that really can or should be treated cinematically?

12

The Power of Presence

Carl Wilkens

We also need to hear that, really, people can do nice things for each other.

—*Gillian*

The document that I have chosen to orient this chapter is a moving letter from a high school student named Gillian. She sent it to me after I visited her school to participate in a Facing History and Ourselves course on the Holocaust and genocide.[1]

Mr. Carl Wilkens,

So, our teacher tells us we're having a speaker come in to talk to us about the Rwandan genocide. So I'm like, shit, way to put a damper on my day. Because, see, I really, really like this class, and maybe it's not exactly fun learning about how people tend to kill each other en masse, but I'm definitely glad to be taking the course.

So I'm taking this class for a reason, you know, but at the same time it's really hard to go from human rights atrocities to physics, or writing, or whatever I have next block—to learn about all this stuff and think about what it means to be human, and judgment, and values, and the legalities of slaughter, and then go work on integrals.

Sometimes it makes it hard to go around and do the school thing knowing that there are people dying out there—we're having a speaker, and if just reading about this stuff has been hard, what's a real live speaker going to be like? What if I have a calculus test the next block? So I wasn't exactly dreading your visit, but I was definitely a bit, uh, apprehensive.

And then you show up, and you start talking, and you're funny, funny as all hell, and everyone's sitting there wondering if we're allowed to laugh at the genocide speaker. And you answered that for us, yes, yes, you have to laugh, you have to look for a bright side. Instead of having a bunch of weeping, depressed teens, you left us a group of hopeful people. I didn't expect that.

So often we are taught this material by shock value, by descriptions of horrors and atrocities, and we need to see that, to learn that, because it's the truth—but then we also need to hear that, really, people can do nice things for each other, even in the middle of those horrors.

So thank you, for flying across the country to tell us what we were all supposed to learn in kindergarten but never really figured out—people are decent—start small—do what you think is right—what you think is kind. It makes a difference to hear it from someone who has been there, seen things none of us can ever imagine, and still comes to talk to a bunch of teenagers and tell us to play nice with each other. Kind of restores my faith in humanity. Your visit was very much appreciated.

—*Gillian*

People often ask why I stayed in Rwanda during the 1994 genocide of the Tutsi, when nearly all of the other foreigners left.* To respond to that

---

* Carl Wilkens (b. 1957), who has appeared in numerous films as well as television and radio interviews, is the former head of the Adventist Development and Relief Agency International in Rwanda. In 1994, he was the only American who chose to remain in the country during the genocide. His choice to stay and try to help resulted in preventing the massacre of hundreds of children over the course of the genocide. Presently, Wilkens directs World Outside My Shoes, a nonprofit educational and professional development organization that equips people to

question, I need to tell you about a reunion at Anitha's place in April 2009, fifteen years after the genocide.[2] This would be nothing unusual for most, but for me it was simply incredible to take in. Just to be there in her cozy little home in Kigali, the capital and largest city of Rwanda, smelling the delicious Rwandan food that she had prepared for us, was like a miracle in so many ways.

I couldn't help but smile as I looked across the living room and watched my wife Teresa sitting there with Anitha, clicking through pictures. The laptop screen would light up, and then Anitha's face would light up again and again, as pictures of our kids popped up. Summer camp, family reunions, our home in the forests of southern Oregon, Shaun's high school graduation: you could see the pride in her eyes as she pointed to that one.

Shaun, our youngest, is now 6'4", but fifteen years ago, when Anitha had said goodbye to him, he was only five. She had lived and worked in our home for as long as Shaun could remember. I wish I had a picture of Anitha saying goodbye to Shaun and his two older sisters, Mindy and Lisa, but four days after the massacres began was no time for pictures. Sadly, I just can't recall the final hug between Anitha and Teresa as my family climbed inside the camper on the back of our little Toyota pickup, and I closed the door on them. My father, who was nearing the end of a three-month visit, slid in behind the steering wheel and drove my family down the road to the home of David Rawson, the American ambassador to Rwanda, which was one of the pre-selected evacuation assembly points for Americans in that section of Kigali.

I do remember very clearly, though, standing barefoot in the middle of our dirt road, watching the "armadillo" (that's what we called our homemade camper) waddle away through the potholes of our street. Dad was sticking like a magnet to the backside of that white United Nations tank escort.

I hadn't remained in the middle of our road just to wave goodbye to my precious family. I was standing there to let all our neighbors

---

resist human rights abuses and genocide. *I'm Not Leaving*, his memoir about the Rwandan genocide, appeared in 2011.—Editors' note.

know—those who turned violent and those who remained courageous—that I was still here. If they had any ideas of busting into our home to go after Anitha, I would be there. I was not sure what I would do if that happened, but I wasn't going anywhere. I was only beginning to learn about the Power of Presence.

Going against the Current

Teresa and I moved our young family to Rwanda in the spring of 1990. I was hired as the director of the Adventist Development and Relief Agency (ADRA) in this small central African country. ADRA is the humanitarian branch of the Seventh-day Adventist Church, and for the four years leading up to the genocide, I kept busy working with the construction of schools and the operation of five clinics around the country. Teresa's days were filled with homeschooling, homemaking, and all the wonderful challenges of raising three children in a developing country. I think we had been in Rwanda less than a year when Anitha came to live and work in our home. When the war between the Tutsi-led Rwandan Patriotic Front (RPF) and the Hutu-dominated government of Rwanda started in the fall of 1990, we at ADRA broadened our work to find ways of partnering with the families displaced by conflict. About one million of Rwanda's seven million people were driven from their homes during this three-year struggle.

Around eight o'clock on the evening of April 6, 1994, we heard a loud explosion. About forty-five minutes later, we learned that the airplane carrying Rwanda's President Juvénal Habyarimana (1937-1994) had been shot down as it prepared to land at Kigali. Not long after that, automatic gunfire began to echo through the hills of our neighborhood and city. While to many it might seem obvious that getting out of town would be the best idea if the country was being shredded by a government-ordered genocide, as turned out to be the case, I'm not sure that it would be so clear-cut if you looked at each individual's particular situation. In our home, Teresa and I actually had two young people working for us: Anitha, who lived and worked inside our home, and Janvier, who joined us as the night watchman. Both carried identity cards labeling them as Tutsi.

The "Tutsi" label in that ID card didn't communicate anything with regard to how much Anitha meant to our family. I think back and realize that our daughter Mindy was about seven, our middle child Lisa about four, and Shaun about two when Anitha moved in. Together we all experienced so much during those three years of the children's growing, so many memories. And then there was Anitha's connection with Teresa. Some know how hard it can be making so many adjustments to living in a foreign country. Teresa and Anitha had a smooth relationship (Teresa found Anitha's soft French so easy to understand), and I can't tell you how many times Teresa talked about missing Anitha in our home after we moved back to the United States.

When the American embassy made the decision—April 8, 1994—to evacuate every single American from the country, the instructions made crystal-clear that no Rwandans could come with us. We were told that we could try to help people from countries other than Rwanda to leave if they had documents proving their citizenship, but for Rwandans there were to be no exceptions. So what were Teresa and I going to do about Anitha and Janvier? There seemed to be no safe place we could take them. The reality was that we probably wouldn't have gotten through more than one or two, possibly three, roadblocks before these two Tutsis would have been pulled from the vehicle and murdered. I don't even want to write about what such a dragging from the vehicle might have looked like, how it would have been for Anitha and Janvier, or what our children would have witnessed. Yet, if we did let our imagination go there, we would have a tiny peek into what it was like for hundreds of thousands of people as they were torn from everyone and everything that meant anything to them in this world.

During this terrible time of dehumanization and extermination, Anitha and Janvier very easily re-humanized the Tutsi people for us. They, along with so many others of our friends and co-workers in Rwanda, put faces and names to individual human beings at a time when many around the world were simply labeling them as Tutsis or "those Africans." I don't know what would have happened if Teresa and I had not shared the same idea of the right thing to do. We both agreed that we had to do something; we simply couldn't do nothing. After much prayer and conversation between the two of us, we decided that I would stay, and Teresa would take the children out of harm's way. It's tough to describe the feelings surrounding this decision. We knew things were very, very bad, but we had no idea how bad it would get or how long it would last.

When I told Teresa goodbye, I quietly said, "I'll see you in two weeks, Love. This thing can't possibly last for longer than that. Then probably in three weeks you will be able to bring our children back." As it turned out, I was unable to leave the house for the first three weeks of the genocide.[3] Only then was I able to get out and meet Colonel Tharcisse Renzaho, the Hutu leader who was in charge of the portion of Kigali where our home was located, the half of the city that was controlled by the genocidal government.[4] On the first of what would be many visits to his office, I asked him how I as a humanitarian might help. Eventually these inquiries led to my working with three orphanages around the city. I would scrounge our ransacked capital for water and food. I would barter with the thieves and killers who controlled various neighborhoods, trying to get the necessities needed to help keep those children alive, but that's another story. Even more important than helping to supply basics such as food and water was the opportunity to supply presence: just being there. That was the key factor in saving the lives of Anitha and Janvier.

"We Are All the Children of God"

I cannot forget Anitha on evacuation day and during the one hundred days of killing that followed. She was always brave and calm, even on the day when three men demanded that I send her from our home and hand her over to them because her ID card said "Tutsi." Pastor Seraya and his wife Foibe, who were an invaluable addition to our home during the genocide, joined the hour-long-through-the-fence discussion. Strangely, no voices were raised during this exchange; in fact, there were some rather long and awkward silences as I tried to persuade the three men to help me with this "problem." We struggled through an intense sixty minutes of life-or-death negotiations, striving to convince these killers to move on and forget about Anitha. After we poked $100 through the chain-link fence, they left without her.

While I had been dealing with those men and their intention to kill Anitha, she stayed inside the house, no doubt thinking about what they would do to her before ending her life. Another survivor shared with me something I will never forget. Vianney had been seventeen in 1994 and survived against all odds by playing dead on a church floor in

Rwamagana.[5] While hundreds around her were being murdered, she had to lie perfectly still, taking shallow breaths as she listened to the screams, the pleas for mercy, and the final whimpers produced by brutal violation. Years later she told me, "We were not afraid of dying. It's what they would do to us before we died that we feared."

During those one hundred long nights, I remember occasionally hearing soft laughter coming from the pantry where Anitha and Foibe slept. They had laid claim to this tiny room in the innermost part of the house, putting several walls between them and the gunshots and shouting outside. They tugged a mattress in there and slept with their heads under the bottom shelf of the pantry. As they were tucked away in that cramped space, lifelong bonds were being formed. I remember Anitha cheerfully preparing meals, sweeping, and washing clothes by hand, while her home-land of Rwanda was engulfed in the worst period of its troubled history. In fact, the genocide in Rwanda was the largest witnessed slaughter of humans by other humans that had taken place in any three-month period of the twentieth century. Anitha went about her work, serving others, much as she had for the three years prior to the genocide while work-ing in our home. I tried to guess what her thoughts were on the inside. Perhaps she was wondering what was happening right that moment to her little sister or to a favorite aunt. I couldn't tell, and I didn't ask.

And now here is Anitha fifteen years later, trying to catch up with the lives of our kids, the life of our whole family. Looking over Anitha's shoul-ders are her two handsome sons and Etienne, her husband, a rock-solid good man. Anyone looking in from the outside would never guess what kind of life journey this family has traveled. At this moment, however, I am simply overwhelmed by the beauty of this family picture. It could have been so very different.

A few minutes later, when Etienne stepped out of the room and Teresa had the boys' attention by showing them more pictures, I took the opportunity to tell Anitha something I wanted only her to hear. I said, "You know, Anitha, people are so inspired by your story. Even though you lost your whole family, had them taken from you, you still chose to marry a man whose ID card before the genocide said 'Hutu.' And I want to be sure I have my facts straight. Before the genocide Etienne's ID card did say 'Hutu,' didn't it?"

Anitha seemed a bit confused; she didn't get the "inspiring" part of this comment. Yes, Etienne's ID card had said "Hutu," but communication became fractured as I stumbled through a series of obvious remarks: her family's killers would have had "Hutu" identity cards, Etienne would have had a "Hutu" ID card, she married him, and that was amazing. But when the light did dawn in her eyes as to what I was getting at, she gracefully removed the awkwardness by simply saying with an open smile, "Mais, nous sommes tous les enfants de Dieu." (But, we are all the children of God.)

The Power of Presence

Whoa! We have all heard that phrase—"We are all the children of God"—but listen to who is saying it! So simple and so profound. Anitha's statement was not some platitude from a person practiced at being interviewed or somehow accustomed to answering awkward questions. But wait, that's probably not true. For years she has had to deal with very difficult questions, at times seemingly unanswerable questions. How could neighbors and friends—no matter the designations on their identity cards—lift a machete or a heavy garden hoe against a boy they had watched take his first steps around the neighborhood, or against a mother with whom they had sung in the church choir as teenagers, or against a neighboring dad who had generously lent them a cow for its milk to help a sick family member recover? How? Why?

I really don't know how Anitha is processing all of this. *Perhaps she spends more time thinking about the fact that we are all God's children than she does about the "whys?" and "hows?" of that indescribable time.* And if this is how she processes what has happened, well, it looks good on paper, but how can a person really do it in daily life?

Reflecting on Anitha's life more than fifteen years after the genocide causes me to look not only at the horrific dehumanizing acts of the torture and rape suffered by so many around her, but also at what potentially could have been taken away even if and indeed because they survived, taken away from all the victims *for the rest of their lives.*

In their acts of physical savagery, were these inhumane violators consciously doing their utmost to:

Take away the victim's sense of worth—*for the rest of her life?*

Take away her chance to have a healthy relationship with anyone—*for the rest of her life?*

Take away her chance to celebrate the wonder and wackiness of a family circle—*for the rest of her life?*

Take away her chance to rest again, securely and deeply rest—*for the rest of her life?*

Take away any possibility of her ever standing silent with her mouth open, incredulously watching the ridiculous antics of her kids—*for the rest of her life?*

Take away the person's chance to explore, learn, love, tease, and even laugh until her sides ache—*for the rest of her life?*

Who knows if the raping attackers thought and planned such things, which could have happened—and often did—even if the perpetrators did not fully intend the devastating implications of their actions. In Anitha's case, against the odds, the dehumanization inflicted by the perpetrators failed. In her case, the perpetrators failed. Anitha was a young woman they had not been able to dehumanize. Having typed those hopeful words, however, my fingers have hardly paused a moment before other thoughts rush through my mind, recollections of all the women, children, and men who have been so mercilessly raped, who had no one "present" to stand up for them. No doubt they looked and hoped and even trusted that someone would stand up for them. But there was *No One*—no one when someone could have been present.

Though I don't know the immediate and long-term thinking of actual rapists toward their victims, I have little doubt regarding the strategic planners of the genocide. These internationally educated, degree-holding desecrators of families knew very well the long-term results they were working towards. This group of men and women were students of history; they watched CNN, listened to the BBC. These executors knew exactly what they wanted to accomplish.

And yet, despite the intentional efforts of those *genocidaires* working ruthlessly and all-too-successfully in the vacuum left by the absence of presence, there are some among those who survived whose lives have not been robbed of everything. They celebrate, they live, they serve in such a way that many would have no idea what certain chapters of their life story hold. And though the memory of those chapters is always close at hand to them, still they miraculously are making it! In fact, they far exceed the standard of "making it"; their lives are inspiring and instructing all who are willing to listen with their hearts and minds. These survivors have moved beyond survival mode. Way, way, way beyond! Maybe you will be able to visit Rwanda one day and see for yourself.

So at this point, *now*, I have to ask myself these questions: What does my presence mean to potential victims? What does my presence mean to perpetrators—both planners and executioners? What does my presence mean to survivors? Taken beyond the specific instance of the situation in Rwanda, what does "presence" mean in other situations? And what does my belief in presence compel me to do on a daily basis, not only in standing up against wrong but also in affirming right, kind, and thoughtful actions?

A Final Thought

Something I experienced again and again during the Rwandan genocide—one of my most lasting lessons from that time—is the following thought sequence: Often seemingly impossible situations threaten to drown, strangle, or even paralyze us. You know what I mean: there is just no imaginable "*good*" solution. These horrible situations go unresponded to just because we think there is nothing we can do, and we absent ourselves from the situation. Then come the catastrophic consequences. It only takes a skimming though current and not-so-current history to point out with alarming accuracy and detail these unresponded-to horrors. What I believe about this, because I've seen it, I felt it, I've smelt it again and again is that nothing changes until we . . . no, not "we," it's not acceptable to hide behind "we." "We" too easily excuses "me." Nothing changes until I decide *this is simply not acceptable!* That's when change starts. Sound too simple? I don't know how many times I have heard, "Well, that's just the way it is.

Life's not fair. The sooner you accept that, the easier life will be." *But that outlook is a lie.* There are solutions, but often they do not materialize until one person says, *This is simply not acceptable!* Even when we are personally threatened (or perhaps especially when we are personally threatened) with some real or metaphorical gun to our head, that crisis cannot be allowed to change our thinking so that the "unacceptable" slides into the "barely tolerable" category.

Doing nothing in a crisis is unacceptable. But going a step further, I have come to the point of redrawing or at least re-examining my own lines about what might be "*somewhat barely tolerable*" and what is—as a friend says—"*absofriknlutely not acceptable!*" Who draws those lines for me? About *what* am I ready to be present and declare—even to the point of being present to death—*this is simply not acceptable*?

For Teresa and me *it was simply unacceptable* to leave Anitha and Janvier alone in the middle of an exploding genocide. Our decision was strongly shaped by our recognizing their "humanness," seeing them in us, us in them. Then with that "*this is simply unacceptable*" declaration in hand, we felt our best response was for one of us to "Be Present." A high school student once asked me, "What did you think you could do? What was your plan when you decided to stay?" Honestly, I had to answer that I didn't have much of a plan. It became clear, however, that once we made the "*this is simply unacceptable*" decision, previously unimagined opportunities appeared. Following that decision and depending on how I had drawn my "lines," different solutions started to materialize. Believe me, solutions will come, hopefully before someone "pulls the trigger," a risk that, unfortunately, sometimes goes with deciding "*this is simply unacceptable*" and accepting the responsibility to "Be Present."

I won't forget and perhaps you will remember that evening in Anitha's home when she generously shared with us so much more than good Rwandan cooking.

Notes

1.   Facing History and Ourselves is an international educational organization, headquartered in Brookline, Massachusetts, whose mission is to "teach civic responsibility, tolerance, and social action to young people, as a way of fostering moral adulthood."

2.   To protect the privacy of real persons, I use the names Anitha, Janvier, and Ettiene, which are fictitious.

3.   The genocide lasted from April to July 1994. In arguably "the most concentrated killing process ever seen in human history," Hutu perpetrators—armed mainly with machetes, clubs, and small arms—murdered about one million people in a few weeks. An estimated 80 percent of the victims, primarily Tutsis but also many moderate Hutus, were slaughtered in what Gérard Prunier aptly has called a "hurricane of death" that took place between mid-April and mid-May 1994. For more detail see Adam Jones, *Genocide: A Comprehensive Introduction*, 2nd ed. (New York: Routledge, 2011), 346-68. The quoted phrases, cited in Jones, 346, are from John Quigley, *The Genocide Convention: An International Law Analysis* (London: Ashgate, 2006), 33, and Gérard Prunier, *The Rwanda Crisis: History of a Genocide* (New York: Columbia University Press, 1997), 261.

4.   On July 14, 2009, the International Criminal Tribunal for Rwanda (ICTR) found Renzaho (b. 1944) guilty of genocide, as well as murder and rape as crimes against humanity. He was sentenced to life imprisonment, subject to appeals.

5.   Rwamagana, the capital of both Rwamagana district and the Eastern Province of Rwanda, is a city located about thirty miles east of Kigali. At the time of the genocide and thereafter the Rwandan population has been predominantly Christian. In Rwanda, the most Christian of African countries, Roman Catholics are the largest group. The Protestant denominations include about ten percent of the Rwandan population that identifies with the Seventh-day Adventist tradition. During the genocide, which was distinctive because so many of the killers and victims alike professed to be Christians, thousands of Tutsis and moderate Hutus sought but did not find refuge in churches. Several genocide memorials, such as those at Kibuye, Ntarama, Nyamata, Nyange, and Nyarubuye are located within or near churches that became places of slaughter. Some church leaders resisted the genocide and, at great risk to themselves, assisted people in need, but others were deeply implicated in the killing process. A few have been convicted of genocide. For more detail on these matters, see Carol Rittner, John K. Roth,

and Wendy Whitworth, eds., *Genocide in Rwanda: Complicity of the Churches?* (St. Paul, MN: Paragon House, 2004).

Further Suggested Reading

Dallaire, Roméo. *Shake Hands with the Devil: The Failure of Humanity in Rwanda.* Toronto: Random House Canada, 2003.

Hatzfeld, Jean. *The Antelope's Strategy: Living in Rwanda after the Genocide.* Translated by Linda Coverdale. New York: Farrar, Straus and Giroux, 2009.

Ilibagiza, Immaculée. *Left to Tell: Discovering God Amidst the Rwandan Holocaust.* Carlsbad, CA: Hay House, 2006.

Power, Samantha. *"A Problem from Hell": America and the Age of Genocide.* New York: Basic Books, 2002.

Wilkens, Carl. *I'm Not Leaving.* Spokane, WA: World Outside My Shoes, 2011.

Questions for Discussion

1. How does the story of Anitha provide inspiration for the reader?

2. How does Carl Wilkens detail the ways he moves toward a greater understanding of the Power of Presence?

3. As you read Wilkens's account, what values and principles seem to guide his thinking and his actions?

4. Have you experienced any situation where your presence made a difference, in either a positive or a negative way?

5. At what point in a particular situation could you imagine yourself saying, *"This is simply not acceptable"*? What consequences would you be prepared to take?

13

Crying Out for Action: Rape-as-Policy and the Responsibility to Protect

John K. Roth

I've learned some new words.

—Nicholas D. Kristof

The *New York Times* op-ed writer Nicholas D. Kristof uses his influence and leverage to call attention eloquently and persistently to human rights abuses that affect women and girls.[1] Kristof cannot eliminate rape-as-policy—intentional and systematic uses of rape as a weapon in war and genocide—at least not single-handedly. Nevertheless, he provides an important example by using his position to oppose atrocities that his words frequently describe so concretely and specifically that the cruelties are never allowed to be abstract and anonymous.

On February 11, 2010, for instance, Kristof published an essay called "The Grotesque Vocabulary in Congo." Four sentences from that article provide one of the two documents that orient this chapter. Beginning with the observation that he had "learned some new words" while in the Democratic Republic of Congo (DRC), Kristof continued his editorial as follows:

> One [of the new words] is "autocannibalism," coined in French but equally appropriate in English. It describes what happens when a militia here in eastern Congo's endless war cuts flesh from living victims and forces them to eat it.

Another is "re-rape." The need for that term arose because doctors were seeing women and girls raped, re-raped and re-raped again, here in the world capital of murder, rape, and mutilation.

When Kristof identified the DRC as "the world capital of murder, rape, and mutilation," he did not exaggerate. "The brutal war here in eastern Congo has not only lasted longer than the Holocaust," Kristof underscored in a *New York Times* editorial dated February 7, 2010, "but also appears to have claimed more lives. A peer-reviewed study put the Congo's war death toll at 5.4 million as of April 2007 and rising at 45,000 a month. That would leave the total today, after a dozen years, at 6.9 million."[2] Although the precise numbers cannot be known, rape and *re-rape* have contributed significantly to those millions of deaths.

The Paramount Need

While the word *re-rape* may be new, the sad reality it denotes is not. For example, this book began by introducing Jeanette Uwimana, a Tutsi woman who was, in Kristof's words, "raped, re-raped and re-raped again" during the Rwandan genocide in 1994. Uwimana is one of many women and girls who have endured such horror before, during, and after that catastrophe. She also is one of not-so-many who survived that ordeal and has testified about it.

One of Uwimana's sisters is a Congolese woman named Jeanne Mukuninwa. She has been caught in the DRC's lethal web and cross fire of violent rivalries that are inescapable as armed and warring factions pursue valuable "conflict minerals": essential smart-phone and DVD-player ingredients such as tantalum, tin, tungsten, and gold. Ruthless struggles to control those lucrative resources dominate the battle-ridden DRC, rendering that state unable or unwilling to protect its own populations. According to Dr. Denis Mukwege, the skilled doctor who saved her life at Panzi Hospital in Bukavu, DRC, multiple rapes left Mukuninwa "completely destroyed inside." Mukwege has done his best to heal Mukuninwa's physical wounds, but he is not sure that his surgery can prevent her from leaking urine, let alone bring wholeness to her mind and spirit. "Sometimes," the doctor told Kristof, "I don't know what I am doing here.

There is no medical solution." Kristof continues: "The paramount need, [Mukwege] says, is not for more humanitarian aid for Congo, but for a much more vigorous international effort to end the war itself. . . . So if we don't act now, when will we? When the toll reaches 10 million deaths? When Jeanne is kidnapped and raped for a third time?"[3]

Linked to the new words that Kristof learned, Mukwege's observation about "the paramount need" and Kristof's question "When will we act?" relate to paragraphs 138 and 139 from the Outcome Document of the United Nations World Summit, which took place in 2005. The second orienting document for this reflection about "Crying Out for Help: Rape-as-Policy and the Responsibility to Protect," those paragraphs state the following commitments:

Responsibility to protect populations from genocide, war crimes, ethnic cleansing and crimes against humanity

138. Each individual State has the responsibility to protect its populations from genocide, war crimes, ethnic cleansing and crimes against humanity. This responsibility entails the prevention of such crimes, including their incitement, through appropriate and necessary means. We accept that responsibility and will act in accordance with it. The international community should, as appropriate, encourage and help States to exercise this responsibility and support the United Nations in establishing an early warning capability.

139. The international community, through the United Nations, also has the responsibility to use appropriate diplomatic, humanitarian and other peaceful means, in accordance with Chapters VI and VIII of the Charter, to help to protect populations from genocide, war crimes, ethnic cleansing and crimes against humanity. In this context, we are prepared to take collective action, in a timely and decisive manner, through the Security Council, in accordance with the Charter, including Chapter VII, on a case-by-case basis and in cooperation with relevant regional organizations as appropriate, should peaceful means be inadequate and national authorities are manifestly failing to protect their populations from genocide, war crimes, ethnic cleansing and crimes against humanity. We stress the need for the General Assembly to continue consideration of

the responsibility to protect populations from genocide, war crimes, ethnic cleansing and crimes against humanity and its implications, bearing in mind the principles of the Charter and international law. We also intend to commit ourselves, as necessary and appropriate, to helping States build capacity to protect their populations from genocide, war crimes, ethnic cleansing and crimes against humanity and to assisting those which are under stress before crises and conflicts break out.[4]

The 2005 United Nations World Summit commemorated the UN's founding sixty years earlier. In the wake of World War II, the United Nations came into existence when its charter was signed in San Francisco on June 26, 1945, and came into force on October 24 of that same year. The charter's preamble affirms that the peoples of the United Nations are determined "to save succeeding generations from the scourge of war, . . . to reaffirm faith in fundamental human rights, in the dignity and worth of the human person, in the equal rights of men and women, and of nations large and small, and . . . to promote social progress and better standards of life in larger freedom."[5] At the same time, the charter stressed that, with the exception of acts of international aggression or actions that threaten or breach international peace, the United Nations is not authorized "to intervene in matters which are essentially within the domestic jurisdiction of any state."[6]

As the latter provisions imply, the United Nations in many ways privileged national sovereignty over human rights, for under the UN charter, massive human rights abuses and even crimes against humanity could take place within a state without those conditions being construed as threats to or breaches of international peace, let alone as acts of international aggression. But if paragraphs 138 and 139 of the Outcome Document of the 2005 United Nations World Summit are honored, then for the following reasons national sovereignty does not trump human rights, at least not as much as it could and did before.

First, paragraph 138 affirms that each individual state has the primary responsibility to *protect* its populations from genocide, war crimes, crimes against humanity, and ethnic cleansing. That responsibility also entails that individual states are obliged to *prevent* those crimes from happening to their populations. Second, paragraph 139 indicates that the international community has the responsibility to help populations threatened by genocide, war crimes, crimes against humanity, and ethnic cleansing. Furthermore, if an individual state is unable or unwilling to protect its populations from these mass atrocity crimes, which definitely include rape used as a weapon of war and genocide, then the international community has the responsibility to take "collective action, in a timely and decisive manner." If peaceful means are inadequate to provide the needed protection, the international community must take stronger measures, including collective use of force authorized by the Security Council under Chapter VII of the United Nations charter.

A New Norm

Gareth Evans, chancellor of the Australian National University, formerly Australia's foreign minister, and from 2000 to 2009 president and chief executive officer of the International Crisis Group, coined the term *responsibility to protect* during his 2000-2001 tenure as co-chair of the International Commission on Intervention and State Sovereignty (ICISS). The responsibility to protect (R2P, as it is sometimes abbreviated) became more than an idealistic concept in September 2005, when heads of state and government agreed to paragraphs 138 and 139 in the Outcome Document of the United Nations World Summit, an action that gave R2P a foothold in international law.[7]

The political scientist Thomas Weiss has argued that "with the possible exception of the prevention of genocide after World War II, no idea has moved faster or farther in the international normative arena."[8] Nevertheless, the potency and status of this new norm are still very much works in progress. The reasons for that uncertainty are multiple and complex. Crucial among them are factors that remain critical more than a decade after the appearance of *The Responsibility to Protect*, the 2001 report of the International Commission on Intervention and State Sovereignty, and its sixth chapter in particular. This report, which was a crucial driving force behind the UN's eventual support for paragraphs 138 and 139 in the 2005 Outcome Document, referred to "conscience-shocking situations crying out for action" (6.36-40, an important section focused on "The Implications of Inaction").[9]

Numerous times the ICISS report refers to rape, including system-atic rape, as among those "conscience-shocking situations crying out for action," especially insofar as rape is part of ethnic cleansing and, by impli-cation, genocide. Speaking about "large scale" losses of life and ethnic cleansing, the ICISS report highlights "acts of terror and rape," as indi-cated in the following propositions:

> Military intervention for human protection purposes is justified in two broad sets of circumstances, namely in order to halt or avert:
>
> • *large scale loss of life, actual or apprehended, with genocidal intent or not, which is the product either of deliberate state action, or state neglect or inability to act, or a failed state situation; or*
>
> • *large scale "ethnic cleansing," actual or apprehended, whether carried out by killing, forced expulsion, acts of terror or rape.*
>
> If either or both of these conditions are satisfied, it is our view that the "just cause" component of the decision to intervene is amply satisfied. (4.19)

As an international norm, R2P is in its infancy. Arguably, if it had existed robustly in, say, 1990, "rape camps" might not have existed in the former Yugoslavia because there would have been forceful interna-tional intervention against ethnic cleansing there, and Jeanette Uwimana might not have been raped and *re-raped* because there would have been forceful international intervention against genocide in Rwanda. More recently, if R2P had existed robustly in, say, 2000, Nicholas Kristof might not have had to learn new words—*autocannibalism* and *re-rape*—because there would have been forceful international intervention to protect Jeanne Mukuninwa and her Congolese sisters. Unfortunately, R2P nei-ther existed robustly then nor does it now, and circumstances, events, and weakness of political will may doom it be an idea whose time has *not* come or worse, like the slogan "Never Again," a banal cliché.

If R2P is to gain traction that can curb if not eliminate rape as a weapon of war and genocide, work in that direction will have to include what the eighth chapter of the ICISS report urges: namely, attention to moral appeals that might prevent, avert, and halt such devastation.

Importantly, the report aptly notes that "getting a moral motive to bite means . . . being able to convey a sense of urgency and reality about the threat to human life in a particular situation" (8.13).

Do the Dead Cry Out for Action?

As this book's chapters bear witness, crying out for action against "acts of terror and rape" can arise in diverse times and places, including especially the courageous examples and testimonies of abused women such as Jeanette Uwimana and Jeanne Mukuninwa. As this book draws to a close, it also worthwhile—even imperative—to ponder how "a sense of urgency and reality" about the threat to human life created by rape as a weapon of war and genocide might be found by remembering the women and girls, and sometimes men and boys, whose testimony seemingly cannot be heard because they are *dead*—killed after or as result of being raped if not raped to death. Arguably, this book has already been too full of pain and heartbreak, but it could scarcely do justice to the "conscience shocking" events and issues it addresses without inviting respectful recollection of and encouraging meditation about the countless persons—predominantly but not only women and girls—who have been "done to death" by rape as a weapon of war and genocide.[10]

Consider, therefore, the following questions: Can the dead themselves, specifically those whose lives have been taken by rape as a weapon of war and genocide, prompt "a sense of urgency and reality" about the importance of protection and resistance against the sexual violence that stole life from them? Can those dead even "cry out for action" in ways that the living never can? Could listening to the dead, those "done to death" by rape-as-policy in war and genocide, improve the odds that moral motives will bite in the ways we need them to do?

Lest my intentions be misunderstood, some explanation is needed before proceeding further. When I speak of "the dead," doing so with specific reference to those whose lives were lost when rape became a weapon of war and genocide, my aim is not to lump individuals together in an anonymous, faceless, genderless, and ultimately disrespectful way. To the contrary, as I think of "the dead," the purpose and point are to underscore that individual girls and women, sometimes boys and men, have been "done to death" by rape-as-policy. If "the dead" can be said to "speak," their "word" comes from individuals who compel respect from us, the living, and also from their "chorus," for every individual who has suffered and died through rape-as-policy is one of many. In both forms—as one and as many—the voices of the dead reverberate in awesome ways if we allow them to do so. Listening, trying to hear what these voices—individual and collective—might say to us as they reach a silent but deeply moving crescendo constitutes one of the most respectful and instructive actions we can take.

Reflection about such listening can be helpfully focused by noting that some of the interviews conducted in 1946 by the American psychologist David P. Boder are among the earliest with persons who survived the Holocaust, a genocide not fueled by rape-as-policy but in which rape nevertheless wrecked and ruined many lives. Using the wire recording technology that was state-of-the-art at the time, Boder interviewed "about seventy people, representing nearly all creeds and nationalities in the DP [displaced persons] installations in the American Zone." He recorded 120 hours of testimony, which was translated, he said, "to keep the material as near to the text of the original narratives as the most elementary rules of grammar would permit."[11] Eight of these interviews were published by the University of Illinois Press in 1949.

Boder ended the introduction to his book with these words: "The verbatim records presented in this book make uneasy reading. And yet," he added, "they are not the grimmest stories that could be told—I did not interview the dead."[12] That last thought-provoking phrase—I did not interview the dead—became his book's title. Boder could not interview the dead because the dead do not speak. Nor, it might be added, should one even imagine interrogating the dead, for to do so would create a temptation that ought to be resisted. It is not the prerogative of the living to speak for the dead. With the Holocaust's murdered Jews foremost on his mind, the Auschwitz survivor Elie Wiesel underscored that point emphatically in his Nobel Peace Prize acceptance speech in Oslo, Norway, on December 10, 1986. "No one may speak for the dead," said Wiesel, "no one may interpret their mutilated dreams and visions."[13]

The living have no right to put words into mouths that death has silenced. Meditation about those who have been "done to death" by rape-as-policy seems to enjoin warnings and imperatives of that kind. They are well worth remembering as one considers listening to what the dead may have to say. Nevertheless, it may be no less important to think twice about such warnings and imperatives, for there are at least two significant issues that deserve attention if ethical senses of urgency and reality are to have a bite to check the forces that may continue to unleash rape as a weapon of war and genocide. First, to what extent is it true that the dead, including people "done to death" by rape-as-policy, do not and cannot speak? Second, to what extent is it sound to say that no one should or even can speak for the dead, including those "done to death" by rape-as-policy?

My response is informed by a study that scarcely alludes to such catastrophes and yet has insights pertinent for reflection on them. I refer to Robert Pogue Harrison's 2003 book *The Dominion of the Dead*. The point of departure for Harrison's eloquent and interdisciplinary study involves deep reflection on a fundamental and distinctive fact about human life: namely, that in one way or another we human beings bury our dead. This action takes place because human beings have memories; it also takes place for memory's sake. Absent memories, the dead would not even be forgotten, they would just be left to decay and disappear. Present memories, however, mean that we do not forget the dead, at least not entirely. In some ways, the dead even have dominion over us and rightly so, for we consciously dispose of their remains in ways that keep them—the dead and usually their remains—with us. Such presence of an absence can profoundly affect people and policies.

Of course, the destruction and death caused by rape-as-policy may make one quarrel with Harrison's account, for such carnage demands and depends upon utterly disrespectful acts. Those "done to death" by rape-as-policy are disrespected many times over. Their lives are trashed, and then their violated, lifeless bodies—most often female, but sometimes male— usually are discarded by the perpetrators, left to decay and rot or disposed of in other degrading ways that maximize the humiliation and terror that rape-as-policy intends. Nevertheless, even taking into account the overwhelming disrespect for the living and the dead shown by the perpetrators of rape-as-policy, Harrison's basic claim still stands: those killed in mass atrocities definitely remain with us, sometimes through memorials that honor them and even retrieve their remains. Their presence-in-absence can and should exercise a distinctive dominion over us, the living.

The presence of the dead, especially in their gendered absence, makes Harrison especially interested in how "we follow in the footsteps of the dead" and what it can mean to speak about what he calls the "indwelling of the dead in the worlds of the living."[14] Much of that "indwelling" pertains to ways, literal and figurative, in which the dead can be said to speak. During his Nobel Peace Prize acceptance speech, Elie Wiesel may have had something akin to this insight in mind, for in addition to contending that no one may speak for the dead, he underscored how much he sensed their presence. The dead do speak, for among the living there are people who can still hear quite directly the voices of family members, friends, or acquaintances who have been "done to death" by rape-as-policy and other mass atrocities, some of them surviving the sexual onslaught for a time and others not. Even if the survivors are no longer alive, their presence can be very real. Their remembered voices, their speaking, can be immensely moving and powerful.

Harrison does not miss the mark when he contends that "the dead are not content to reside in our genes alone, for genes are not *worlds*, and the dead seek above all to share our worlds" (84). Here it might be objected that Harrison enlivens the dead, that he gives them an existence that they do not and cannot have. But this objection does not hold because human existence cannot be what it is apart from our dying, from our awareness that our lives, at least on this earth, do not last forever, and that unavoidably, if not from desire, our being here leaves its mark, faint and trace-like though that mark may be. What we leave behind when we die and after we are dead reveals—a corpse alone can do so—that the dead do seek to share the worlds of the living. To a considerable extent, moreover, that sharing works. No human identity is possible without the dead; they inform us profoundly. Insofar as the chapters in this book make us think of those "done to death" by rape in war and genocide, that claim not only can be confirmed but also our own identities may be changed by encounters with those dead ones. "As human beings," Harrison writes, "we are born of the dead" (xi). In that sense, the dead have an afterlife. Although it does not depend on immortality or resurrection, the afterlife of the dead is nonetheless one that can and does speak.

Long ago, the Jewish sage Maimonides (1138-1204) suggested that there are voices that can be heard only in silence.[15] But can that really be the case if the focus is on the dead victims of rape-as-policy? Are Maimonides's claim and Harrison's analysis credible when one considers, for example, the silence enshrouding the lifeless bodies of those "done to death" by rape in war and genocide? Contrary to the direction in which such questions seem to go, the points made by Maimonides and Harrison are arguably even more deeply applicable, at least in some of their dimensions, in cases that involve persons who are nameless strangers to persons such as me or you.

Absent the presence of those who have been killed after or as result of being raped, if not raped to death, and the silence surrounding that presence, the reality of rape as a weapon of war and genocide would still be horrific, but its magnitude, its degree of unfathomable and irremediable loss, the extent of the despair and loss of trust in the world that such rape causes would be very different. Both in their individual particularity and in their collective enormity, the unfathomable number of girls and women, sometimes boys and men, "done to death" by rape-as-policy, their presence in the midst of silence, grounds much of our awareness of what such atrocity has been and continues to be. Beyond that recognition, what those "done to death" by rape-as-policy communicate, if anything, is another matter. But that those dead, anonymous to us or intimately known, communicate with and inform the living can scarcely be denied without denying the atrocities themselves.

No One's Death Should Come That Way

If those "done to death" by rape-as-policy in war and genocide can and do speak in and through their silence, what do they say? To what extent, moreover, is even the raising of that question a temptation to speak for the dead, a temptation that ought to be resisted? Such questions are important, especially in the context of Harrison's *Dominion of the Dead*, which proposes something intriguingly and profoundly paradoxical, namely, that the dead-in-their-muteness still speak.

Harrison contends that "some truths are glimpsed only in the dark." To discern those truths as fully as possible means turning to "those who can see through the gloom." Among them are the dead, he suggests, including the dead-in-their-muteness, who "possess a nocturnal vision" that involves such seeing through, such enduring that may keep the darkness of death from being all there is at the end of the day (158-59). Again, objections come to the fore, especially when the dead from mass atrocities are at attention's center. Their eyes do not see; every flicker of life is long gone from them. Far from seeing through the gloom, these dead constitute that darkness of oblivion. Apart from legal fictions, it is even problematic to say that they possess anything, least of all vision. Harrison's view, it seems, is not insightful because it is not true.

As with other aspects of Harrison's account, a second glance is important here too. In a sense of *owning* that is distinctively theirs, the dead, including the dead-in-their-muteness do *possess* something of the utmost significance. They do so because they *embody*, as only they can, a facticity that is *nocturnal,* if by such words one alludes to the darkness that death itself signifies. Without sharing the nocturnal vision that only the dead can give us, and in that sense they possess it, the living are blind—at least we are to what befalls us and may await us with regard to death's realities, which are always specific and often hideously so, something those "done to death" by rape-as-policy may make us see like no others.

Even granting Harrison this much, however, is it still not misleading and mystifying to suggest, as he does, that the dead are among "those who can see through the gloom" and that "in moments of extreme need" one ought to turn to them because "some truths are glimpsed only in the dark"? The dead, we may say, are simply dead. But to say even that is far from being as simple as it may seem. A person's death is not hers or his exclusively or alone. It belongs to others as well, which becomes evident in the fact that there is a gendered corpse to dispose of, or at least awareness that every human death involves a female or male body, even if no one disposes of it. When one dies, and those "done to death" by rape-as-policy are no exception to this fact, a person unavoidably gives her or his death to others, who do with it what they will. In Harrison's view, this means that the dead have ways of seeing through the gloom because they can "speak from beyond the grave as long as we lend them the means of locution; they take up their abode in books, dreams, houses, portraits, legends, monuments, and graves as long as we keep open the places of their indwelling" (153).

Keeping those places open entails fidelity to the dead, which, in turn, requires both concentration on the darkness that only the dead can make one see and courage to resist reluctance to see that darkness honestly and insightfully, a shortsightedness that blinds the living. In addition, fidelity to the dead may require bearing witness for them, a responsibility that may sometimes require speaking for the dead while always remembering that no one can fully recall or interpret their mutilated dreams and visions for them. Meanwhile, the dead, even in their muteness, can speak through us. Indeed, if we do not allow them to speak through us, we betray one of the most penetrating ways in which those "done to death" by rape-as-policy want to indwell our worlds.

In our seeing them, in our discerning of what their presence-as-absence in our lives may mean, the sight of the dead "done to death" by rape-as-policy may penetrate through the gloom of death. The nocturnal vision that is theirs can help us to see, in the dark, truths that are always ignored at our peril, not least because such ignorance tends to expand the abysmal count of those whose lives have been wasted by violence, brutality, genocide, and all the other practices of mass atrocity. It should go without saying that there is nothing triumphal or necessarily redemptive in these angles of vision. The sight/site of the dead withholds, in Harrison's words, "a presence at the same time as it renders present an absence. The disquieting character of its presence-at-hand comes precisely from the presence of a void where there once was a person" (92-93). Yet the truths that can be glimpsed and most profoundly heard only in the dark of that presence of a void may have much to teach, including, Harrison suggests, restraint of "our destructive impulses" (158).

To amplify possibilities of that kind, Harrison stresses that a debt, an "essentially insoluble" one, is owed to the dead (154). This claim makes sense because no one is "self-authored," and we all "follow in the footsteps of the dead" (ix). But if that insight encompasses those "done to death" by rape-as-policy, what is the debt that perhaps can be glimpsed fully only in the dark of the presence of a void? How could one start to respond to that debt and its obligations, keeping in mind that it is impossible to pay and meet them completely because the dead are dead?

Here, I believe, a combination of cautious restraint and bold statement must remain in respectful tension with one another. Restraint is needed because the bold responses that are right and good are also likely to sound like clichés if they are articulated. Silence followed by action that resists death's waste may be the wisest course. But silence, even when accompanied by action that resists death's waste, may be insufficient and irresponsible.

Those "done to death" by rape-as-policy in war and genocide can and do cry out for action. Perhaps one way to interpret their cry, one way to state their truths glimpsed only in the dark, is not-so-simply to say: Yes, we all are dying and will soon be dead, but no one's death should come *that way*. What *that way* was and means is partly knowable because we have testimony, memoirs, trial records, historical research, and even new words such as *autocannibalism* and *re-rape* that state and document the butchery. What *that way* was and means is also unutterable, for one cannot interview the dead. But because the latter realization persists, revealing as it does that, in David Boder's words, "the grimmest stories" are not the ones that are told, responses in word and deed that join with the dead to "see through the gloom" may be found. Such seeing would not dispel the gloom of atrocity. Nothing, not even a robustly normative responsibility to protect can do so, at least not completely. But *seeing through* might suggest a much-needed combination: namely, a linking of *seeing through* as enduring to the end, however bitter it may be, with a *seeing through* that entails doing as much as one/we can to find the ways that keep the gloom from overwhelming us. If the responsibility to protect is not one of those ways, nothing could be. It emanates from atrocity's dead, and fulfilling that responsibility, even if imperfectly, is arguably one of our best ways to respect and hear them.

Harrison draws his book to a close by observing that the dead can be "our guardians. We give them a future," he says, "so that they may give us a past. We help them live on so that they may help us go forward" (158). That description can fit those "done to death" by rape-as-policy in war and genocide and our relationship to them. By remembering them, by allowing them to indwell our worlds, by allowing them to speak to and through us, we may be able to thwart the conditions that destroyed them. Such action would not bring back those "done to death" by rape as a weapon of war and genocide, but it would create a present and a future—and even a past—more worth having. Or, as a responsibility-to-protect reading of Maimonides might suggest, improving the odds that moral motives will bite in needed ways depends significantly on respecting and heeding the "conscience shocking" calls for action crying out like no others from "voices that can be heard only in silence."

Notes

1.   In addition to Kristof's many *New York Times* editorials on these topics, see Nicholas D. Kristof and Sheryl WuDunn. *Half the Sky: Turning Oppression into Opportunity for Women Worldwide*. New York: Alfred A. Knopf, 2009.

2.   Nicholas D. Kristof, "The World Capital of Killing," *New York Times*, February 7, 2010. The peer-reviewed study cited by Kristof is "Mortality in the Democratic Republic of Congo: An Ongoing Crisis," which is a special report by the highly respected International Rescue Committee. The report is available at: http://www.rescue.org/sites/default/files/migrated/resources/2007/2006-7_congomortalitysurvey.pdf. Accessed December 6, 2011.

3.   The statements quoted in this paragraph are from Kristof, "The World Capital of Killing." Mukwege and the Panzi Hospital are discussed in more detail by Lee Ann De Reus in chapter 9 above.

4.   These paragraphs are from "2005 World Summit Outcome," a report from the General Assembly of the United Nations, dated October 24, 2005. The document is available at: http://www.un.org/summit2005/documents.html. Under Main Documents, click the link for 2005 World Summit Outcome (September 15, 2005). Accessed December 5, 2011.

5.   The Charter of the United Nations is available at: http://www.un.org/en/documents/charter/intro.shtml. Accessed December 6, 2011.

6.   See Chapter I, Article 2, Paragraph 7. The qualifications pertain to the conditions enumerated in Chapter VII.

7.   A good source for further information about these developments is the internet site for the International Coalition for the Responsibility to Protect, which is available at: http://www.responsibilitytoprotect.org/index.php/about-rtop. Accessed December 6, 2011.

8. See Thomas G. Weiss, "R2P after 9/11 and the World Summit," *Wisconsin International Law Journal* 24 (2006): 741.

9. See *The Responsibility to Protect: Report of the International Commission on Intervention and State Sovereignty* (Ottawa: International Development Research Centre, 2001). Citations refer to the report's internal enumeration of sections and paragraphs. The report can be found at: http://responsibilitytoprotect. org/ICISS%20Report.pdf. Accessed December 6, 2011. See also Gareth Evans, *The Responsibility to Protect: Ending Mass Atrocity Crimes Once and For All* (Washington, DC: Brookings Institution Press, 2008).

10. The phrase "done to death" is George Steiner's. See his *Language and Silence: Essays on Language, Literature, and the Inhuman* (New York: Atheneum, 1967), 157. I am indebted to Paul C. Santilli for this reference. Santilli's thought about the importance of encountering the dead, especially the murdered dead, has influenced mine. See especially Paul C. Santilli, "Philosophy's Obligation to the Human Being in the Aftermath of Genocide," in *Genocide and Human Rights: A Philosophical Guide*, ed. John K. Roth (New York: Palgrave Macmillan, 2005), 220-32.

11. David P. Boder, *I Did Not Interview the Dead* (Urbana, IL: University of Illinois Press, 1949), xiii. For a significant study of Boder and his work, see Alan Rosen, *The Wonder of Their Voices: The 1946 Holocaust Interviews of David Boder* (New York: Oxford University Press, 2010).

12. Boder, *I Did Not Interview the Dead*, xix.

13. See the speech as it is reprinted in Elie Wiesel, *Night*, trans. Marion Wiesel (New York: Hill and Wang, 2006), 117-20, especially 118

14. Robert Pogue Harrison, *The Dominion of the Dead* (Chicago: University of Chicago Press, 2003), ix, x. Subsequent references to Harrison's book are indicated in parentheses.

15. I take this idea to mean more than that a listener must be quiet to hear such voices and what they are saying. I take the idea to mean that the voices heard and what they are saying are inseparable from silence or that the voices speak only in silence. The paradox here is as inescapable as the insight it contains.

Further Suggested Reading

Autesserre, Séverine. *The Trouble with the Congo: Local Violence and the Failure of International Peacebuilding.* New York: Cambridge University Press, 2010.

Brudholm, Thomas, and Thomas Cushman, eds. *The Religious in Responses to Mass Atrocity: Interdisciplinary Perspectives.* New York: Cambridge University Press, 2009.

Human Rights Watch. "'If You Come Back We Will Kill You': Sexual Violence and Other Abuses against Congolese Migrants during Expulsion from Angola," May 21, 2012. Available at: http://www.hrw.org/reports/2012/05/21/if-you-come-back-we-will-kill-you. Accessed May 30, 2012.

Knight, W. Andy, and Frazer Egerton, eds.   *The Routledge Handbook of the Responsibility to Protect.* New York: Routledge, 2012.

Orford, Anne. *International Authority and the Responsibility to Protect.* New York: Cambridge University Press, 2011.

Totten, Samuel, and Paul R. Bartrop. *Dictionary of Genocide.* 2 vols. Westport, CT: Greenwood Press, 2008.

Questions for Discussion

1.   Considering all that you have read in this book, what words—new or old—become increasingly important?

2.   If you could speak to those "done to death" by rape-as-policy, what would you say?

3.   If those "done to death" by rape-as-policy "speak" to you, what are your responses likely to be?

4.   During your lifetime, do you expect the "responsibility to protect" to grow or diminish in strength with regard to rape as a weapon of war and genocide?

5.   What is the most important action that you/we could take to strengthen the "responsibility to protect"?

SELECTED BIBLIOGRAPHY

The contributors to this book have provided full citations for the many books and articles that are referenced in their chapters. They have also made suggestions for further reading that is relevant for the topics they have addressed. This selected bibliography supplements that information by citing additional publications of importance that may be helpful to readers who want to study further.

Addressing Conflict-Related Sexual Violence—An Analytical Inventory of Peacekeeping Practice. New York: United Nations (UNIFEM), 2010.

African Rights. *Rwanda—Not So Innocent: When Women Became Killers.* London: African Rights, 1995.

———. *Rwanda: Broken Bodies, Torn Spirits, Living with Genocide, Rape, and HIV/AIDS.* London: African Rights, 2004.

Amnesty International. *Sudan, Darfur: Rape as a Weapon of War; Sexual Violence and Its Consequences.* London: Amnesty International, 2004.

———. *Liberia: No Impunity for Rape. A Crime against Humanity and a War Crime.* London: Amnesty International, 2004.

———. *Lives Blown Apart: Crimes against Women in Times of Conflict.* London: Amnesty International, 2004.

———. *Casualties of War: Women's Bodies, Women's Lives. Stop Crimes Against Women in Armed Conflict.* London: Amnesty International, 2004.

Bartels, Susan, M. Van Rooyen, Jennifer Leaning, J. Scott, and Jocelyn Kelly, *"Now, the World Is Without Me": An Investigation of Sexual Violence in Eastern Democratic Republic of Congo.* Cambridge, MA: Harvard Humanitarian Initiative and Oxfam International, 2010.

Bellamy, Alex J. *Global Politics and the Responsibility to Protect: From Words to Deeds.* New York: Routledge, 2011.

———. *Responsibility to Protect: The Global Effort to End Mass Atrocities.* Cambridge, UK: Polity Press, 2009.

Card, Claudia. *Confronting Evils: Terrorism, Torture, Genocide.* New York: Cambridge University Press, 2010.

Carpenter, Charli. *Innocent Women and Children: Gender, Norms and the Protection of Civilians.* Farnham, Surrey, UK: Ashgate, 2006.

Carpenter, Charli, Kai Greig, Donna Sharkey, and Giulia Baldi. *Protecting Children Born of Wartime Rape and Exploitation in Conflict Zones: Existing Practice and Knowledge Gaps.* Pittsburgh: University of Pittsburgh GSPIA/Ford Institute of Human Security, 2005.

De Vito, Daniela. *Rape, Torture and Genocide: Some Theoretical Implications.* Hauppauge, NY: Nova Science Publishers, 2010.

De Temmerman, Els. *Aboke Girls: Children Abducted in Northern Uganda.* Kampala, Uganda: Fountain Publishers, 2001.

DelZotto, Augusta, and Adam Jones. "Male-on-Male Sexual Violence in Wartime: Human Rights' Last Taboo?" Available at: http://adamjones.freeservers.com/malerape.htm . Accessed November 10, 2011.

Durham, Helen, and Tracey Gurd, eds. *Listening to the Silences: Women and War.* Leiden, The Netherlands: Martinus Nijhoff, 2005.

El-Bushra, Judy, and Ibrahim Sahl. *Cycles of Violence, Gender Relations and Armed Conflict.* Nairobi, Kenya: ACORD—Agency for Co-operation and Research in Development, 2005.

Enloe, Cynthia. *Maneuvers: The International Politics of Militarizing Women's Lives.* Berkeley, CA: University of California Press, 2000.

Ensler, Eve. *Necessary Targets: A Story of Women and War.* New York: Villard, 2001.

———. *The Vagina Monologues.* New York: Villard, 2008.

Frederick, Sharon. *Rape: Weapon of Terror.* Hackensack, NJ: World Scientific Publishing Co., 2000.

Gardner, Judith and Judy El-Bushra. *Somalia—the Untold Story: The War Through the Eyes of Somali Women.* London, UK: Pluto Press, 2004.

Gbowee, Leymah. *Mighty Be Our Powers: How Sisterhood, Prayer and Sex Changed a Nation at War.* New York: Beast Books, 2011.

Giles, Wenona and Jennifer Hyndman, eds. *Sites of Violence: Gender and Conflict Zones.* Berkeley, CA: University of California Press, 2004.

Gingerich, Tara, and Jennifer Leaning. *The Use of Rape As a Weapon of War in the Conflict in Darfur, Sudan.* Cambridge, MA: Harvard School of Public Health, and Physicians for Human Rights, 2005.

Goldhagen, Daniel Jonah. *Worse Than War: Genocide, Eliminationism, and the Ongoing Assault on Humanity.* New York: Public Affairs, 2009.

Goldstein, Anne Tierney. *Recognizing Forced Impregnation as a War Crime Under International Law.* New York: The Center for Reproductive Law & Policy, 1993.

Guatemala: Memory of Silence, Report of the Commission for Historical Clarification. Guatemala City, Guatemala, February 1999.

Gutman, Roy. *A Witness to Genocide.* New York: Simon and Schuster, 1993.

Hagay-Frey, Alona. *Sex and Gender Crimes in New International Law.* Leiden, The Netherlands: Brill Publishers, 2011.

Hardi, Choman. *Gendered Experiences of Genocide: Anfal Survivors in Kurdistan, Iraq.* Farnham, Surrey, UK: Ashgate, 2011.

Hatzfeld, Jean. *Into the Quick of Life: The Rwandan Genocide—The Survivors Speak.* Translated by Gerry Feehily. London: Serpent's Tail, 2005.

———. *Life Laid Bare: The Survivors of Rwanda Speak.* Translated by Linda Coverdale. New York: Other Press, 2006.

Heineman, Elizabeth, ed. *Sexual Violence in Conflict Zones: From the Ancient World to the Era of Human Rights.* Philadelphia: University of Pennsylvania Press, 2011.

Hicks, George. *The Comfort Women: Japan's Brutal Regime of Enforced Prostitution in the Second World War.* New York: W. W. Norton, 1995.

Hobson, M. *Forgotten Casualties of War: Girls in Armed Conflict.* London: Save the Children, 2005.

Human Rights Watch. *"My Heart Is Cut": Sexual Violence by Rebels and Pro-government Forces in Côte d'Ivoire.* New York: Human Rights Watch, 2007.

———. *The War within the War: Sexual Violence in Eastern Congo.* New York: Human Rights Watch, 2002.

———. *"We'll Kill You If You Cry": Sexual Violence in the Sierra Leone Conflict.* New York: Human Rights Watch, 2003.

Intimate Enemy: Images and Voices of the Rwandan Genocide. Photographs by Robert Lyons. Introduction and Interviews by Scott Straus. New York: Zone Books, 2006.

Jacobs, Susie, Ruth Jacobson, and Jennifer Marchbank, eds. *States of Conflict: Gender, Violence and Resistance*. London: Zed Press, 2000.

Jones, Adam. *Gender Inclusive: Essays on Violence, Men, and Feminist International Relations*. New York: Routledge, 2008.

———, ed. *New Directions in Genocide Research*. New York: Routledge, 2012.

Kelly, Jocelyn. *Rape in War: Motives of the Militia in DRC*. Washington, DC: U. S. Institute for Peace, 2010.

Leatherman, Janie L. *Sexual Violence and Armed Conflict*. Cambridge, UK: Polity Press, 2011.

Lentin, Ronit, ed. *Gender and Catastrophe*. London: Zed Books, 1997.

Li, Donke. *Echoes of Chongqing: Women in Wartime China*. Chicago: University of Illinois Press, 2010.

Mananzan, Mary John, Mercy Amba Oduyoye, Elsa Tamez, J. Shannon Clarkson, Mary C. Grey, Letty M. Russell, eds. *Women Resisting Violence: Spirituality for Life*. Maryknoll, NY: Orbis Publishers, 1996.

Médecins Sans Frontières. *The Crushing Burden of Rape: Sexual Violence in Darfur*, Amsterdam: March 2005.

Mertus, Julie A. *War's Offensive on Women: The Humanitarian Challenge in Bosnia, Kosovo, and Afghanistan*. Bloomfield, CT: Kumarian Press, 2000.

Mojzes, Paul. *Balkan Genocides: Holocaust and Ethnic Cleansing in the Twentieth Century*. Lanham, MD: Rowman & Littlefield, 2011.

Moser, Caroline N.O., and Fiona Clark, eds. *Victims, Perpetrators or Actors? Gender, Armed Conflict and Political Violence*. London: Zed Books, 2001.

Naimark, Norman M. *The Russians in Germany: A History of the Soviet Zone of Occupation, 1945-1949*. Cambridge, MA: Harvard University Press, 1995.

Nikolic-Ristanovic, Vesna. *Women, Violence, and War: Wartime Victimization of Refugees in the Balkans*. Budapest: Central European University Press, 2000.

Nottage, Lynn. *Ruined*. New York: Theatre Communications Group, 2009.

Parrot, Andrea, and Nina Cummings. *Forsaken Females: The Global Brutalization of Women*. Lanham, MD: Rowman & Littlefield, 2006.

Penn, Michael L., and Rahel Nardos. *Overcoming Violence Against Women and Girls*. New York: Rowman & Littlefield, 2003.

Physicians for Human Rights. *War-related Sexual Violence in Sierra Leone: A Population-based Assessment.* Boston: Physicians for Human Rights, 2002.

Pilch, Frances T. *Rape as Genocide: The Legal Response to Sexual Violence.* New York: Center for Global Security and Democracy, Columbia University International Affairs On-line, 2002.

Prescott, Jordan A., and Adrian M. Madsen, eds. *Sexual Violence in Africa's Conflict Zones.* Hauppauge, NY: Nova Science Publishers, 2011.

Ramet, Sabrina P., ed. *Gender Politics in the Western Balkans: Women and Society in Yugoslavia and the Yugoslav Successor States.* University Park, PA: Pennsylvania State University Press, 1999.

Rape as a Weapon of War: Accountability for Sexual Violence in Conflict. Washington, DC: BiblioGov, 2010.

Reese, Willy Peter. *A Stranger to Myself: The Inhumanity of War: Russia, 1941-1944.* New York: Farrar, Straus and Giroux, 2005.

Rehn, Elisabeth, and Ellen Johnson Sirleaf. *Women, War, Peace: The Independent Experts' Assessment.* New York: UNIFEM, 2002.

San Pedro, Paula. *Sexual Violence in Columbia: Instrument of War.* Oxford: Oxfam International, 2009.

Sharratt, Sara. *Gender, Shame and Sexual Violence: The Voices of Witnesses and Court Members at War Crimes Tribunals.* Burlington, VT: Ashgate Publishing Co., 2011.

Skjelsbaek, Inger. *The Elephant in the Room: An Overview of How Sexual Violence Came to be Seen as a Weapon of War.* Oslo, Norway: Peace Research Institute, 2010.

————. *The Political Psychology of War Rape: Studies from Bosnia-Herzegovina.* New York: Routledge, 2012.

Snyder, David Raub. *Sex Crimes under the Wehrmacht.* Lincoln: University of Nebraska Press, 2007.

Staub, Ervin. *Overcoming Evil: Genocide, Violent Conflict, and Terrorism.* New York: Oxford University Press, 2011.

Stemple, Lara. "Male Rape and Human Rights." *Hastings Law Review* 60 (2009): 605-647.

————. "The Hidden Victims of Rape." *New York Times,* March 2, 2011, 24.

Storr, Will. "The Rape of Men." *The Guardian Observer Magazine* (UK), July 17, 2011, 36.

Tanaka, Yuki. *Hidden Horrors: Japanese War Crimes in World War II*. Boulder, CO: Westview, 1996.

Totten, Samuel. *An Oral and Documentary History of the Darfur Genocide*. Santa Barbara, CA: Praeger Security International, 2011.

Totten, Samuel, and Rafiki Ubaldo. *We Cannot Forget: Interviews with Survivors of the Genocide in Rwanda*. New Brunswick, NJ: Rutgers University Press, 2010.

Turshen, Meredeth, and Clotilde Twagiramariya, eds. *What Women Do in Wartime: Gender and Conflict in Africa*. London: Zed Books, 1998.

Vandenberg, Martina. *Kosovo: Rape as a Weapon of "Ethnic Cleansing"*. New York: Human Rights Watch, 2000.

Ward, Jeanne. *If Not Now, When? Addressing Gender-Based Violence in Refugee, Internally Displaced, and Post-Conflict Settings: A Global Overview*. New York: Reproductive Health for Refugees Consortium, 2002.

Ward, Jeanne, et al. *The Shame of War: Sexual Violence Against Women and Girls in Conflict*. Nairobi: OCHA/IRIN, 2007.

Ward, Jeanne and Mendy Marsh. "Sexual Violence Against Women and Girls in War and Its Aftermath: Realities, Responses, and Required Resources." Brussels, Belgium: UNFPA, 2006. Available at: http://www.unfpa.org/emergencies/symposium06/docs/finalbrusselsbriefingpaper.pdf. Accessed December 9, 2011.

Weaver, Gina Marie. *Ideologies of Forgetting: Rape in the Vietnam War*. Albany, NY: State University of New York, 2010.

Weine, Stevan M. *When History is a Nightmare: Lives and Memories of Ethnic Cleansing in Bosnia-Herzegovina*. New Brunswick, NJ: Rutgers University Press, 1999.

Williams, Paul D. *War and Conflict in Africa*. Cambridge, UK: Polity Press, 2011.

WEBSITES

Excellent sources of up-to-date information, reports, and documents about the use of rape as a weapon of war and genocide can be found at the websites of humanitarian organizations, research institutes, and international organizations. The following is a selection of reputable and reliable websites that can be consulted by scholars, students, and others interested in this book's topics.

Amnesty International: www.amnesty.org

Crimes of War: www.crimesofwar.org

Doctors Without Borders: www.doctorswithoutborders.org

Gendercide Watch: www.gendercide.org

Harvard Humanitarian Initiative: www.hhi.harvard.edu

Human Rights Watch: www.hrw.org

International Committee of the Red Cross: www.icrc.org

International Crisis Group: www.crisisgroup.org

International Rescue Committee: www.rescue.org

IRIN Global: www.irinnews.org

Lessons from Rwanda: www.un.org/preventgenocide/rwanda

Oxfam International: www.oxfam.org

Physicians for Human Rights: www.physiciansforhumanrights.org

Refugees International: www.refintl.org

Sexual Violence Research Initiative: www.svri.org

Stop Rape Now: UN Action Against Sexual Violence in Conflict: www.stoprapenow.org

United Nations: www.un.org

UN Women: www.unwomen.org

U. S. Institute for Peace: www.usip.org

V-Day: A Global Movement to End Violence Against Women and Girls: www.vday.org/home

Women for Women: www.womenforwomen.org

Women, War & Peace: www.pbs.org/wnet/women-war-and-peace/

FILMS, VIDEOS, AND CLIPS

What follows is a selective listing of films, videos, and film/video clips available through film production companies, national and international news organizations, and on YouTube. All of these items are either in English, or they are subtitled in English. Some are full-length feature films; those listed supplement the filmography provided by Paul Bartrop in chapter 11. Other entries below are documentary films or docudramas; still others are news reports. In almost all instances, the material is difficult viewing and should be used with discretion with all age groups, but especially with high school students.

The Abandoned (*Ostavljenl*) (2010). Directed by Adis Bakrač. HEFT Production.

"Art from the Ashes of Ruin" (2010). Available at: http://www.pbs.org/wnet/women-war-and-peace/tag/ruined/. Accessed November 5, 2011.

City of Life and Death (2011). Directed by Lu Chuan. Kino International.

The Devil Came on Horseback (2007). Directed by Annie Sundberg and Ricki Stern. Docurama Films.

Duhozanye: A Rwandan Village of Widows (2011). Directed by Karoline Frogner. Women Make Films.

Esma's Secret—Grbavica: The Land of My Dreams (2006). Directed by Jasmila Zbanic. Strand Releasing.

Fighting the Silence (2007). Directed by Ilse van Velzen and Femke van Velzen. Women Make Movies.

Genocidal Rape in Višsegrad, "Javna Tajna" (2009). BHTV.

The Greatest Silence: Rape in Congo (2008). Directed by Lisa F. Jackson. Women Make Movies.

In the Land of Blood and Honey (2011). Directed by Angelina Jolie. GK Films. See also Christiane Amanpour's interview with Jolie (December 5, 2011), which is available at: http://abcnews.go.com/Nightline/video/angelina-jolie-motherhood-career-15093113. Accessed January 10, 2012.

Intended Consequences (2008). By Jonathan Torgovnik. MediaStorm. Available at: http://mediastorm.com/publication/intended-consequences. Accessed November 12, 2011.

Keepers of Memory (2004). Directed by Eric Kabera. Link Media Productions.

Libya: War and Rape (2011). Al Jazeera English. Available at: www.youtube.com. Accessed: November 5, 2011.

Lumo—One Young Woman's Struggle to Heal in a Nation Beset by War (2007). Directed by Bent-Jorgen Perlmutt et al. A Goma Film Project.

Nguyen ThiTe's Rape and Torture by Soldiers (1981). Open Vault. WGBH Media Library and Archives.

Operation Fine Girl: Rape Used as a Weapon in Sierra Leone (2001). Directed by Lilibet Foster. Oxygen Media LLC.

People & Power—Bosnia's Broken Promises (2009). Al Jazeera English. Available at: www.youtube.com. Accessed November 5, 2011.

Rape: A Crime of War (1996). Directed by Shelley Saywell. National Film Board of Canada.

Rape, A Weapon of War: Destroying the Glue of a Society (2011). Available at: Economist.com/video. Accessed November 4, 2011.

Rape As a Weapon of War (2011). Directed by Ewelina Kotowska. Available at: Vimeo.com/18809745. Accessed November 4, 2011.

Rape as a Weapon of War in the Democratic Republic of the Congo (2010). PBS. Available at: www.youtube.com. Accessed November 5, 2011.

"Rape as a Weapon of War in Shan State" (2011). Available at: www.youtube.com. Accessed November 5, 2011.

"Raped by Red Army Soldiers, They Talk for the First Time" (2009). Available at: www.youtube.com. Accessed November 5, 2011.

Riz Khan—Rape: A Weapon of War (2009). Al Jazeera English. Available at: www.youtube.com. Accessed November 5, 2011.

Until the Violence Stops (2003). Directed by Abby Epstein. V-Day Productions.

Valentina's Story (1997). By Fergal Keane. BBC Panorama.

War Against Women (2008). CBS News, 60 Minutes.

Weapon of War (2009). Directed by Ilse van Velzen and Femke van Velzen. Women Make Movies.

Witnessing Darfur: Genocide Emergency (2004). Committee on Conscience, United States Holocaust Memorial Museum.

Women, War & Peace: A Five-Part Special Series (2011). By Abigail E. Disney et al. THIRTEEN and Fork Films.

- I Came to Testify
- Pray the Devil Back to Hell
- Peace Unveiled
- The War We are Living
- War Redefined

Worse Than War (2010). Directed by Mike Dewitt. JTN Productions and WNET Thirteen.

About the Editors and Contributors

Editors

Carol Rittner, RSM, is Distinguished Professor of Holocaust and Genocide Studies and the Dr. Marsha Raticoff Grossman Professor of Holocaust Studies at The Richard Stockton College of New Jersey, where she has taught since 1994. She is the author, editor, or coeditor of numerous publications, including *Different Voices: Women and the Holocaust* (Paragon House), *Will Genocide Ever End?* (Aegis/Paragon House), and *Genocide in Rwanda: Complicity of the Churches?* (Aegis/Paragon House). Rittner's current research interests include rescue during the Holocaust and in post-Holocaust genocides.

John K. Roth is the Edward J. Sexton Professor Emeritus of Philosophy and the Founding Director of the Center for the Study of the Holocaust, Genocide, and Human Rights (now the Center for Human Rights Leadership) at Claremont McKenna College, where he taught from 1966 through 2006. His numerous books include *Genocide and Human Rights: A Philosophical Guide* (Palgrave Macmillan), *Ethics During and After the Holocaust: In the Shadow of Birkenau* (Palgrave Macmillan), and *The Oxford Handbook of Holocaust Studies* (Oxford University Press). In 1988, Roth was named U.S. National Professor of the Year by the Council for Advancement and Support of Education and the Carnegie Foundation for the Advancement of Teaching.

Contributors

Paul R. Bartrop, the 2011-2012 Ida E. King Distinguished Visiting Professor of Holocaust and Genocide Studies at The Richard Stockton College of New Jersey, is Professor of History and Director of the Center of Judaic, Holocaust, and Human Rights Studies at Florida Gulf Coast University. Formerly the Head of History at Bialik College, Melbourne, Australia, Bartrop also has taught at the University of South Australia and Deakin University in Australia. His books include *Fifty Key Thinkers on the Holocaust and Genocide* (Routledge), *The Genocide Studies Reader* (Routledge), and *Dictionary of Genocide* (Greenwood Press). His current projects include two additional books: *An Encyclopedia of Contemporary Genocide Biography: Portraits of Evil and Good* and *Genocide Goes to the Movies: An Annotated Filmography of the Holocaust and Genocide.*

Roselyn Costantino is Associate Professor of Spanish and Women's Studies and Coordinator of Women's Studies at Pennsylvania State University, Altoona. In 2011, she was a Fulbright Fellow in Guatemala, where she advanced a project titled *"There are many ways to kill a woman": Structural Deformities, Femicide, and Transformative Collaboration in Guatemala's Narrative of Extreme Gendered Violence.* Costantino is the co-editor of *Holy Terrors: Latin American Women Perform* (Duke University Press). In addition to her work on femicide and Guatemalan women's creative resistance, she has published on Latin American feminist thought, theater, performance, and fiction and on pedagogies of peace and social justice.

Lee Ann De Reus is Associate Professor of Human Development and Family Studies and Women's Studies at Pennsylvania State University, Altoona. The author of many research articles and book chapters, she has been a Carl Wilkens Fellow with the Genocide Intervention Network. She frequently travels to Panzi Hospital in the war-torn, eastern Democratic Republic of Congo (DRC) to conduct research, develop programs for rape survivors, and inform her advocacy work in the United States. Based on interviews with rape survivors in the eastern DRC, *Negotiating the*

Stigma of Rape and Traumatic Fistula in the Democratic Republic of Congo is one of her current projects. An activist scholar, De Reus co-founded and serves as president of the board of directors of The Panzi Foundation, USA, which supports the hospital's work in the DRC.

Eva Fogelman is a social psychologist, psychotherapist, author, and filmmaker. In private practice in New York City, she works extensively with Holocaust survivors and their children. Co-founder of the Jewish Foundation for Christian Rescuers, Fogelman is the author of many articles and books, including *Conscience and Courage: Rescuers of Jews during the Holocaust* (Anchor Books) and *Children during the Nazi Reign: Psychological Perspective on the Interview Process* (Praeger). The award-winning PBS documentary *Breaking the Silence: The Generation after the Holocaust* is among her film credits.

Dagmar Herzog is Professor of History and Daniel Rose Faculty Scholar at the Graduate Center, City University of New York. She has published extensively on the histories of sexuality and gender, theology and religion, Jewish-Christian relations, and Holocaust memory. Her books include *Sex after Fascism: Memory and Morality in Twentieth-Century Germany* (Princeton University Press), *Brutality and Desire: War and Sexuality in Europe's Twentieth Century* (Palgrave Macmillan), and *Sexuality in Europe: A Twentieth Century History* (Cambridge University Press).

Jessica A. Hubbard, trained in sociology and women's studies, pursues research in conflict analysis, sexual violence and genocide, gender and disaster response, feminist research methodologies, and issues in higher education. She is the author of *Understanding Rape as Genocide: A Feminist Analysis of Sexual Violence and Genocide* (VDM Verlag), which focuses on women who were raped in the Rwandan genocide, and *Emergency Management in Higher Education: Current Practices and Conversations* (Public Entity Risk Institute).

Julie Kuhlken has served as Assistant Professor of Philosophy at Misericordia University, teaching courses in political philosophy, ethics, the philosophy of law, and environmental philosophy. Her publications include articles entitled "The Nation-State and the Potential for Earthly Dwelling," "Extending Extensionist Environmental Virtue Ethics," "Nietzsche's Dabbling in the Political," and "Heidegger's Political Philosophy: The Distinction between Nationalism and Patriotic Orientation." Her interest in issues of rape and genocide and, in particular, her concern about economic aspects of rape as an instrument of war and genocide grow out of her research in ecofeminist political philosophy.

Christina M. Morus is Assistant Professor of Comparative Genocide and Communication Studies at The Richard Stockton College of New Jersey. A 2009-10 Fulbright Fellow in Serbia, she also works as a volunteer with Serbia's feminist activist groups Women in Black and DAH Theatre. Morus's research focuses on contemporary pre- and post-conflict discourses in the Balkans, Rwanda, Cambodia, and South Africa, with an emphasis on women and war, memory in the wake of mass violence, and locally originating grassroots peace activist organizations.

Tazreena Sajjad is a Professorial Lecturer in the School of International Service (SIS) at American University. Her professional experience includes working for the Global Rights' Asia Program in Afghanistan and for the National Democratic Institute for International Affairs' South Asia division. She has also served as an independent consultant for the Afghanistan Research and Evaluation Unit (AREU) in Kabul. Her scholarly research and publications examine questions of human rights and conflict, transitional justice, the experience of women in war, and post-conflict reconstruction.

James E. Waller is the Cohen Chair of Holocaust and Genocide Studies at Keene State College. He is also an affiliated scholar at the Auschwitz Institute for Peace and Reconciliation. Waller's many publications include *Becoming Evil: How Ordinary People Commit Genocide and Mass Killing* (Oxford University Press), *Face to Face: The Changing State of Racism across America* (Insight Books), and *Prejudice across America* (University Press of Mississippi). Among his current projects is *Genocide: Ever Again* (forthcoming, Oxford University Press), which reviews the history of modern genocide and addresses issues about intervention, justice, religion, and remembrance.

Carl Wilkens, the director of World Outside My Shoes, a non-profit humanitarian and educational organization, served as an aid worker with the Adventist Church, and moved his young family to Rwanda in the spring of 1990. When the genocide erupted in April 1994, he refused to leave and became the only American to remain in the country throughout that catastrophe. Wilkens has been featured in several documentaries about the Rwandan genocide. Committed to building resistance against mass atrocity crimes, he spends much of his time speaking to students. Based largely on tapes he made for his wife and children during the genocide, not knowing whether he would see them again, *I'm Not Leaving* (World Outside My Shoes) is Wilkens's book about his experiences in Rwanda.

INDEX

A

Abortions, 146

Abu Ghraib, xlv, 93

Action
  needed for Mwamaroyi and her Congolese sisters in the Democratic Republic of Congo, 151–53
  victims of sexual violence becoming architects of their own empowerment, 130–32
  See also Crying out for action

Action against Sexual Violence in Conflict, 161

Activist scholarship, xviii, 142

Adventist Development and Relief Agency International (ADRA), 196, 198

Advocacy, problematic approaches in the Democratic Republic of Congo, 150–51

Afghanistan, 75

Against Our Will, 173–74

Agreement for the Prosecution and Punishment of the Major War Criminals of the European Axis and Charter of the International Military Tribunal (IMT), 76

AIDS, x
  See also HIV-positive status

Akayesu, Jean-Paul, xiv, xvii, xxi–xxii, xl, 69, 71, 103, 105, 110, 113, 170

al-Bashir, Omar, xxxvi, xlviii

al-Obeidy, Eman, lii

Al Qaeda, xliv

Algeria, xli

Allies occupying Germany, xxvi–xxvii

American military
  fighting Native Americans, 191
  leading Iraq invasion, xliv
  notorious for raping Vietnamese women, 65
  See also Abu Ghraib

Améry, Jean, xiv–xv

Amin, Idi, xxxii

Amnesty International, xxxviii, 84

Anonyma—Eine Frau in Berlin (movie)
  See A Woman in Berlin (movie)

Anonymity, guiding principle of, 152

Antonijević, Peter, 184–85

Arājs, Viktors, 15–16, 18

Ararat (movie), genocide and rape in, 189

Archdiocese of Guatemala, Human Rights Office, 126–27

Arendt, Hannah, 164, 168

Argentina, xxxiii

Armenian genocide, 189–91

Arrow in the Sun, 191

"Aryan" ideal, 23

Index

torture at Flossenbürg, 29–44
Shakespeare, William, 183
Sharlach, Lisa, 105
Shattered Lives: Sexual Violence during the Rwandan Genocide and its Aftermath, 101–103, 109
Shiva, Vandana, 165
Shoah Foundation, Institute of Visual History and Education, 15
Sierra Leone, xxxvi, li, 69–71, 74–75, 86
Significance of women, and the economic and ethical elements of rape, 164–66
Singer, Flora, 20–21
Sino-Japanese war, xxv
Sirleaf, Ellen Johnson, lii
"Situational Diagnosis of the Violent Deaths of Women in Guatemala," 128
16 Days of Activism Against Gender Violence campaign, xxxvi
Slavery
    See Sexual enslavement
Slim, Hugo, 167
Smardzic, Nedjo, 73
Social contexts of cruelty, 92–96
    binding factors of the group, 95–96
    group identification, 93–95
    professional socialization, 92–93
    and rape as a tool of "othering" in genocide, 92–96
Social networking, xix
Social pressure, 24

Social reality, women needing full human status in, xv–xvi, 1–13
Socio-cultural norms, leaving victims invisible, 74
Sofsky, Wolfgang, 39
Soldier Blue (movie), genocide and rape in, 191
Solzhenitsyn, Aleksandr, 157, 161
Soviet soldiers raping German women, 4–5
Spanish conquest, of Guatemala, 122
Srebrenica massacre, lii
SS, Protection Squad (*Schutzstaffel*), 33
    homosexuality within, 35
Stanford University, 23–24
Stangl, Franz, 15, 25
Stankovic, Radovan, 72–73
Sterilization experiments, 35
Stockholm Declaration on Genocide, xlv
Stone, Oliver, 184
Stories of suffering, survival, and hope in the Democratic Republic of Congo, 139–56
    making a difference for Mwamaroyi and her Congolese sisters, 151–53
    perpetrators, mass destruction, resilience, religion, and hope, 147–50
    problematic approaches to advocacy and policy, 150–51
    "the worst place in the world to be a woman," 142–44
    the wounds and children of rape, 144–47